MONUMENTS
IN THE
LANDSCAPE

EDITED BY PAUL RAINBIRD

TEMPUS

The contributors dedicate this book to Andrew Fleming

First published 2008

Tempus Publishing
Cirencester Road, Chalford,
Stroud, Gloucestershire, GL6 8PE
www.tempus-publishing.com

Tempus Publishing is an imprint of NPI Media Group

British Library Cataloguing in Publication Data.
A catalogue record for this book is available from the British Library.

ISBN 978 0 7524 4283 9

Typesetting and origination by NPI Media Group
Printed in Great Britain

CONTENTS

LIST OF ILLUSTRATIONS

13 The study area in Wales, with a detailed map showing the topography of lowland north Ceredigion and the main ceremonial complexes (squares) and other sites (circles) described here. Main complexes: (1) Pant-y-Peran (2) Plas Gogerddan (3) Dollwen (4) Pyllau-isaf (5) Llanilar. Other sites: (A) Pen-y-Garn (B) Llangorwen Church (C) Garreg Fawr, Llanbadarn Fawr (D) Lovesgrove (E) Penllwyn. *Crown Copyright, All rights reserved. RCAHMW. Licence number 100017916, 2007*

14 The main Neolithic and Bronze Age ceremonial complexes; cropmark evidence. Pant-y-peran and Plas Gogerddan – the shaded area illustrates the extent of the excavation. *Crown Copyright, All rights reserved. RCAHMW. Licence number 100017916, 2007*

15 Dollwen, Goginan and Pyllau-isaf. *Crown Copyright, All rights reserved. RCAHMW. Licence number 100017916, 2007*

16 The cropmark of the Dollwen concentric enclosure: a ground view from the west with the lush growth over the buried ditches contrasting with the surrounding drought-ridden pasture. The landowner provides a scale in the centre of the monument. The position of the enclosure, on a very level river terrace at the head of the valley, surrounded on all sides by rising ground, is also apparent in this view *Crown Copyright RCAHMW, DS2006_212_008*

17 Cairn or Carn? The weathered entrance grave (second from right) on Samson North Hill, Isles of Scilly resembles its neighbours. *Photograph by Mary Ann Owoc*

18 Davidstow Moor Site V. *From Christie 1988; reproduced here with permission from The Cornwall Archaeological Society*

19 Schematic of mound construction at Crig-a-Mennis using variously textured and coloured materials

20 Part of the dramatic visual 'burst' of tor-topped hills seen once the summit cairn on Tolborough Tor is climbed. Roughtor's southern tor pokes over Brown Willy's shoulder and appears to merge with its descending line of tors

21 The line of sight to Roughtor from the NW end of the Searle's Down row

22 Ceremonial niche. *Courtesy of Parreira and Morán*

23 Alcalar 7 (Mexilhoeira Grande, Algarve)

24 Alcalar 7, detail of entrance

25 Location of ancient field systems and burons studied in the Canton of Pierrefort

26 Sketch plan of a buron at Montagne de la Mouche A (X 637.5E Y 200.3N). 1, 10: shallow depressions; 2: circular platform; 3: banked linear depression; 4-9: probable mazucs; 11: hollowed pathway

27 Sketch plan of a buron at Montagne de la Mouche B (X 638E Y 200.7N). 1: ditch or leat; 2-6, 9: mazucs; 7, 8: collapsed burons

28 Plan of the field systems in fields 2 and 3 at Chabridet (EDM survey by Rupert Featherby and Steve Marsden)

LIST OF CONTRIBUTORS

John Barnett
Peak District National Park Authority
Bakewell, Derbyshire

Brian Boyd
C/- Department of Anthropology
Columbia University, New York

Richard Bradley
Department of Archaeology
University of Reading

C. Stephen Briggs
Llanddeiniol, near Aberystwyth

Ivone Canavilhas
Civilhã, Portugal

John Collis
Department of Archaeology
University of Sheffield

Zoë Crossland
Department of Anthropology
Columbia University, New York

Robert A. Dodgshon
Institute of Geography & Earth Sciences
University of Wales, Aberystwyth

Toby Driver
Royal Commission on the Ancient and
Historical Monuments of Wales
Aberystwyth

Chris Fenton-Thomas
On Site Archaeology Ltd
York

Michael Freeman
Ceredigion Museum
Aberystwyth

Michael Fulford
Department of Archaeology
University of Reading

Tom Gledhill
Rural Development Service (North East
Region)
Natural England

Yannis Hamilakis
Department of Archaeology
University of Southampton

Peter Herring
Historic Environment Service
Cornwall County Council

Paula Jones
Department of Archaeology &
Anthropology
University of Wales, Lampeter

Ros Nichol
C/- Tom Gledhill

Mary Ann Owoc
Department of Anthropology
Mercyhurst College, USA

Mike Parker Pearson
Department of Archaeology
University of Sheffield

Mark Pluciennik
School of Archaeology & Ancient
History
University of Leicester

Paul Rainbird
Department of Archaeology &
Anthropology
University of Wales, Lampeter

Sarah Tarlow
School of Archaeology & Ancient
History
University of Leicester

Dr Jane Webster
School of Historical Studies
(Archaeology)
University of Newcastle upon Tyne

Tom Williamson
School of History
University of East Anglia

Alex Woolf
School of History
University of St Andrews

Rob Young
Northumberland National Park
Authority
Hexham

ACKNOWLEDGEMENTS

My thanks to all of the contributors for their patience and assistance during the preparation of this volume. Paula Jones assisted in the editing of the volume and I thank her and the University of Wales, Lampeter, for allowing this assistance. Thanks also to Peter Kemmis Betty of Tempus for his enthusiasm and desire to publish this book.

The contributors to this book all have one thing in common, they have been influenced by Andrew Fleming, now Professor Emeritus of the University of Wales, Lampeter. Both in Sheffield and Lampeter Andrew has taught innumerable students in the classroom and the field, but it is in the field where, if you can keep up with his long stride, his enthusiasm for landscape archaeology is keenly felt. Others in this volume have been colleagues of Andrew's and have not only appreciated his academic skills, but also his willingness to be a mentor and friend and to offer sagely advice. Others know Andrew through his publications and contributions to seminars and conferences, especially his role as a founder of the Theoretical Archaeology Group and the extremely successful TAG conferences held annually. Despite the myriad ways in which Andrew is known to the authors of this volume, they all share a desire, realised through their writings presented here to express a gratitude to Andrew now that he has retired from formal academic duties and to wish him the very best for the future. We know, with anticipation, that his engagement with monuments and landscapes is by no means at an end and we look forward to hearing much more from him for many years to come. Thank you Andrew.

Paul Rainbird
Lampeter
July 2007

1

MONUMENTS IN THE LANDSCAPE
Paul Rainbird

Much ink as been spilt, both academic and popular, in writing about and presenting images of monuments in the landscape. For example, prehistoric megaliths, such as standing stones, stone circles and tombs (*1*) have found themselves as contested space where alternative interpretations, both academic and from outside of academia vie with one another for public attention and the recognition of various interest groups. Although certainly not limited to this place, perhaps the best known in Britain generally is the site of Stonehenge, and Barbara Bender (1998) has shown the various claims to authority over this ancient site from, amongst others, archaeologists, government officers and druids. Similarly, like monuments, landscapes can be contested spaces, whether the aesthetics of a vista, that is, the possession of a view, or the ownership of property and expectations of the rights of that ownership. There can be a variety of demands on such places, and certainly in Britain as we shall see, even the wildest upland moorlands of the National Parks is not the unchanging landscape so often assumed. Prior to exploring these issues further I want first to define the key terms, monuments and landscape, and return to issues of the natural by way of introducing the papers in this book.

MONUMENTS

Monuments as physical entities come in a variety of forms. Most commonly, perhaps, monuments are envisaged as memorials, things related to a person or past events, such as graveyard furniture, follies, war memorials or statues. Although apparently straight-forward in their purpose, even modern memorials, such as that in Broken Hill, New South Wales, Australia commemorating those who fought in the First World War can have contested meanings, in this case a proud monument for a newly formed nation

1 Dyffryn Ardudwy. Dolmen complex, Merioneth

or for others a symbol of capitalist war-mongerers (Rainbird 2003). Monuments then are sites for interpretation and have potential for a variety of meanings. Interpretation, at least on first view, can depend on direction of approach, distance of observation and other variables, including weather conditions. Even monuments which are not yet built have the ability to be affective where a community has the expectation that one should be built and a person or event has not been marked properly until this is done or where a space exists, such as the empty fourth plinth in Trafalgar Square, London, which has caused a huge amount of debate regarding an appropriate permanent monument.

In archaeology monuments can be monumental in scale, but they do not have to be. A preferred definition is that a monument is a physical residue of past human activity. Mike Parker Pearson's paper in this volume considers the social context of Neolithic and Early Bronze Age Wessex in relation to both the evidence for the upstanding monuments of earth and stone and the excavated features at and between the upstanding sites which had no surface trace but, included the rare evidence of houses from this period. Residues of past human activity are the basic elements for archaeology whether upstanding, excavated or surface finds. The monumental suite also consists of written documents and the chapters in this volume by Alex Woolf and Bob Dodgshon take these as primary source materials; Yannis Hamilakis draws on the records provided in photographic form. Zoë Crossland and her co-authors in tracing the fascinating context of a graveyard monument note in passing that the Welsh language has too been considered a monument, this time representing the nation of Wales.

Although the sites may no longer be visible as upstanding monuments, Chris Fenton-Thomas and Toby Driver show us how in prehistory the sites could be the focus of activity over long periods, with people remembering them and returning over generations, something that recent work on some of the still-standing and monumental structures of Wessex long barrows is, perhaps paradoxically, indicating did not always happen (see, e.g., Whittle and Bayliss 2007). Mary-Ann Owoc shows that where some sites may be obvious upstanding monuments it is only through excavation that the complexities of their histories and in particular the reasons for their siting at specific locations can be understood. In her paper regarding Portuguese megalithic tombs Ivone Canavilhas draws inspiration from observations made by Andrew Fleming early in his publishing career that megalithic tombs could say much about the local social conditions in which they were constructed, rather than being generalised types reflecting received ideas as they were passed from one community to the next.

LANDSCAPE

Given the developed nature of some of the projects reported in this volume it may be surprising for some readers to realise that the sub-discipline of landscape archaeology is a relatively recent phenomenon. Recent reviews by Fleming (2006) and Johnson (2007) illustrate a move in Britain from site-based archaeology, to the recording of 'field archaeology' and a developing recognition of an archaeology of landscape in the 1970s and early 1980s. As Briggs's paper in this volume shows, it is not that the upstanding archaeology was ignored by antiquarians, the seventeenth-century recording of Avebury by William Stukeley being an early example, but it was the evolution of a set of techniques of field survey and mapping, allied to aerial photography, which gave a coherence to 'humps and bumps' (more than the obvious monuments) and which allowed for their interpretation (to a certain extent) in their own right, without the requirement of excavation. There was a recognition of a stratigraphy to be found in the observation of surface features, what a number of authors in this volume (see Bradley and Fulford; Williamson; Barnatt; Gledhill and Nichol; and Young and Webster) call a 'palimpsest', like the writings on a page re-used many times where the underlying scribbles can still be partially ascertained, leading to a knowledge of the multiple layers that have gone before.

Collis (this volume) illustrates well how landscape archaeology is a typically British tradition, but Fleming (2006) has illustrated a concern that landscape archaeology

2 Dartmoor reave, truncated by road and picked out in snow melt

has become fragmented in its short life, with what he calls 'post-processual landscape archaeology', mostly conducted by British prehistorians, reading much more into the landscape. This issue is picked up in the very different chapters by Owoc dealing with prehistoric monuments in south-west England and Pluciennik looking at modern landscapes in central Sicily and with both illustrating, I think, that the 'traditional' baby has not been thrown out with the bathwater. The critical field and desk skills of landscape archaeologists are still essential to all varieties of landscape archaeology, but the interpretive framework can have widely divergent influences.

A number of chapters in this book look at specific parcels of landscape in England, from Salisbury Plain (Bradley and Fulford), through East Anglia (Williamson), the Peak District (Barnatt) and on to County Durham (Gledhill and Nichol; Young and Webster) and all of the authors recognise the influence of Fleming's work in identifying the traces of abandoned houses and fields in the uplands of Dartmoor and Swaledale. The earlier of the two projects was on Dartmoor where the Bronze Age antiquity and extent of ancient field boundaries (locally known as 'reaves') (2) was identified over several seasons of fieldwork (see also Collis, this volume). Although there are numerous academic publications related to this project (see final chapter, this volume) the subsequent book, *The Dartmoor Reaves: investigating prehistoric land divisions*, was awarded the British Archaeology Book of the Year Award for 1990 and, in recognition of its influential status, has since been published in a second edition (Fleming 2007).

Work on the uplands of England and then later the Atlantic island of St Kilda has led Fleming to consider perceptions of marginality and mobility. That the uplands may not be permanent centres of settlement at various times in the past has meant consideration of transhumance when domestic animals may have been taken to the uplands for summer grazing (see also Collis this volume for examples in France). Peter Herring (this volume) postulates the use of prehistoric stone alignments as guides, among other functions, to upland common pastures on Bodmin Moor, whereas Sarah Tarlow and Mark Pluciennik use the archaeology of inland areas to identify different histories of inland areas often perceived as marginal to the centres of settlement and use.

'NATURAL' MONUMENTS

Fleming's third major fieldwork project has taken him over several seasons to the archipelago of St Kilda, located approximately 65km west of the Outer Hebrides islands of Scotland in the Atlantic Ocean. In 1930 the inhabitants of St Kilda were evacuated from the island following fears for the viability and safety of the community. The islanders of St Kilda became renowned through popular literature for the egalitarian nature of their social organisation, a supposed response to the apparent isolation of the archipelago, and the dare devil climbing skills of the men in collecting extensive archive research, has led to Fleming in various publications, but especially in the book *St Kilda and the Wider World: tales of an iconic island* (2005), to challenge the popular perception of isolation and bring St Kilda strongly into debates concerning the issue as to whether islands have a peculiar role in shaping local communities (see, e.g., Rainbird 2007).

Islands may have had other roles in the past and Gabriel Cooney (2004) has proposed that some islands, for example, the distinctive dome-shaped island of Ailsa Craig in the Firth of Clyde, Scotland, may have been thought of as monuments by prehistoric communities. This idea is related to a more general point that the distinction between constructed monuments and features already in the landscape may not be as clearly defined as it is often stated to be in modern western societies (see Owoc, this volume). In the Preseli Mountains of south-west Wales, the source of the Stonehenge bluestones, piles of stones normally associated with freestanding prehistoric cairns have been piled against and around distinctive stone outcrops (themselves named 'carns'). The constructed cairn and the stone outcrop may have been of equal significance to the prehistoric peoples of the area. A number of these have been recorded in archaeological survey of this upland area and given the type name of 'outcrop cairns' (Darvill, Morgan Evans and Wainwright 2003). Elsewhere in Wales, and western Britain more generally, there appear to be clear associations between ancient megalithic monuments and stone outcrops beyond a direct source of quarry stone (3). Peter Herring (this volume) provides an example of how stone alignments may have led prehistoric peoples to specific views of the variety of distinctive granite tors on Bodmin Moor. Working in the same area Barbara Bender and colleagues also showed that the framing of views to distinctive hill and ridge top features, either constructed cairns or stone outcrops, could be found through the doorways of round houses and was thus not restricted to 'ceremonial' monuments (Bender, Hamilton and Tilley 1997).

British prehistorian Richard Bradley in a number of publications (see, e.g., 1993; 1998a; 1998b; and 2000) has discussed the 'monument as landscape' recognising that in the stone worlds of the Neolithic and Early Bronze Age distinctions between piles of stone created by geological and geomorphological processes and those piles made by humans may not have been clearly defined. Certainly there are many claims of specific alignments made between the entrances of megalithic tombs and landscape features, or the perceived preference for an inter-visibility between monuments of similar types, but Bradley (1998a) has also noted that in their construction prehistoric monuments can be seen to have two potential differences, one where a key concern for the builders was the landscape context and the second where the key concern was the skyscape. Above we have seen many examples of terrestrial monuments, but celestial monuments are those constructed with heavenly bodies in mind, particularly the sun and the moon, once again the prime example

3 Coetan Arthur. Megalithic tomb on St David's Head, Pembrokeshire

being Stonehenge. A recent rediscovery of a midsummer sunrise alignment is that of the megalithic passage grave of Bryn Celli Ddu on Anglesey, Wales (Burrow 2006; see also Owoc, this volume).

MONUMENTS IN THE LANDSCAPE

As this volume and previous works illustrate, monuments in the landscape come in many forms. Monuments built of marble and deriving from Classical Greece are at one end of the spectrum, but the megalithic tombs or 'squatter' houses of the Welsh uplands are no less monuments. We also need to be aware that monuments may only be a construction of the mind, particularly in relation to the myths generated in regard to sacred geographies. For example, Uluru (Ayers Rock) in central Australia is a great sandstone monolith, but although not erected by human hands, forms a very strong part of the origin stories (sometimes glossed 'Dreamtime') for the Aboriginal communities of the region. Monuments in the landscape provide pathways to multiple histories and some, influenced more or less by Andrew Fleming, are presented in this volume.

BIBLIOGRAPHY

Bender, B., 1998 *Stonehenge: making space*. Oxford: Berg.

Bender, B., Hamilton, S. & Tilley, C., 1997 Leskernick: stone worlds; alternative narratives; nested landscapes. *Proceedings of the Prehistoric Society* 63, 147-78.

Bradley, R., 1993 *Altering the Earth. The origins of monuments on Britain and Continental Europe.* Edinburgh: Society of Antiquaries of Scotland.

Bradley, R., 1998a *The Significance of Monuments. On the shaping of human experience in Neolithic and Bronze Age Europe.* London: Routledge.

Bradley, R., 1998b Ruined buildings, ruined stones: enclosures, tombs and natural places in the Neolithic of south-west England. *World Archaeology* 30, 13-22.

Bradley, R., 2000 *An Archaeology of Natural Places.* London: Routledge.

Burrow, S., 2006 *The Tomb Builders in Wales 4000-3000 BC.* Cardiff: National Museum of Wales.

Cooney, G., 2004 Neolithic worlds; islands in the Irish Sea. In Cummings, V. & Fowler, C. (eds), 145-59.

Cummings, V. & Fowler, C. (eds), 2004 *The Neolithic of the Irish Sea: materiality and traditions of practice*, 145-59. Oxford: Oxbow.

Darvill, T., Morgan Evans, D. & Wainwright, G., 2003 Strumble-Preseli ancient communities and environment study (SPACES): second report 2003. *Archaeology in Wales* 43, 3-12.

Fleming, A., 2005 *St. Kilda and the Wider World: Tales of an iconic island.* Macclesfield: Windgather Press.

Fleming, A., 2006 Post-processual landscape archaeology: a critique. *Cambridge Archaeological Journal* 16, 267-80.

Fleming, A., 2007 *The Dartmoor Reaves: investigating prehistoric land divisions*, second edition. Macclesfield: Windgather.

Johnson, M., 2007 *Ideas of Landscape*. Oxford: Blackwells.

Rainbird, P., 2003 Representing nation, dividing community: the Broken Hill War Memorial, New South Wales, Australia. *World Archaeology* 35, 22-34.

Rainbird, P., 2007 *The Archaeology of Islands.* Cambridge: Cambridge University Press.

Whittle, A. & Bayliss, A. 2007 The times of their lives: from chronological precision to kinds of history and change. *Cambridge Archaeological Journal* 17, 21-8.

2

TIME AND TIME AGAIN: LIVING IN THE NEOLITHIC LANDSCAPE AT SEWERBY COTTAGE FARM, BRIDLINGTON, EAST YORKSHIRE

Chris Fenton-Thomas

East Yorkshire is one of the key areas in Britain for Neolithic archaeology. The Yorkshire Wolds in particular has a range of ceremonial monuments with enough variety and complexity to rival anything known from Wessex. Despite the many monuments and the hundreds of thousands of artefacts, there are very few known occupation sites. As a result, we know very little about where the people that built and used the monuments were actually living. Recent excavations in Bridlington have discovered extensive Neolithic remains including buildings, dump layers and pits spread out across the landscape. We will consider the nature of this habitation and in particular the ways in which people revisited this place, over several centuries throughout the second half of the fourth millennium BC (*c.*3500-3000 BC).

Bridlington lies at the mouth of the Gypsey Race stream whose valley is littered with Neolithic ceremonial monuments. Duggleby Howe is close to the stream's source and it is one of several great round barrows along the valley. Further monuments are known at Rudston, seven kilometres west of Bridlington, where a group of cursus monuments converge on a bend in the Gypsey Race. Because of the ready availability of good quality knapping-flint, the ploughsoils of the north-eastern Wolds are strewn with struck flakes (Durden 1995). In most cases these durable artefacts are all that is left of the sites where flint production must have taken place during the period between *c.*4000 and 2500 BC.

NEOLITHIC SETTLEMENT IN EAST YORKSHIRE

Neolithic occupation sites in the region are rare. Three sites were excavated in the 1950s and 1960s where pottery, flint and other artefacts were found alongside hearths, hollows and pits (Moore 1964; Manby 1957, 1958). Two were close to Driffield and

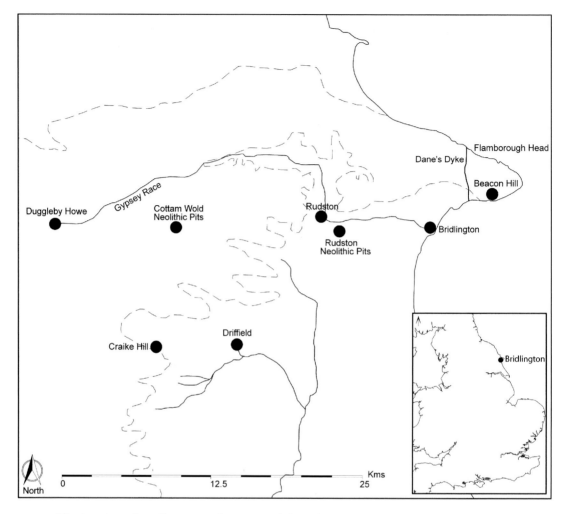

4 The location of Bridlington within East Yorkshire showing various sites mentioned in the text. The contour is at 60m AOD

a third at Beacon Hill lay on top of the cliffs between Flamborough Head and Bridlington. There was no evidence for any actual buildings on these sites but the combination of hearths and artefacts was the closest thing to actual occupation activity. The ephemeral nature of the features and un-structured character of the remains stands in contrast to the formal deposition and massive constructions of the monuments. As well as these sites there are clusters of Neolithic pits known from the ridge to the south of Rudston village (*4*). Others are concentrated on higher ground around Cottam or along the valley floor of the Garton-Wetwang Slack, just west of Driffield. The pits produced rich assemblages of pottery and flint as well as charred plant remains (Manby 1975). They date from periods throughout the Neolithic.

When Terry Manby first discussed the pits he thought that they represented occupation sites. He argued that the contents of the pits were made up of rubbish and 'hearth sweepings' gathered up and placed in the ground (Manby 1975, 48). A decade or so later, another view became dominant. Julian Thomas (1999) and others argued that Neolithic pits should be understood more for their symbolic meaning than their functional role. They argued that the pits had been deliberately backfilled with selected material as a means of marking special events or places in the landscape. Several more recent discussions have concluded that, whilst the pits were deliberately backfilled, the material used to fill them may have actually been regular rubbish gathered up from larger middens (Garrow et al. 2005; Harding 2006). This view takes nothing away from the symbolism inherent in digging and filling pits. However, it does imply that the pit-sites were not simply ceremonial places but were inhabited. The pits themselves may be all that is left of the places where people were living.

DWELLINGS IN NEOLITHIC BRITAIN

The lack of archaeological evidence for houses or dwellings is a common theme in Neolithic archaeology. For England and Wales there are a relatively small number of houses (Darvill and Thomas 1996) in contrast to places like Orkney, Ireland and parts of Scotland (Armit et al. 2003). Despite certain differences in emphasis, the prevailing model for Neolithic habitation in England is that groups were not living in fixed permanent settlements but instead were moving around from place to place (Whittle 1997). This much is generally accepted although the nature of this mobility has by no means been agreed upon. The small number of known buildings has been explained by the fact that they were temporary structures and therefore did not leave durable traces in the archaeological record. We could ask therefore, what of the houses that have survived: should they be seen as evidence for unusual examples of more fixed occupation? Well not necessarily, as disagreement reigns around whether the known buildings were actually dwellings (Thomas 1996) or indeed whether the scant remains for some of the buildings have actually been over-interpreted (Gibson 2003). In many cases buildings exist in exceptional preserving conditions as at Trelystan where they were preserved beneath later barrows (Gibson 1996). Recent discoveries at Durrington Walls show that people here were living amongst the monuments and the build up of an extensive midden suggests a long period of occupation (Parker Pearson et al. 2005; and Parker Pearson this volume). This may not of course have been continuous and many questions remain unanswered.

The lack of a wide range of good quality evidence for Neolithic habitation means that interpretations remain generalised, vague and at best hopeful. Several recent discussions point to the 'temporality' of occupation as a key area for debate (Pollard 1999; Garrow et al. 2005). Put simply, temporality is the degree to which occupation was mobile or fixed. This is not only the length of time spent at one place by a resident group but also the time that passed between visits to the same place. It concerns the rhythm of settlement mobility in the landscape. A proper understanding of temporality should give equal weight to the seasonal movements within a single year, the annual changes from year to year, the shifts of lifetimes or between generations and the long-term ancestral cycles that are played out across centuries and more. The quality of dating and phasing of Neolithic occupation sites is rarely good enough to differentiate between these overlapping time scales. Pollard (1999) points out that we should not expect a single model of temporality across Britain but a complicated set of overlapping practices. The recent discussion of pits at Kilverstone emphasises the point. Here, groups came back to the same place intermittently over several centuries (Garrow *et al.* 2005).

SEWERBY COTTAGE FARM SITE

If people and groups were 'moving on and moving around' (Whittle 1997) then how can we see their occupation sites archaeologically? If the buildings they erected were ephemeral structures like tents or yurts, which left little impression below the ground, how will the sites register on the archaeological record? The discoveries at Sewerby Cottage Farm do not challenge the conventional wisdom about Neolithic habitation but they may allow us to explore this idea of the 'temporality' of occupation more fully. The remains do include some buildings but there were many more ephemeral features that could not be reconciled into actual structures. The Neolithic archaeology, which also included pits and dump layers, reflected occupation activity spread over at least 500 years (Fenton-Thomas forthcoming). This was not continuous however as several distinct phases were recognised. In one part of the site, trench 17, the occupation sequence was represented by over a metre of stratigraphy where layers and features were overlain upon each other within a large natural hollow (5). This seems to reflect a series of visits to the same place. However, it was very hard to establish the length of each episode or the gap between each visit.

The nature of the Neolithic archaeology was different between two areas of the site, separated from one another by about 300m. The northern zone produced distinctive groups of pits, which were often rich in finds of pottery and flint. By contrast, trench 17, in the southern part of the site, contained none of these artefact-rich pits. Here the bulk of the finds were abraded or broken and came from extensive dump layers. On the site as a whole, people did not live here permanently but tended to move on and then return. The two questions we will address both relate to the temporality of that occupation during the second half of the fourth millennium BC. The first is how long people stayed in one place and the second is whether we can see different forms of occupation across the landscape.

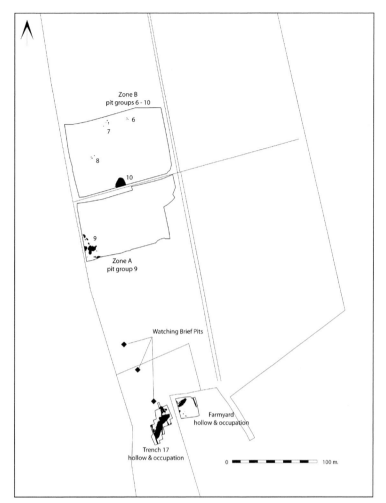

Zone B
pit groups 6 - 10

6

7

8

10

9

Zone A
pit group 9

Watching Brief Pits

Farmyard
hollow & occupation

Trench 17
hollow & occupation

0   100 m.

5 The area covered by the excavations at Sewerby Cottage Farm showing former field boundaries. The Neolithic pits were found in zones A and B in the north of the site whilst the Neolithic buildings and dumps were found in the hollow of trench 17, to the south

The site covered an area of 16 hectares on the northern outskirts of Bridlington and had previously been farmland. Most of the fields were arable but a small paddock next to the farmhouse was pasture. The ridge and furrow earthworks in this field showed that it had escaped the deeper ploughing of recent times. The most well-preserved Neolithic remains were found in this paddock in trench 17, where the deposits and features were contained within a natural hollow in the clay subsoil. Another smaller hollow was investigated in the old farmyard 10m east of here. In both of the hollows there were groups of postholes and pits, which were sealed by layers containing flint flakes and pottery. In the trench 17 hollow there were four phases of activity each one separated from the next by dump layers. According to the small number of radiocarbon dates, the earliest of these phases dated from the middle of the fourth millennium BC (*c*.3500) whilst the final phase took place at the beginning of the third millennium BC (*c*.3000).

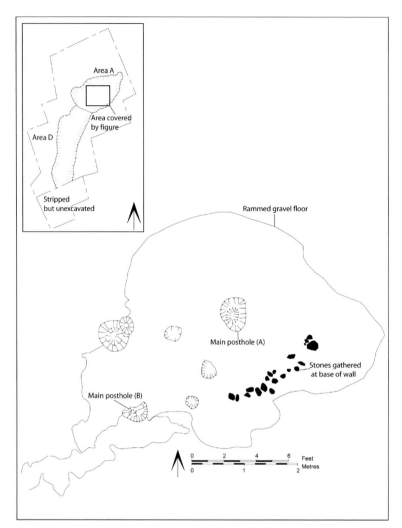

6 The earlier of the two buildings mentioned in the text. The main postholes (A) and (B) are marked as is the line of stones that may have gathered along the base of the perishable wall

The clearest evidence for buildings came from the third phase in the trench 17 sequence, phase 1c. The remains came from the northern end of the hollow. The main building was oval in plan and measured roughly 5m x 4m (6). It was defined by a rammed gravel surface that had been laid in the centre of the hollow. This surface was interpreted as the floor of the building. Given that there were no surviving remains of the walls, the extent of the floor was the best indication of the limits of the structure. Two successive layers had built up on top of this surface and all three deposits occupied roughly the same spatial extent (7). The implication was that the surface and the layers were all laid down at different times but within the walls of the same building. This probably took place when the structure was re-built, which seems to have happened at least once. The oval building had two main structural supports, both of which had been cut through this floor. An arc of four less substantial postholes probably supported

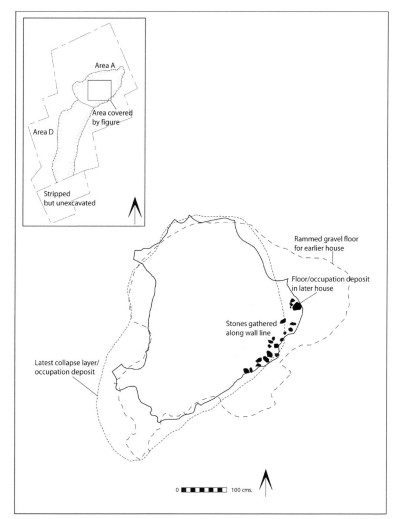

7 The continuity of buildings evident through the overlapping floor layers and occupation deposits. The latest layer was probably a collapse layer following the abandonment of the later house

an internal screen. On the south side of the floor there was a line of stones and this matched with the edge of the layer that had built up above the gravel surface. Our interpretation of this was that the layer had built up within the walls of the building, either as a later floor or as an occupation deposit, and that the stones had gathered here at the base of the now perished wall. The two main supports could have supported a domed frame of flexible poles, which may have been covered in hides or thatch. This would have left little impression in the ground around the edges of the building.

Both of the main postholes were re-cut indicating that new structural timbers had been erected in almost exactly the same positions (8). The structure was re-built but the construction method was altered slightly. The earlier building was supported by two central timber uprights whilst the second structure was built around a small timber frame represented by a cross pattern of five postholes. The deepest posthole

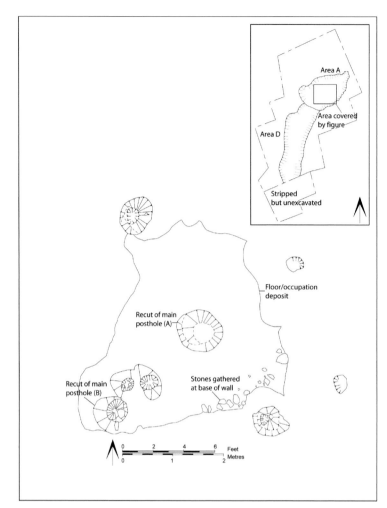

Area A

Area covered by figure

Area D

Stripped but unexcavated

Floor/occupation deposit

Recut of main posthole (A)

Recut of main posthole (B)

Stones gathered at base of wall

0   2   4   6   Feet
0   1   2   Metres

8 The later of the two buildings, built on exactly the same spot. The main postholes (A) and (B) were re-cut and the same wall lines appear to have been used, although this building was supported by a timber frame evident from the cross pattern of postholes

(posthole A) at the centre of the cross pattern had also been the main posthole for the earlier structure. Although the actual walls did not survive their limits were fossilised by deposits that had built up within them. This continuity and the re-cutting of the main postholes suggest this was a modification of an existing structure rather than a new building. This obviously raises questions about the permanence of settlement. Our first impression of this re-build was that people had lived here for several years and re-built the structure when it had needed repairing. However, we do not know exactly how much time had elapsed between re-builds. It is possible that people had returned to the structure following a short period of abandonment. This would fit with the movements of an itinerant group who moved around the landscape returning to familiar locales time and again. The dating evidence was not precise enough to say, but the similarity in the location of the walls between the two structures suggested that the gap between re-builds was tens of years rather than hundreds. It could, of course, have been considerably less than this. Whilst the sequence of building was fairly well understood, the function of the buildings was not so clear. Crucially, despite the good preservation of floor layers there was no evidence of any hearths.

In the northern part of the site, 300m away from trench 17 and the farmyard, the Neolithic archaeology was very different. Here there were five groups of pits, each one spatially distinct from the next. Four of the groups had between three and five pits and some produced relatively large assemblages of pottery and worked flint. Each pit within a group had been dug and filled around the same time, whereas the groups were not contemporary with one another. The radiocarbon dates from hazelnuts and carbonised residues on the pottery showed that each group was quite different in date and that, where dating evidence existed, the pits from the same group were broadly contemporary. The styles of pottery were often the same *within* groups and different *between* groups. The earliest cluster, for instance, contained sherds of Towthorpe Ware whilst later groups produced Peterborough Ware or Grooved Ware. The pits ranged in date from between the middle of the fourth millennium BC and the early centuries of the third millennium. In the southern areas, none of the pits contained pottery and few even produced flint. The pottery from trench 17 and the farmyard came instead from dump layers. The sherds in these layers were abraded with many different styles from different periods mixed together in the same deposit.

TIME AND TIME AGAIN

So why was the archaeology so different between the two parts of the site? With Julian Thomas's ideas in mind, it was tempting to see the northern area occupied by the pits as a ceremonial space, in contrast with the occupation areas to the south. However, recent discussions have argued that pit assemblages like these are likely to reflect occupation activity (Garrow *et al.* 2005; Harding 2006). The contents of the pits at Kilverstone, for instance, have been closely analysed. Duncan Garrow has reached the conclusion here that each artefact was not individually selected and placed in the pit. Instead, the pits contained groups of broken pottery and flint gathered from nearby residue piles, following breakage and discard as part of regular habitation. At Sewerby Cottage Farm, the pottery from the pits was unabraded with large sherds in fresh condition often from the same vessel in the same pit. However, there were no complete vessels in any of the pits and it also appears to be material that had first been dumped on middens or rubbish piles. Handfuls or baskets full of this midden material were probably gathered up and placed in the pits. So if the pits did reflect occupation, how can we explain the difference between the two parts of the site? Was the nature of occupation different? In the pits, the fresh condition of the pottery, the presence of joining sherds and some refitting flints suggested that this material had not been placed on the midden for long before it was put into the pit.

This may be the crucial difference then between the north and south of the site. In the northern area, the residues of occupation were first put on a rubbish pile. Some of this material was then placed in a pit but this must have happened fairly quickly. In the southern area, the finds were mixed, broken and abraded. Here, the middens must have been manipulated, moved about and re-deposited several times before the dumps containing the finds were made in the hollows.

We know that the trench 17 hollow was re-visited and re-occupied several times between the middle of the fourth millennium BC and the beginning of the third. Here, occupation took place on the same site as previous habitations leading to stratified archaeology. In the northern areas however, the occupation sites did not overlap. Each visit chose a separate and slightly different locale. The occupation represented by the northern pits may have been much more temporary than that to the south. The northern pit groups contained unabraded and often joining sherds that were relatively large in size. By contrast, the dumps from trench 17 and the farmyard produced broken, abraded and mixed assemblages of finds. The differences in the finds may have been caused by the varying lengths of time they spent on middens. This could in turn reflect a different temporality of occupation between the two areas. In the northern area, the periods of habitation were short and discrete. In the southern area, periods of habitation were longer and tended to occupy the same location each time.

The significance of this site is that there was a variety of evidence spread out across the landscape indicating several different temporalities of occupation. The discoveries suggest that occupation was mobile and that people did not live here continuously but stayed here for varying lengths of time. In spite of this, there was a strong fixedness to certain places that persisted for centuries. These places were not continuously occupied and they must have been grassed over and empty of people for long periods. When they were not being lived in, however, they were still known about as people kept coming back to them. This project has looked at a small piece of a landscape that was probably full of people. Even in this small window we have been able to see several different scales of temporality played out over time and across space. If this pattern were projected across the country, the Neolithic landscape would have been busy with different groups inhabiting a series of places in many different ways.

BIBLIOGRAPHY

Armit, I., Murphy, E., Nelis, E. & Simpson, D., 2003 *Neolithic Settlement in Ireland and Western Britain*. Oxford: Oxbow Books.
Brück, J. & Goodman, M. (eds), 1999 *Making Places in the Prehistoric World: Themes in Settlement Archaeology*. London: UCL Press.
Darvill, T. & Thomas, J. (eds), 1996 *Neolithic Houses in North West Europe and Beyond*. Oxford: Oxbow.
Fenton-Thomas, C., forthcoming *A Place by the Sea: Neolithic, Late Iron Age and Romano-British occupation at Sewerby Cottage Farm, Bridlington*. Leeds: Yorkshire Archaeology Society.

Garrow, D., Beadsmore, A. & Knight, M., 2005 Pit Clusters and the temporality of occupation: an earlier Neolithic site at Kilverstone, Thetford, Norfolk. *Proceedings of the Prehistoric Society* 71, 139-57.

Gibson, A., 1996 The later Neolithic structures at Trelystan, Powys, Wales: ten years on. In Darvill, T. & Thomas, J. (eds), 133-41.

Gibson, A., 2003 What do we mean by Neolithic settlement? Some approaches, ten years on. In, Armit, I., Murphy, E., Nelis, E. & Simpson, D. (eds), 136-45.

Harding, J., 2006 Pit-digging, occupation and structured deposition on Rudston Wold, Eastern Yorkshire. *Oxford Journal of Archaeology* 25, 109-26.

Manby, T.G., 1957 A Neolithic site at Driffield, East Riding of Yorkshire. *Yorkshire Archaeological Journal* 39, 169-78.

Manby, T.G., 1958 A Neolithic site at Craike Hill, Garton Slack, East Riding of Yorkshire. *Antiquaries Journal* 38, 223-36.

Manby T.G., 1975 Neolithic occupation sites on the Yorkshire Wolds. *Yorkshire Archaeological Journal* 47, 23-59.

Moore, J.W., 1964 Excavations at Beacon Hill, Flamborough Head. *Yorkshire Archaeological Journal* 41, 191-202

Parker Pearson, M., Pollard, J., Tilley, C., Thomas, J., Richards, C. & Welham, K., 2005 *The Stonehenge Riverside Project: Interim Report 2005.* www.shef.ac.uk/archaeology/research/land-env/index.html

Pollard, J., 1999 These places have their moments: thoughts on settlement practices in the British Neolithic. In Brück, J. & Goodman, M. (eds), 76-93.

Thomas, J., 1996 Neolithic houses in mainland Britain and Ireland – a sceptical view. In Darvill, T. and Thomas, J. (eds), 1-12.

Topping, P. (ed.), 1997 *Neolithic Landscapes.* Oxford: Oxbow.

Whittle, A., 1997 Moving on and moving around: Neolithic settlement mobility. In Topping, P. (ed.), 14-22.

3

CHIEFTAINS AND PASTORALISTS IN NEOLITHIC AND BRONZE AGE WESSEX: A REVIEW

Mike Parker Pearson

As Fleming (2004) rightly observes, the issue of social organisation in Neolithic and Bronze Age Wessex at the time of Stonehenge has been contentious ever since the 'Explanation of Culture Change' conference in Sheffield in 1972. I'm not sure I agree, however, with Fleming's explanation for the growing critique of the chiefdom interpretation during the 1980s as representing 'the most easily identifiable archaeological expression of Thatcherism' (2004, 144). I think that it may have more to do with the inter-generational antipathy of the New Archaeologists and the post-processualists, exacerbated by the growing gulf between British and American archaeologists' uses of social theory at that time. It's always an attractive – and necessary – strategy to locate archaeological trends within their political and economic context, but for me the big divide that hit archaeology in the early 1980s was founded on the break from functionalist and social evolutionist thinking that was made in the other humanities in the previous decade – archaeology is always the last to jump on the bandwagon.

I think that the chiefdom question also came to be perceived as being all about form and not about content. Focusing on chiefs and social organisation meant that we no longer had to worry about what Stonehenge was actually *for*, since all that mattered was the level of evolutionary complexity that enabled its construction. This concern with social evolution stopped us from examining the more tantalising questions about meaning and purpose, or from developing more fully contextual investigations in which architecture, art, ceramics, food preparation, gender, technology and many other aspects of Neolithic life had important contributions to make to our understanding of the society of prehistoric Wessex.

Of course, the other problem has been the annoying ambiguity of the archaeological evidence for social organisation in prehistoric Wessex. I can remember back in the late 1970s, Arthur ApSimon, one of our lecturers at Southampton University, pouring scorn on our professor, Colin Renfrew's claims that the necessary mobilisation of labour for monument building was evidence for group-oriented chiefdoms – for him this was a leap of faith which had little support from the archaeological evidence. When compared to the classic chiefdom formulations for Mesoamerica, Hawaii and even Bronze Age Denmark in terms of large-scale craft specialisation, strong evidence for social status distinctions, large settlements with chiefly residences etc. (Earle 1991), the impoverished material culture record from Wessex hasn't produced any particularly strong evidence for a chiefdom society, except for the monuments themselves. Perhaps it is no wonder that Tim Earle didn't include Wessex as a case study in his book *Bronze Age Economics* (2002). As Fleming (2004) spotted, I've always been ambivalent about the inference of chieftains and social hierarchies in Wessex in the later third millennium BC.

Yet the issue is something of an archaeological standoff in which the supporters of theories of prehistoric 'elites' are ranged against those who downplay social distinctions and chiefdom-style organisation as the mechanism for megalith building. Reading Brian Hayden's cultural ecological explanation of Stonehenge as a product of elite competition (2003), I find it somewhat ironic that a North American should be so prepared to attribute monument building to class division, whereas British colleagues such as Mark Edmonds (1999), Josh Pollard (Pollard and Reynolds 2002, 121) and Julian Thomas (1999) have downplayed its influence in prehistory.

I think we need to re-examine the evidence for social distinction in southern Britain between 2500 and 2000 cal. BC.

MEGALITHS AND MANAGERS

I've attended some pretty chaotic megalith raisings in my time: everyone shouting, the old ones standing at the back shaking their heads ('you don't want to do it like that!'), and the young men drunk and pulling in different directions. That was how it was when we put up a standing stone in Ankiliabo in southern Madagascar in 2000. Yet there was always someone in charge: someone had to choose the date and send out messages to call the kin together; someone was providing the animals for sacrifice, feeding the vast crowd, and directing – however ineffectively – the moving of large stones. Mobilising labour and moving megaliths requires authority, be it temporary, personal control of the event in question or a long-term and institutionalised structure. As I've written about elsewhere (1998; 2000; 2003; Parker Pearson and Godden 2002), this example of contemporary megalith building in southern Madagascar takes place in a community strongly egalitarian in ethos; the hierarchical nature of clan structure and kinship organisation is considerably diminished from the former slave-based chiefdoms in previous centuries. Those powerful and warlike chiefdoms of the seventeenth to mid-nineteenth centuries in southern Madagascar were, however, not

9 Stonehenge continues to raise questions about the level of social organisation required to build it. *Photograph by Julian Thomas*

megalith building societies. Furthermore, it would be hard for an archaeologist to find clear evidence of the social distinctions between chiefs, commoners and slaves in that hierarchical chiefdom society without the ethnohistorical records. This is just one of no doubt many examples where chiefdom organisation does not appear plainly in the diet, burial record, artefactual assemblages or architecture. The cautionary message is clear – just because we can't recover the evidence doesn't mean that it wasn't so.

So what can we make of Stonehenge and associated monuments and labour mobilisation? (9). The sheer size of the Stonehenge sarsens is so much greater than those dragged in contemporary or recent times in places such as Madagascar, Toraja and Sumba (Parker Pearson and Ramilisonina 1998; Hoskins 1986). The distances (up to 20 miles for the sarsens and 140 miles for the much smaller Welsh bluestones) are also considerably further than their equivalents in other parts of the world.

Our current view is that Stonehenge was just part of a much larger programme of construction in the twenty-sixth century BC which also involved the building of the Southern Circle at Durrington Walls (*10*). The stone phase at Stonehenge is probably even older than some prehistorians have thought, dating to 2620-2480 cal. BC (Allen and Bayliss 1995; Bayliss *et al.* 1977; Parker Pearson *et al.* forthcoming), well before the elaborate burials of Wessex I (*c.*2200-1800 BC) and even before Beaker burials of *c.*2400-2000 BC, such as that of the Amesbury Archer (Fitzpatrick 2000).

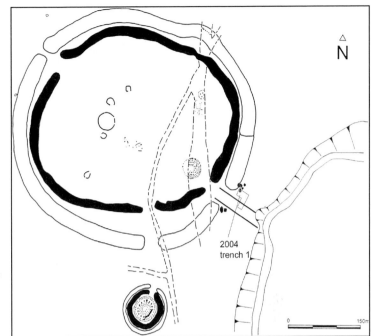

10 Durrington Walls is a henge enclosure with four suspected entrances, two of which were blocked in prehistory. *Drawn by Irene de Luis*

The preparation of equipment and materials for the construction of Stonehenge and Durrington Walls (ropes, timber posts, axes, antler picks, sledges and cradles) must have taken many people many years. That's before we even think about the quarrying, dragging, dressing, erection and raising of upright and lintel stones, and equivalent tasks with timber posts – activities requiring a cast of thousands over many years.

How might we arrive at a more detailed understanding of the necessary social organisation, beyond that of person-hours of labour investment? The carriage of bluestones from South Wales to Wessex is currently reckoned to have been a human achievement (but see Burl 2006 for continuing support for the glacial hypothesis) and it must have required long-distance organisation for unimpeded passage whether by land or water.

Julian Richards has demonstrated that each of the Stonehenge sarsens could be transported by a team of 200 (Richards and Whitby 1997). Perhaps more intriguingly, our recent investigation of the banked and ditched henge enclosure at Durrington Walls gives some notion of how work parties may have been arranged to co-operate in a collective venture.

The geophysical surveys of the henge have highlighted the uneven nature of the sides of its ditch (Payne 2003). In plan the ditch appears something like a string of 40m-long sausages, suggestive of the gang-digging that is inferred for the causewayed enclosures of an earlier millennium (Edmonds 1999). In 2005-6 we excavated the henge bank at one of these breaks and found that both gang-dug segments were built contemporaneously, with chalk deposited near contemporaneously either side of the ditch demarcating the division between the two work gangs. In 1967, Geoff Wainwright excavated one of these ditch segments in the south terminal of the east entrance and found 57 antler picks left on the ditch bottom; it seems likely these were tools downed at the end of the job (Wainwright with Longworth 1971). If that represents 57 pick workers, then maybe there were three or four times that number in the work gang, with one to hold the antler pick whilst another hammered it in and the rest moving chalk and constructing the bank. The geophysical survey indicates that there are probably 22 ditch segments; if all sections were indeed dug together, that would suggest the involvement of between 3700 and 5000 workers, not to mention those making the sandwiches. The Durrington Walls ditch is interrupted by four entrances, creating four groups of ditch segments; it may be worth envisaging each group being allotted to a particular, geographically defined community, itself divisible into a series of work-gangs each responsible for their ditch section. This idea of a segmentary and tiered management structure is, of course, not new when discussing Stonehenge (Renfrew 1973) but its inscription in the layout of Durrington Walls presents it more clearly and in a way that may be amenable to further investigation (as I shall outline later).

It is a feasible hypothesis that Stonehenge and Durrington Walls were constructed by segmentary groups recruited from different geographical areas, organised into four larger groupings. Not only would this have been a major organisational challenge but it must also have endured over decades. Quite possibly, people spent entire lives engaged in this overall undertaking of moving stones and timbers, erecting lintels, dressing stones and digging ditches. Someone had to organise it – was it a hereditary chief (or even a dynasty) looking for a means of self-aggrandisement or, as John Barrett (1994) suggested for Avebury, a community-led task that created hierarchy out of its implementation? Equally, was the leadership a temporary phenomenon of just a few decades or centuries or was it henceforth established in perpetuity?

DEAD MEN AND WOMEN'S TALES

As I have indicated above, we must examine all the archaeological evidence, not just the megaliths alone. What can we infer about social organisation from the remains of the dead? We often have to rely heavily on the evidence of grave goods which are relatively poor indicators of social difference (Carr 1994). As we all know, just because a grave has few or no goods makes it no certain index of that person's low social standing. Since the dead don't bury themselves it is hard to distinguish between the status of the mourners and of the deceased. Additionally, Ann Woodward (2000) has made a strong case for many Early Bronze Age grave goods being heirlooms – perhaps items that would normally be inherited ended up in the ground only because there was no suitable recipient.

Ellen Pader (1982) pointed out many years ago that we should avoid the term 'rich' when describing grave good assemblages. What may appear to be a large and elaborate grave good group – arrowheads, dagger, and antler and bone artefacts – might only have taken a few days or weeks to manufacture. Quantity of such items is no measure of social status. Many archaeologists fall into this error; in a recent example Volker Heyd (in press), in an otherwise excellent paper, infers that some of the child burials from the Beaker period in central Europe were indicators of hereditary, ascribed rank on the basis of above-average inclusions of grave goods; in fact the grave goods present generally would have required little time or effort to obtain or make.

Child burials under large mounds may indicate either hereditary social standing, or the acquired wealth/rank of the family. In prehistoric – and historical – societies with high infant mortality, we need to find an explanation for investment of labour in very few child burials. We cannot presume a difference is being expressed in the experience of grief; such burials indicate an anomalous expression of grieving, given that most infant deaths are archaeologically invisible, and, by ethnographic analogy, likely to have been interred with no great ceremony. Consequently, it is likely that the mourners were of sufficient social standing to provide a lavish burial but it does not necessarily follow that the dead child held rank of any significance (cf. Metcalf and Huntington 1991).

If we concentrate on grave goods and examine quality rather than quantity, it does seem that certain materials such as gold, copper, amber and jet had special value for people of the third millennium BC. Yet how do we judge the occurrence of just one or two items of such materials in a grave? Heyd (in press) has documented the number of gold and amber items in Beaker-period burials in central Europe and decided that these are evidence of a stratified society even though most are small and single items. Only in two instances (out of some 600 Beaker burials) in southern Germany do multiple gold artefacts co-occur in the same grave. In Britain, only a handful of Beaker-period burials have gold accoutrements; for both Britain and Europe, the sparse use of rare materials in graves leaves open the question of whether such burials are those hereditary chiefs, 'big men' or merely wealthy farmers.

What does the mortuary evidence for the third millennium BC reveal about social organisation? Firstly, few burials dating to 3000-2500 BC have yet been found in Britain. There are tiny numbers of cremations and a few river and cave finds of human bones from this period. The two largest cremation cemeteries are Dorchester-on-Thames (Atkinson *et al.* 1951) and Stonehenge (Cleal *et al.* 1995) though neither has burials that have yet been dated closely. Other than simple stone tools and bone skewer pins (which may have been personal ornaments rather than items used to contain the ashes in a bag; Cleal *et al.* 1995), grave goods are largely absent. There are no burial accompaniments to make a case for these as the remains of elite individuals, despite this being the time frame in which Stonehenge went through most of its transformations. On the other hand, perhaps the mere fact of being buried at Stonehenge was a mark of esteem merited by these few in contrast to the vast majority whose passing has left no trace whatsoever.

There are several possibilities for explaining the dearth of burials:

1) They may have been a random cross-section of the population, being the only ones to be found amongst many others buried.
2) They may have been amongst the very few who merited burial because of their high status, the majority of the dead being disposed of in an archaeologically invisible manner.
3) They may have been amongst the very few who merited burial but this was to do with circumstances of death or other factors not related to social status.

The problem of representativity also affects our grasp on the second half of that millennium. All of the inhumation and cremation graves known to date to after 2500 BC can only represent a small proportion of the dead; the majority are absent. As Alex Gibson (in press) points out, so many of these surviving burials have complex pre-interment histories, making the epithet of 'rest in peace' inapplicable for the many partial or disturbed bodies placed in graves. Burial was not the dominant rite in this period and may have been adopted by particular sections of society besides the elite if there was one. We have to be prepared for the possibility that burial was a selective fashion, adopted by some but not by all.

The Amesbury Archer has had a profound impact on our perceptions of wealth, and therefore status, after 2400 BC. Here was a great world traveller buried with the trappings of his long-distance trade relationships and sporting every type of grave good known for this period. There were over 100 non-perishable items placed in the grave, including gold earrings and three copper daggers (Fitzpatrick 2000) – this was incontrovertibly a 'rich' burial. He has been called the 'king of Stonehenge' by the popular press but he was buried the wrong side of the river, suggesting something of an outsider status. The multiple sets of goods have caused speculation that he was inserted into a re-used grave (John Barrett pers. comm.) but this is unlikely given the absence of any bones from other individuals. He and/or the funeral hosts were wealthy enough that all of these items could be discarded.

Yet these objects were trappings of wealth rather than wealth *per se*. Cattle were probably the most valuable form of currency – it is hard to see how he might have brought such wealth with him from his birthplace in the Alps (whilst cattle herds are highly mobile, we may reasonably assume some geographical limits to the movement of large numbers). To find evidence of cattle wealth in funerary contexts, we can look to the East Midlands where the 180 cattle skulls on top of a barrow at Irthlingborough

(Davis and Payne 1993) and the bones of more than 300 cattle in the ditches of a slightly later barrow at Gayhurst (Deighton 2005) provide evidence for considerable commemorative feasting. These two remarkable barrow burials demonstrate that certain families were able to draw upon considerable resources during funerary performances.

Are Amesbury, Irthlingborough and Gayhurst our missing chieftains? They might be but equally they could also have been individuals of renown – *primi inter pares* – within a society with no overall leaders. They appeared not at the time that the great public building works of Wessex and southern Britain were in full flow but when they were coming to an end. The Amesbury Archer, struggling on his gammy leg all the way from the Alpine foothills, certainly missed the erection of the sarsens at Stonehenge but may have arrived in time to witness the re-locating of the bluestone oval at Stonehenge (Phase 3iv; 2280-1930 BC) and perhaps even the building of Silbury Hill. From 2400 BC onwards, public works were replaced on the monumental front by round barrows, expressions of lineage and family ties rather than of wider allegiances.

One of the dimensions of status that has been under-estimated is that of gender. The first results of our Beaker People Project are demonstrating a clear nutritional difference between the sexes. This distinction gives new insight into the gender differences in inhumation burials first noticed by Leckie Shepherd in 1975 (Tuckwell 1975). Our more recent studies confirm that men were normally buried on their left sides and women on their right sides in the Beaker period. She had also noticed that beakers placed with men are often slightly different in form to those placed with women. The initial dietary information from the Beaker People Project, derived from dental microwear and δ^{15} N and δ^{13} C isotope measurements, confirms that gender distinctions in death were grounded in lifelong social and economic practices rather than merely (mis)represented in funerary ritual. The oppositional treatment of men and women in death was thus founded on profound notions of difference and *actual* difference within daily life. Was gender a more significant structuring principle of power relations than any hierarchical arrangement of elite and commoners?

In the as yet undated period of Wessex I (Piggott's (1938) gold-rich burial horizon thought to date to around 2000 BC), hierarchy is clearly visible within the funerary record. Commentators since Piggott have referred to the Bush Barrow burial and other gold-associated graves as those of aristocrats, elites and chieftains (Piggott 1938; Ashbee 1960; Burgess 1980). New finds such as the Lockington barrow deposit (Hughes 2000) confirm the widespread extent of personal wealth well beyond Wessex. That some of the Wessex goldwork may have been produced from a restricted supply of gold by a small coterie of gold-workers is suggested by the close metallurgical links that have recently been demonstrated for Bush Barrow and nearby graves (Taylor 2005).

There are many graves of the Wessex I period without spectacular grave goods which were probably those of high-status individuals. For example, of more than 70 tree-trunk coffin burials from across Britain that probably date to c.2200–1800 BC, only a handful such as Hove (Needham *et al.* 2006) and Stoborough (Ashbee 1960) had items of exotic materials, but about one in five of these burials did include a bronze dagger against the average of around 1 per cent of Early Bronze Age graves containing such items. Of course, we must ask how common were bronze daggers? Does their appearance as grave goods indicate the disposal of real wealth? Or were they sufficiently common that they were easily expendable within graves? Sheridan and Cowie's observation (in Baker *et al.* 2003), that those daggers found in Scottish EBA graves are normally associated with men over 40, corroborates with the less well studied evidence for England. They would seem to have been markers of status for senior males.

Tree-trunk coffins were used for cremations as well as inhumations and osteological evidence for sex is often unexamined or in need of review. None the less, there appear to be many more men than women in tree-trunk coffins, with the men continuing to be placed on their left sides as seen in the earlier Beaker graves.

The distribution of tree-trunk burials is concentrated in three areas: Wessex, Yorkshire and the Lower Nene and Welland valleys, all largely deforested by the Early Bronze Age. This regionalisation may point to specific polities or centres of power although these three concentrations are perhaps more likely to have been local traditions of funerary practice. Once again, were these men (for there are few children in tree-trunk burials) chiefs or merely local worthies of 'big man' status? There were no great monuments being constructed at this time (with the possible exception of Silbury Hill which might have been built as late as 2000 BC although an earlier date around 2300 BC is preferred – Whittle, Bayliss and McEvoy 2007).

In terms of earthmoving, round barrows represent the greatest communal effort in that period and these were probably kin-based projects for no more than a couple of hundred people in each instance. It is reasonable to assume that they were kin-based monuments whose builders were drawn from small pools of labour within relatively small kin groups. This localised kin-based labour mobilisation was a radical change from the previous major public works in which kin-based groups were organised within far larger gatherings of builders.

FANCY GOODS

Another category of evidence are the portable items of material culture which have been claimed as elite items on the basis of the rarity of their materials and/or the labour involved in their production. Much has been made of symbols of power in the second half of the third millennium BC (e.g. Clarke *et al.* 1985). Gold, amber and jet were formed into vessels and ornaments with considerable artistic skill. Some of the shaped and polished stone, chalk, jet and shale artefacts were beautifully made. As J.D. Hill has asked for the Early Iron Age in Britain, we may have elite objects but do we necessarily have an hereditary elite? Many of the superlative finds such as the Ringlemere Cup (Needham *et al.* 2006) are from deposits that are not associated with graves (Needham 1988; Woodward 2000). Yet there are enough in grave contexts to satisfy the sceptic that many were personal property, in death as well as in life.

Where these elite items can be dated, they mostly belong to the last few centuries of the third millennium BC. When we examine the items from the time of Stonehenge's main building phases (*c.*2600-2500 BC), the impression is radically different. This is considered to have been before the adoption of copper metallurgy in Britain (even though it was at least half a millennium after the Ötztal man dropped his copper axe in an Alpine snowfield – Spindler 1994). However, it is possible that copper axes were in use in Britain during the mid-third millennium BC; there is an almost total absence of stone axes or their re-sharpening flakes within the substantial lithic assemblage of this period from Durrington Walls. This was a site where timber was worked into many different shapes and sizes for houses and ceremonial circles so the presence of just two axe fragments from a lithic assemblage of over 80,000 items is suspicious. This discrepancy reminds us to expect that precious items, particularly in their innovative periods of use, were recycled or passed down as heirlooms rather than deposited under the ground.

The 'prestige goods' of the mid-third millennium BC do not amount to much in the way of elite items, in contrast to the goldwork from burials towards the end of this millennium. There is a small gneiss macehead from Stonehenge. The carved bone pendant from Skara Brae can be matched by a newly found incomplete example from Durrington Walls, although neither is as well decorated as the antler macehead from Garboldisham in Norfolk (Clarke *et al.* 1985). A couple of newly discovered spherical beads from Durrington Walls are among the few indicators that strings of beads, like those found at Skara Brae (Clarke *et al.* 1985), were worn. The only items of bodily ornament to be found in any quantity from this period are bone pins (Wainwright with Longworth 1971), with many new examples to add to Wainwright's finds from 1967. Of course, the absence of suitable funerary contexts limits our appreciation of what may have been worn on the body at this time. We would do well to remember that earlier individual graves of the late fourth millennium BC, notably Duggleby Howe, contained sliders and beads of jet, beads of shale, fine stone and antler maceheads, exquisitely polished flint knives and polished boars' tusks (Mortimer 1905; Kinnes 1979).

Yet I am still reluctant to wholly attribute this poverty of non-perishable expression in personal adornment to the problems of archaeological visibility. What makes me suspicious is the restricted repertoire of artistic representation from this period. There is certainly lots of it – the highly decorated Grooved Ware pottery, the Passage Grave art (at least in the western zones of the British Isles), the few decorated portable artefacts of bone and stone, and the growing number of carved chalk plaques and blocks – but the repertoire is restricted to a small range of abstract designs. The human/owl face from Rothley Lodge Farm, Leicestershire (Pitts 2005) and the Folkton chalk drums (Greenwell 1890), the latter entirely undated, are the only representations of naturalistic forms other than the phalli fashioned from chalk and flint nodules (Wainwright 1979; Thomas 1996; Ann Teather, pers. comm.). For all of the doodles on carved chalk that we have found at Durrington Walls in the last two years, why are they all so dull and formulaic?

Is the mid-third millennium BC one of those moments in human history when individual creativity and free expression were repressed by regimes of fundamentalist austerity? Might individual and lineage concerns have been sublimated to the greater good of the monument-building masses? This does not necessarily imply a Stalinist-style communism or a religiously fundamentalist regime of social control but it may be rather stronger supporting evidence for the power of a centralised authority than we have previously suspected. Colin Renfrew's (1973) concept of a 'group-oriented chiefdom' may not be too wide of the mark except that perhaps he under-estimated the religious and spiritual basis of this authority.

HOUSES AND THE SOCIAL ORDER

Back in 1918 Percival Farrer suggested that Durrington Walls was the settlement for the priests who worshipped at Stonehenge. Euan MacKie's (1977) elite of astronomer-priests also had their base at Durrington Walls. Even Bernard Cornwell (1999), author of the *Sharpe* series, set Durrington Walls as the settlement in his period novel *Stonehenge*. Until recently there has been a case for envisaging the great timber circles of Durrington Walls (the Southern Circle and Woodhenge) as roofed communal buildings and the smaller post structures such as the Northern Circle (Wainwright with Longworth 1971) and Durrington 68 (Pollard 1995) as houses (Darvill 2006), even as priests' halls and homes (MacKie 1977).

The new excavations of 2004-6 have radically changed this picture. Work on the Southern Circle has revealed that the outer two rings of posts are incomplete on the north-west side. This absence of full circuits of posts in the Southern Circle and its lack of a floor other than the partially surviving chalk pathway, which can now be understood to have led into the centre of the circle, are strong indications that it was not a roofed building. Eight houses recently excavated at Durrington Walls, roughly square in plan and between 16 and 30 square metres in area, are much smaller than the formerly suspected houses of the Northern Circle and Durrington 68 which can now be understood as monumentalised versions of the ordinary dwelling, with a probably ceremonial purpose. The good state of preservation of the ordinary

11 House 547 at Durrington Walls, showing a beam slot along the northern edge (nearest the camera) of its clay floor. *Photograph by Mike Parker Pearson*

12 House 851 at Durrington Walls, showing beam slots along its northern and eastern (nearest the camera) edges of its clay floor, as well as the stake holes forming its walls. *Photograph by Bob Nunn*

dwellings provides a clear appreciation of their characteristics: with wooden beds and storage units around the wattle-and-daub walls, enclosing a central space in the middle of which was an oval hearth. Two of the houses display internal distinctions of cooking to the south of the hearth and craftworking to its north. Another two houses were found within the western half of Durrington Walls, sitting on a terrace looking down upon the Southern Circle, enclosed within circular palisades within their own small henges; their lack of associated domestic rubbish (paralleled by the Northern Circle and Durrington 68) suggests a non-domestic purpose even though they had central hearths.

Probably all of these new-found houses (*11, 12*) were inhabited before the henge enclosure of Durrington Walls was built. Their interior layouts are similar to Orcadian households of the third millennium (Richards 2005) and the Durrington Walls houses show no sign of being occupied by households that were other than family groups. Yet these were not carrying out the full range of domestic activities: evidence for grain processing is absent and stone tools such as scrapers, burins and awls are under-represented within the large lithic assemblage. The large proportion of articulated and unbroken animal bone further underlines the special purpose of this settlement as a place of feasting. The unusually high concentration of arrowheads from the settlement is suggestive of a sporting or martial element. With many arrowhead tips embedded in pig bones (Albarella and Serjeantson 2002; more have been found in the new excavations), it is likely that archery was part of the corporate activities. My preferred interpretation is that these were the temporary homes of the celebrants and builders of Stonehenge rather than the dwellings of an elite, whether religious or secular.

PASTORAL CARE

Were the great round barrow cemeteries of Wessex material expressions of pastoralists' territories (Fleming 1971)? Did a rise in pastoralism lead to the build-up of economic and social stratification (Fleming 1972)? How well have these ideas fared? As Fleming said in the 1970s, the pastoralist hypothesis has been hard to demonstrate from archaeological evidence but we now have the scientific methods and settlement evidence to begin to assess its veracity.

The huge numbers of cattle whose bones were placed on round barrows at Irthlingborough and Gayhurst are strong support for pastoralism being a dominant form of subsistence at this time. Environmental studies of the Stonehenge environs present a picture for the third millennium BC of an extensively grazed, largely treeless landscape without any evidence so far for cultivation of this chalkland before the Middle Bronze Age (Cleal et al. 2004). Stonehenge's small faunal assemblage is dominated by cattle, as are those of many third millennium sites (Serjeantson 1995; Albarella and Sergeantson 2002). Yet Durrington Walls and the other henge enclosures of Wessex are dominated by pig bones. Pigs are notoriously difficult to herd even with the employment of swineherds and are, according to the ethnographic evidence, not generally kept by pastoralists; Late Neolithic Wessex may be a rare example of pig-based pastoralism. Pigs also thrive in woodland and are less suited to the treeless chalklands (Grigson 1981). I don't think that many people would choose to interpret Durrington Walls and Stonehenge as contemporaneous outposts of a 'pig culture' and a 'cattle culture' and I've argued elsewhere that they formed compatible components of one and the same economy, slaughtered for different festivals and functions (Parker Pearson et al. in press).

Perhaps the most interesting avenue for future research is the study of human and animal migration and movement by measuring strontium isotopes in teeth. As a pilot study for the Beaker People Project, Janet Montgomery, Jane Evans and Rachel Cooper have already identified a pattern for Early Bronze Age human burials in East Yorkshire which shows that five out of eleven analysed individuals derived varying amounts of strontium from the Yorkshire Wolds chalk and from the carboniferous coal measures of the Pennines, suggesting a transhumant movement between the two geologies. The Beaker People Project should provide further illuminating results in the next few years. Strontium isotopic analysis of cattle teeth, and perhaps of pigs too, should provide information on where they were reared. In the context of Durrington Walls, for example, we may be able to establish where the stock were brought from and whether there is any spatial patterning in the henge of animal bones from domestic stock brought there from different regions. For example, the distinctive curvilinear motifs on Grooved Ware pottery at Durrington Walls are found only in the south-east quadrant of the Southern Circle and in the south-east quadrant of the henge; were the workers in the four quadrants brought from four different regions? Only time and isotopes will tell.

Without prejudging the results of future work, my opinion is that these third millennium societies were not wholly pastoralist societies but exploited off-chalk valleys for cereal cultivation. As David Field has suggested, the ceremonial landscapes of Stonehenge, Avebury, Cranborne Chase and Dorchester may have been one end of the transhumant range for many groups who moved back and forward on the east side to the lowlands of the Hampshire basin, and on the west side to the lowlands of west Dorset and Somerset (Field 2004). Pastoralist societies can be conspicuously hierarchical and may strictly enforce strong gender differences. Although it might seem a contradiction, they can also be strongly egalitarian in ethos despite considerable differences in the personal and lineage ownership of cattle. Hierarchical pastoralist societies with autocratic rulers are well documented in other parts of the world (e.g. Evans-Pritchard 1956; Kent 1970).

CONCLUSION

So, in answer to the question of whether there were chiefdoms in Neolithic Wessex, my answer is a qualified 'yes but'. Can we really be sure that the political economy of Wessex was that of a 'stable state' chiefdom with hereditary rulers over half a millennium, rather than a complex history of political struggles with hierarchical and anti-hierarchical movements? As Alasdair Whittle's (e.g. Whittle and Bayliss 2007) project on dating monument building in the fourth millennium BC demonstrates, we need to be aware of the possibility that the apparent sequences of events which are archaeologically detectable during the third millennium BC may have been exceptional within the long durée, brief events within chronological limits spanning less than half a century. The phases of monument building may seem to us to dominate the history of these societies but they were probably brief episodes – flashes in the pan – which were soon over. We may never attain the chronological detail to establish whether the more elaborate Beaker burials or the graves of Wessex I and II were short-lived horizons or legitimation crises although we will be able to date the events at Durrington Walls with satisfactory precision.

The building of Stonehenge in bluestone and sarsen, probably during the twenty-sixth century BC, required a hierarchical authority structure which was geographically far-ranging and robust enough to successfully implement and complete this massive project over many years. The exercise was largely about 'muscle' – dragging, shaping and erecting stones, and lifting certain stones on top of others – and has to have carried hearts and minds. I'm less inclined to see this as the work of despotic chieftains with whip-wielding subordinates exploiting a cowed labour force, than of charismatic leaders – possibly over a single lifetime only – directing a motivated populace in work of spiritual and supernatural necessity. What emerged from this may well have been a chiefdom-style rule over a region of Britain, the size of which we can only guess at (although the strontium analysis of animal teeth from the Wessex henge enclosures may help establish whether each was a separate polity or parts of a greater whole). With the Great Pyramid of Kephren (Khafra or Cheops) being built within the same century, it is apposite to recall the adage that the Pharaohs built the pyramids and then the pyramids built the Pharaohs (Metcalf and Huntington 1991).

Thereafter, I suspect that this austere and increasingly anachronistic power structure was overthrown in the period 2400-2200 BC.

- Ideologically, religious beliefs in the passage in the afterlife from the transient world of the living to the collective ancestral eternity, expressed by the principle of lithification were challenged by metal technologies involving pyrotechnic transformation and by new beliefs arriving from continental Europe.
- Economically, lineages were able to withdraw from large-scale labour mobilisations and establish more decentralised power bases.
- Socially, new modes of dress and adornment permitted 'big men' to flaunt their wealth, particularly through funerals and commemorative rites for their direct ancestors.

Perhaps Silbury Hill really was one great round barrow, caught at the transition from the centralised power of a royal dynasty to the hierarchical yet decentralised Beaker pastoralist societies.

Around 2000 BC, the Wessex I burials represent a second political transformation in which wealth differences in stock (such as Gayhurst) and in portable valuables expressed extreme social inequalities. It is interesting that women's graves from this period do occasionally contain precious grave goods of gold and amber; perhaps this marks the emergence of true class differences between elites and commoners, over-riding previous gender inequalities. The concentration of 'big man' and 'big woman' burials around Stonehenge around 2000 BC (for example, at Normanton Down, Wilsford and Upton Lovell – Piggott 1938) illustrates the continuing power of these Wessex elites, but these barrows may have been the final swan song of a regional group rapidly being left behind by regions in eastern England and the Lower Thames which were economically more productive in the Middle and Late Bronze Age (Bradley 1984).

ACKNOWLEDGEMENTS

I'd like to acknowledge my colleagues in the Beaker People Project, particularly Mandy Jay, Patrick Mahoney, Janet Montgomery and Mike Richards for their new results, and also my colleagues in the Stonehenge Riverside Project.

ADDENDUM

In 1979, while I was a PhD student, I received a letter from Andrew Fleming to which I did not reply. In the letter Andrew is concerned to make sure that my own research does not overlap too much with one of his own students working in south-west England. Here I offer a belated reply to that letter:

Dear Professor Fleming

Thank you for your letter of 13 June 1979. It seems to have been in my in-tray for some time now. I'm sorry to be so late in replying but I've been a bit busy, as I'm sure you have too. I haven't done much more work on the prehistory of SW England so I doubt any research of mine has overlapped with that of your prospective student. How did he/she get on?

And how have you got on? You were busy working on the Dartmoor Reaves back then with some theory that those field boundaries that everyone said were medieval might actually be Bronze Age. I'm sure I heard that you found some evidence for this?

In the 1990s I think I saw you a few times in the Outer Hebrides, striding about in the distance over the wild moorland of South Uist while Niall Sharples, Jacqui Mulville, Helen Smith and I were on the beach excavating prehistoric settlements. You are still remembered with fondness by the islanders as 'the Viking', particularly in the public bar of the Borrodale Hotel.

I gather you went off to St Kilda after that. I thought a British archaeologist couldn't get much more remote in their study area than South Uist but you're obviously happy to work on an island so tiny that it's hardly more than a lump of rock with grass on top. I think I'd suffer from whatever claustrophobic condition might be the island equivalent of cabin fever!

I see you are still busy in retirement. That article about post-processual landscape archaeology (Fleming 2006) has sent some fur flying!

Anyway, my plans for the future (you were kind enough to ask in your letter) were somewhat derailed by my PhD supervisor. I was planning to work on the Bronze Age of Britain and Europe, focusing on the topic of exchange in the Alps, but my supervisor – a chap called Hodder (young and dynamic) – directed me down the morbid path of ethnoarchaeological and archaeological studies of funerary practices. I thought it might be a dead end at the time but over the years it's paid the bills.

So, Professor Fleming, in regard to Wessex, I'd say that there were chiefdoms but within an oscillating political history in which we see a collapse of centralised power around 2300 BC followed by two or three centuries of 'big man' politics and finally the emergence of a class-based elite by 2000 BC. I'm sure that the climatic downturn of 2354-2345 BC, interpreted by Mike Baillie (1999) as resulting from the impact of a comet, could be fitted into this nicely if one wanted. It is certainly food for thought as to whether a sun-worshipping chiefdom might find recruitment and loyalty difficult over nine years of bad harvests and sun-obscuring cloud!

Yours sincerely,
Professor Parker Pearson

BIBLIOGRAPHY

Albarella, U. & Serjeantson, D., 2002 A passion for pork: meat consumption at the British Late Neolithic site of Durrington Walls. In Miracle, P. & Milner, N. (eds), 33-49.

Allen, M. & Bayliss, A., 1995 Appendix 2: the radiocarbon dating programme. In R.M.J. Cleal, K.E. Walker & R. Montague (eds), 511-35.

Ashbee, P., 1960 *The Bronze Age Round Barrow in Britain*. London: Phoenix.

Atkinson, R.J.C., Piggott, C.M. & Sandars, N., 1951 *Excavations at Dorchester, Oxon*. Oxford: Ashmolean Museum.

Baillie, M., 1999 *Exodus to Arthur: Catastrophic Encounters with Comets*. London: Batsford.

Baker, L., Sheridan, A. & Cowie, T., 2003 An Early Bronze Age 'dagger grave' from Rameldry Farm, near Kingskettle, Fife. *Proceedings of the Society of Antiquaries of Scotland* 133, 85-123.

Bayliss, A., Bronk Ramsey, C. & McCormac, F.G., 1997 Dating Stonehenge. In Renfrew, C. & Cunliffe, B. (eds), 39-59.

Bayliss, A., Whittle, A. & McEvoy, F., 2007 The world recreated: redating Silbury Hill in its monumental landscape. *Antiquity* 81, 26-53.

Barrett, J., 1994 *Fragments from Antiquity: an archaeology of social life in Britain, 2900-1200 BC*. Oxford: Blackwell.

Bradley, R., 1984 *The Social Foundations of Prehistoric Britain*. Harlow: Longman.

Burgess, C., 1980 *The Age of Stonehenge*. London: Orion.

Burl, A., 2006 *Stonehenge: a new history of the World's greatest stone circle*. London: Constable.

Carr, C., 1995 Mortuary practices: their social, philosophical-religious, circumstantial, and physical determinants. *Journal of Archaeological Method and Theory* 2, 105-200.

Cherry, J., Scarre, C. & Shennan, S. (eds), 2004 *Explaining Social Change: studies in honour of Colin Renfrew*. Cambridge: McDonald Institute.

Clarke, D.V., Cowie, T. & Foxon, A., 1985 *Symbols of Power at the Time of Stonehenge*. Edinburgh: HMSO.

Cleal, R.M.J., Allen, M. & Newman, C., 2004 An archaeological and environmental study of the Neolithic and later prehistoric landscape of the Avon Valley and Durrington Walls environs. *Wiltshire Archaeological and Natural History Magazine* 97, 218-48.

Cleal, R.M.J., Walker, K.E. & Montague, R. (eds), 1995 *Stonehenge in its Landscape: twentieth-century excavations*. London: English Heritage.

Cornwall, B., 1999 *Stonehenge: a novel of 2000 BC*. London: HarperCollins.

Darvill, T., 2006 *Stonehenge: the biography of a landscape*. Stroud: Tempus.

Davis, S. & Payne, S., 1993 A barrow full of cattle skulls. *Antiquity* 67, 12-22.

Deighton, K., 2005 Gayhurst: reconstructing the burial rite of an Early Bronze Age lord. *Current Archaeology* 195, 114-18.

Downes, J. & Pollard, A. (eds), 1998. *The Loved Body's Corruption: archaeological contributions to the study of human mortality*. Glasgow: Cruithne Press.

Earle, T. (ed.), 1991 *Chiefdoms: power, economy and ideology*. Cambridge: Cambridge University Press.

Earle, T., 2002 *Bronze Age Economics: the beginnings of political economies*. Boulder: Westview.

Evans-Pritchard, E.E., 1956 *Nuer Religion*. Oxford: Oxford University Press.

Edmonds, M., 1999 *Ancestral Geographies of the Neolithic: landscapes, monuments and memory*. London: Routledge.

Farrer, P., 1918 Durrington Walls, or Long Walls. *Wiltshire Archaeological and Natural History Magazine* 40, 95-103.

Field, D., 2004 *Use of Land in Central Southern England during the Neolithic and Early Bronze Age*. Unpublished PhD thesis, University of Reading.

Fitzpatrick, A.P., 2002 'The Amesbury archer': a well-furnished Early Bronze Age burial in southern England. *Antiquity* 76, 629-30.

Fleming, A., 1971 Territorial patterns in Bronze Age Wessex. *Proceedings of the Prehistoric Society* 27, 138-66.

Fleming, A., 1973 Models for the development of the Wessex culture. In Renfrew, C. (ed.), 571-85.

Fleming, A., 2004 Hail to the chiefdom? The quest for social archaeology. In Cherry, J., Scarre, C. & Shennan, S. (eds), 141-7.

Fleming, A., 2006 Post-processual landscape archaeology: a critique. *Cambridge Archaeological Journal* 16, 267-80.

Gibson, A. in press A Beaker veneer? Some evidence from the burial record. In Larsson, M. & Parker Pearson, M. (eds).

Greenwell, W., 1890 Recent researches in barrows in Yorkshire, Wiltshire, Berkshire etc. *Archaeologia* 52, 1-72.

Grigson, C., 1981 Fauna. In Simmons, I. & Tooley, M. (eds), 191-9.

Hayden, B., 2003 *Shamans, Sorcerers and Saints*. Washington: Smithsonian Books.

Heyd, V., in press Families, treasures, warriors and complex societies: Beaker groups and the third millennium BC along the upper and middle Danube. *Proceedings of the Prehistoric Society* 73.

Hoskins, J.A., 1986 So my name shall live: stone-dragging and grave-building in Kodi, west Sumba. *Bijdragen tot de Taal-, Land- en Volkenkunde* 145, 430-44.

Hughes, G., 2000 *The Lockington Gold Hoard: an Early Bronze Age barrow cemetery at Lockington, Leicestershire*. Oxford: Oxbow.

Kent, R., 1970 *Early Kingdoms in Madagascar, 1500-1700*. New York: Holt.

Kinnes, I., 1979 *Round Barrows and Ring-ditches in the British Neolithic*. London: British Museum.

Larsson, M. & Parker Pearson, M. (eds), in press *From Stonehenge to the Baltic: Cultural Diversity in the Third Millennium BC*. Oxford: BAR.

MacKie, E., 1977 *Science and Society in Prehistoric Britain*. London: Paul Elek.

Metcalf, P. & Huntington, R., 1991 *Celebrations of Death: the anthropology of mortuary ritual*. Second edition. Cambridge: Cambridge University Press.

Miracle, P. & Milner, N. (eds), 2002 *Consuming Passions and Patterns of Consumption*. Cambridge: McDonald Institute.

Mortimer, J.R., 1905 *Fifty Years' Researches in British and Saxon Burial Mounds of East Yorkshire*. London: A. Brown & Sons.

Needham, S., 1988 Selective deposition in the British Early Bronze Age. *World Archaeology* 20, 229-48.

Needham, S., Parfitt, K. & Varndell, G. (eds), 2006 *The Ringlemere Cup: precious cups and the beginning of the Channel Bronze Age*. London: British Museum.

Pader, E., 1982 *Symbolism, Social Relations and the Interpretation of Mortuary Remains*. Oxford: BAR.

Payne, A., 2003 *Durrington Walls Henge, Wiltshire. Report on Geophysical Surveys, January 1996 and April 2003.* Centre for Archaeology Report Series 107/2003. Portsmouth: English Heritage.

Parker Pearson, M., 1998 Fearing and celebrating the dead in southern Madagascar. In Downes, J. & Pollard, A. (eds), 9-18.

Parker Pearson, M., 2000 Eating money: a study in the ethnoarchaeology of food. *Archaeological Dialogues* 7, 217-32.

Parker Pearson, M., 2003 Materiality and ritual: the origin of stone tombs in southern Madagascar. *Michigan Discussions in Anthropology* 14, 127-57.

Parker Pearson, M. & Godden, K., 2002 *In Search of the Red Slave: shipwreck and captivity in Madagascar.* Stroud: Sutton.

Parker Pearson, M. & Ramilisonina, 1998 Stonehenge for the ancestors: the stones pass on the message. *Antiquity* 72, 308-26.

Parker Pearson, M., Richards, C., Allen, M., Payne, A. & Welham, K., 2004 The Stonehenge Riverside Project: research design and initial results. *Journal of Nordic Archaeological Science* 14, 45-60.

Parker Pearson, M., Pollard, J., Richards, C., Thomas, J., Tilley, C., Welham, K. & Albarella, U., 2006, Materializing Stonehenge: the Stonehenge Riverside Project and new discoveries. *Journal of Material Culture* 11, 227-61.

Parker Pearson, M., Cleal, R., Marshall, P., Needham, S., Pollard, J., Richards, C, Ruggles, C., Sheridan, A., Thomas, J. Tilley, C., Welham, K., Chamberlain, A., Chenery, C., Evans, J., Knüsel, C., Montgomery, J. & Richards. M., forthcoming The age of Stonehenge. *Antiquity.*

Piggott, S., 1938 The Early Bronze Age in Wessex. *Proceedings of the Prehistoric Society* 4, 52-106.

Pitts, M., 2005 Stone plaque is first Neolithic face in over a century. *British Archaeology* 84, 9.

Pollard, J., 1995 The Durrington 68 timber circle: a forgotten Late Neolithic monument. *Wiltshire Archaeological and Natural History Magazine* 88, 122-5.

Pollard, J. & Reynolds, A., 2002 *Avebury: the biography of a landscape.* Stroud: Tempus.

Renfrew, C., 1973 Monuments, mobilisation and social organisation in Neolithic Wessex. In Renfrew, C. (ed.), 539-58.

Renfrew, C. (ed.), 1973 *The Explanation of Culture Change: models in prehistory.* London: Duckworth.

Renfrew, C. & Cunliffe, B. (eds), 1997 *Science and Stonehenge. Proceedings of the British Academy 92.* Oxford.

Richards, C., 2004 *Dwelling amongst the Monuments: excavations at Barnhouse and Maes Howe.* Cambridge: McDonald Institute.

Richards, J.C. & Whitby, M., 1997 The engineering of Stonehenge. In Renfrew, C. & Cunliffe, B. (eds), 231-56.

Serjeantson, D., 1995 Animal bones. In Cleal, R.M.J., Walker, K.E. & Montague, R. (eds), 437-51.

Simmons, I. & Tooley, M. (eds), 1981 *The Environment in British Prehistory.* London: Duckworth.

Spindler, K., 1994 *The Man in the Ice.* London: Weidenfeld & Nicolson.

Taylor, J.J., 2005 The work of the Wessex master goldsmith: its implications. *Wiltshire Archaeological and Natural History Magazine* 96, 316-26.

Thomas, J., 1996 *Time, Culture and Identity: an interpretive archaeology.* London: Routledge.

Thomas, J., 1999 *Understanding the Neolithic.* London: Routledge.

Tuckwell, A., 1975 Patterns of burial orientation in the round barrows of east Yorkshire. *University of London Bulletin of the Institute of Archaeology* 12, 95-123.

Wainwright, G.J., 1979 *Mount Pleasant, Dorset: excavations 1970-1971.* London: Society of Antiquaries.

Wainwright, G.J. with Longworth, I.H., 1971 *Durrington Walls: excavations 1966-1968.* London: Society of Antiquaries.

Whittle, A. & Bayliss, A., 2007 The times of their lives: from chronological precision to kinds of history and change. *Cambridge Archaeological Journal* 17, 21-8.

Woodward, A., 2000 British *Barrows: a matter of life and death.* Stroud: Tempus.

4

SACRED MONUMENTS IN A CHANGING LANDSCAPE: PLOUGH-LEVELLED NEOLITHIC AND BRONZE AGE COMPLEXES ALONG THE NORTH CEREDIGION COASTAL VALLEYS

Toby Driver

INTRODUCTION

The coastal valleys inland of Aberystwyth preserve a variety of plough-levelled ritual and burial complexes which are difficult to parallel along the west coast of Wales between the Caernarfonshire and Pembrokeshire peninsulas. They are unusual in their complexity and excavations have demonstrated activity ranging between the Neolithic and early medieval periods. Aerial photographs taken during the drought summer of 2006 yielded a further unexpected ritual complex (Dollwen) and numerous plough-levelled barrows, adding to the corpus of monuments. The lowland complexes share distinctive topographic settings, sited conspicuously on level plateaux above the valley floors, or occupying localised gravel ridges at valley junctions. Their occurrence, coupled with the quality of recorded artefacts from the early Bronze Age in north Ceredigion, including fine urns from Penllwyn and Llanilar (see below) and the Banc Tynddol sun-disc (Timberlake *et al.* 2002), may suggest a particular concentration of activity in north Ceredigion during the Early Bronze Age. The present-day profile of these lowland complexes remains low; some have been omitted from county surveys while others have been unwittingly disturbed by building works in the recent past. As new aerial survey, field walking and small-scale excavation has revealed the extent and quality of these lowland complexes, they can be compared with better-studied prehistoric ceremonial landscapes such as those around Four Crosses and Dyffryn Lane in lowland Montgomeryshire (Warrilow *et al.* 1986; Gibson 1994) or Glandy Cross in south-west Wales (Kirk and Williams 2000). This paper is not about the Bronze Age of Ceredigion as a whole, a subject which has already been thoroughly documented by Briggs (1994) and recently revisited by Cook (2006). Instead, it aims to introduce, and begin initial discussion about, the lowland prehistoric ceremonial complexes of north Ceredigion. Both Llanilar and Plas Gogerddan have benefited from thorough published excavation reports (Murphy 1992; Briggs 1997) so this paper will chiefly concern itself with descriptions of the remaining cropmark evidence.

THE NEOLITHIC AND BRONZE AGES OF THE NORTH CEREDIGION COASTAL VALLEYS

The coast of north Ceredigion describes a wide, concave arc, backed by the high ground of the Plynlimon range (752m) which overlooks some of the most desolate moorland tracts in Britain. To the west a network of valleys dissects a fertile coastal plain predominantly set down to grass for grazing. Four major rivers descend from the mountain, through the hill-fringe zone to the coast, being (from north to south) the Afon Rheidol, the Afon Ystwyth (both have their confluence at Aberystwyth), the Afon Aeron (issuing at Aberaeron) and the Afon Teifi (issuing at Cardigan) (13).

It was once thought that this area of the west coast of Wales had seen comparatively little settlement or monument building during the Neolithic, and that little Bronze Age activity had been focussed in the lowlands and valleys (Briggs 1997). Despite a paucity of visible monuments, a series of antiquarian finds had long indicated a high degree of social complexity in this coastal region. One example is the Penllwyn urn, unearthed by a grave-digger in 1926 from a cist in the grounds of Penllwyn Chapel, some seven kilometres inland (east) of Aberystwyth (Briggs 1994). This Encrusted Urn is described by Briggs (1994, 153) as 'one of the most spectacular urns from Wales…'; the site was apparently invisible at ground level.

In the last two decades, new excavations at Plas Gogerddan and Gwarfelin, Llanilar have demonstrated the extent of the buried evidence which can survive. Work at Plas Gogerddan by Murphy (1992) uncovered a multi-period burial and ritual complex comprising a Bronze Age standing stone and standing timbers, round barrows, Iron Age cremation deposits and early medieval special graves. The earliest activity on this site was a deposit of carbonised grains – a Neolithic 'muesli' – from a pit indicating cereal cultivation close by. The chronological range of activity at this one site indicated a considerable significance being attached to a prominent gravel spur, sited at a valley junction opening from a main valley, and extending into wetter lowlands. Other sites lie close by, including a buried cremation cemetery discovered during building works and grave-digging at Llangorwen Church, Clarach, in the nineteenth century (Briggs 1994). Further work since Murphy's publication has extended the complexity of Plas Gogerddan ceremonial landscape. Additional cropmark discoveries show a pair of oval enclosures to the north of the excavated site, potentially of Neolithic or Bronze Age date given finds of high quality flintwork nearer the first, western enclosure (Driver 2002). Limited campaigns of field walking in the Clarach Valley and in the environs of Plas Gogerddan (Driver and Charnock 1999; 2001) located 'special' lithic tools above a plough-levelled concentric barrow north-west of the Plas Gogerddan excavations

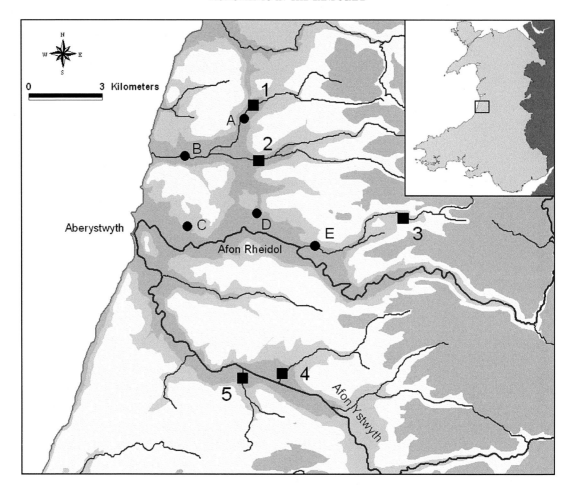

13 The study area in Wales, with a detailed map showing the topography of lowland north Ceredigion and the main ceremonial complexes (squares) and other sites (circles) described here. Main complexes: (1) Pant-y-Peran (2) Plas Gogerddan (3) Dollwen (4) Pyllau-isaf (5) Llanilar. Other sites: (A) Pen-y-Garn (B) Llangorwen Church (C) Garreg Fawr, Llanbadarn Fawr (D) Lovesgrove (E) Penllwyn. *Crown Copyright, All rights reserved. RCAHMW. Licence number 100017916, 2007*

and provided contextual evidence for open settlement with finds of Neolithic and Bronze Age cores, blades and burnt flint, largely manufactured of pebble flint (Driver and Charnock 2001).

Further advances were made in our knowledge of the later prehistory of lowland Ceredigion with the publication of a long programme of excavation at Gwarfelin, Llanilar to the south, in the lower Ystwyth Valley (Briggs 1997). At a bend in the river, on a north-facing alluvial terrace at the foot of, and backed by, rising hillslopes to the south, was found evidence for Neolithic settlement and burial, possibly associated with buildings. This activity was disturbed and overlain by a Bronze Age cremation cemetery with burials interred in a polygonal-ditched enclosure up to 20m in diameter, possibly once an upstanding barrow mound. The Later Neolithic Peterborough Ware was the first major collection from west Wales and together with the Grooved Ware sherds represented a crucial, and hitherto unexpected, extension of Neolithic settlement evidence. The Early Bronze Age burials yielded fine ceramics, including an Enlarged Food Vessel. Briggs (1997, 33) carefully noted how elusive such un-monumental, or plough-levelled, remains may be in valley environments and how the numerous enigmatic cropmark sites discovered in considerable numbers since the 1960s may have '...settlement pedigrees going back to the Neolithic'.

THE MAIN CROPMARK COMPLEXES

Pant-y-peran (Llandre), Rhydypennau

The complex of burial monuments at Pant-y-peran, Rhydypennau occupies the Y-fork of a major lowland valley (14). To the north is a group of five large ring ditches, probably representing former barrows of some considerable size (ranging between 30-35m in diameter). This plough-levelled barrow cemetery is sited on a striking riverine terrace with a level summit and a steep slope on the west side which drops down to a minor river valley. In essence this is a great stage set, backed by rising ground and set at the junction of three valleys. Some 200m to the south-east and away from the terrace edge is a small, close-set group of up to five barrows carefully sited on one of several undulating gravel ridges hereabouts. These range between 6-10m in diameter and central grave pits are visible in three. A rectangular enclosure close to the main barrow cemetery is probably prehistoric, and may be contemporary.

The surviving plough-levelled complex, discovered in the drought of 1975 (St Joseph 1975), is regionally unusual, but there is additional evidence for wider ceremonial use of the lowlands immediately around Rhydypennau. Some 200m north-east of the bridge at Rhydypennau is the find spot of a flat axe (Grimes 1939; Briggs 1994); 600m north-east at Dole is a pair of burnt mounds, steadily being ploughed away, while to the south at Pen-y-garn a large barrow was removed sometime in the early years of the nineteenth century. The former presence of this monument, recorded by place-name evidence alone (garn = cairn), was documented by Williams (1867, 287). He noted:

> ... a large carn removed about fifty years ago [c.1817?] in making the turnpike road: at a place which still retains the name of Penygarn. From this an immense number of human bones (unburnt) were removed to Llanbadarn Churchyard. To the same ground were also removed, about the same time, other unburnt bones from a smaller carn...

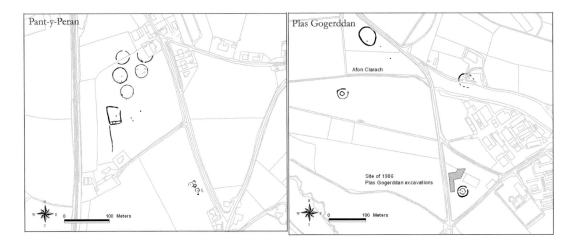

14 The main Neolithic and Bronze Age ceremonial complexes; cropmark evidence. Pant-y-peran and Plas Gogerddan – the shaded area illustrates the extent of the excavation. *Crown Copyright, All rights reserved. RCAHMW. Licence number 100017916, 2007*

Initially this is a vivid description, but the presence of large quantities of unburnt bone is an anomaly in a region where acidic soils destroy bone, and for a period where cremation was the dominant burial practice. The tale may have been embellished; alternatively a Bronze Age mound could have been re-used for early medieval or later inhumations as at Plas Gogerddan to the south. The striking topographic setting of the barrow is still visible today, as the road reaches the highest point of an elevated lowland plateau.

Dollwen, Goginan

Prior to the summer of 2006, the pronounced lowland basin around the upper reaches of the Afon Melindwr at Goginan was devoid of any pre-Iron Age archaeology. Like many other river corridors in north Ceredigion, the Afon Melindwr cuts a broad lowland swathe into the hillfringe, providing fertile grazing land in what is effectively an upland zone, the surrounding ridges quickly rising to 300m and more. During the drought of July 2006, aerial reconnaissance identified a complex of Early Bronze Age monuments in the valley bottom (Driver 2006) which graphically illustrates the major discoveries which are still possible in the Welsh landscape (*15*).

The Dollwen complex comprises a large concentric enclosure *c*.43.6m in diameter, with 1.4-1.9m wide ditches (measurements were taken from the cropmark while it still showed on the ground) (*16*). Only 20m to the south-east, cropmarks show a large circular depression or pit, likely to be a pond barrow. Fifteen metres to the north-east is an upstanding barrow, only discovered as a parched mound at the time of the cropmark discovery. Ring ditches are also visible to the south of the concentric enclosure, and across the river to the north. Other cropmarks of former boundaries could represent

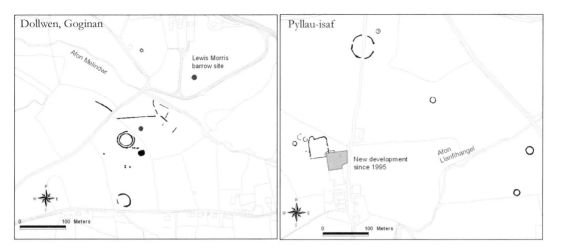

15 Dollwen, Goginan and Pyllau-isaf. *Crown Copyright, All rights reserved. RCAHMW. Licence number 100017916, 2007*

16 The cropmark of the Dollwen concentric enclosure: a ground view from the west with the lush growth over the buried ditches contrasting with the surrounding drought-ridden pasture. The landowner provides a scale in the centre of the monument. The position of the enclosure, on a very level river terrace at the head of the valley, surrounded on all sides by rising ground, is also apparent in this view *Crown Copyright RCAHMW, DS2006_212_008*

a contemporary field system. Of additional interest is the reconstructed position of a 'barrow' or 'tump' illustrated by the mine surveyor Lewis Morris in a view of Goginan mine in 1744, and on a later survey of the Manor of Perverth in 1789 (see Bick and Wyn Davies 1994). The barrow was subsequently incorporated into spoil tips of the adjacent mine, and the area was later cleared to form a present-day small golf course and gardens. The barrow's position was reconstructed from early mapping, and seen to lie in direct alignment with the concentric enclosure and upstanding barrow, according with a circular parchmark seen in 2006 which might represent the vestigial foundations of the levelled mound.

Like the Pant-y-peran barrow cemetery, the Dollwen monuments are carefully sited on elevated river terraces at the narrowing eastern end of the valley, at an (asymmetric) Y-fork where the valley splits. The monuments would have been highly conspicuous when extant, especially to visitors descending from high-ground along well-travelled mountain routes to the east. It is perhaps significant that they straddle a stream valley. The Dollwen enclosure is of considerable interest. For a Welsh barrow it is large and exceeds the diameter of the largest Pant-y-peran barrow by nearly 9m; it is exceeded by the Precelly Farm barrow at the Glandy Cross complex (Kirk and Williams 2000) which measures *c.*51m in diameter. One possible interpretation of the Dollwen enclosure is of an open, hengiform monument providing a focus for rituals in the Later Neolithic and Early Bronze Age landscape. However, complex, concentric structures are known from within upstanding barrows, for example, at Sites 1 and 5, Four Crosses (Warrilow *et al.* 1986); at Plas Gogerddan both the upstanding Gogerddan barrow and two cropmark barrows to the west and north have concentric plans, but none exceeds 30m in diameter (see Driver and Charnock 2001).

Pyllau-isaf, Llanfihangel y Creuddyn

The Pyllau-isaf complex is sited centrally on a wide alluvial fan which opens at the junction of the minor Afon Llanfihangel tributary with the major lowland valley corridor of the Afon Ystwyth. The level expanse is bordered by low hills on all but the south side. Set across the Ystwyth Valley to the south-west is the Llanilar settlement and burial complex (Briggs 1997). In the nineteenth century an urn within a cairn was discovered here, recorded on the gravestone of William Hughes in Llanbadarn Fawr churchyard. Although the discovery has since become confused with Penyberth (Gloucester Hall) to the north (see Briggs 1994), Briggs (1994) notes that the epitaph is the earliest and clearest account of an urn being found in 1840 in a field called Cae'r-odyn on the farm of Pyllau-isaf. The urn (now in the National Museum of Wales) is a fine vessel with corded decoration standing about 20cm high.

This antiquarian discovery is put into a fuller context by a series of cropmark discoveries made at Pyllau-isaf between 1995 and 2006. The complex comprises two enclosures, one square, the other circular, and at least seven plough-levelled round barrows. The square enclosure (41 metres square) is an anomaly in such a very low-lying situation on the floodplain of the Ystwyth. Square enclosures are a relatively common site type among the defended enclosures of Iron Age Wales; they have been the subject of a recent campaign of survey and excavation in southern Ceredigion (Murphy *et al.* 2004), while a polygonal earthwork enclosure (58m square) with a substantial bank lies just 900m to the south-west, on the slopes below Pen-y-castell Hillfort, Llanilar. The Pyllau-isaf enclosure may not be Iron Age; it is narrow-ditched, with irregular corners, one rounded, the others squared, with a simple entrance on the east side. A cemetery of up to four plough-levelled round barrows lies on the west side but one is 'incorporated' into the boundary of the enclosure, forming a semi-circular apse. This may be a form of mortuary enclosure, highly unusual on the west coast of Wales. Some 180m north is a circular enclosure (50m in diameter), originally thought to be a later prehistoric settlement (Driver 2005) but with a very broad putative 'entrance' – 15m wide – and enlarged ditch terminals terminating in a large pit to the north. Again, this is not entirely standard for the regional Iron Age where one would expect a more narrow entrance. A series of barrows extend the Pyllau-isaf complex across the Afon Llanfihangel, the largest being around 19m in diameter.

DISCUSSION

The lowland topography of the north Ceredigion river valleys clearly provided distinct, and recurrent, landforms and loci at which Neolithic and Early Bronze Age settlement and activity was focussed, notably prominent gravel ridges, level or prominent alluvial terraces and significant valley junctions. One of the very few probable Neolithic chambered tombs in Ceredigion is Garreg Fawr, a large slab divorced from other structural stones nearby, which sits in the village square at Llanbadarn Fawr, Aberystwyth (Houlder 1994). The tomb occupies the opening of a steep minor stream valley into the main lower valley of the Afon Rheidol, backed by rising ground, and would once have commanded an alluvial terrace; the location was later adopted by the early Christian Church. The find site of the impressive Penllwyn Urn is similar, positioned at the edge of an alluvial terrace, backed by rising ground and commanding a flat, steep-edged river terrace. These criteria are repeated at the Llanilar and Pyllau-isaf complexes. Rivers conspicuously bisect most complexes, although the main Pant-y-peran barrow cemetery overlooks a dry valley. At other complexes the surrounding valley topography was harnessed, particularly prominent valley-junctions and the openings of side valleys from main 'thoroughfares', with complexes placed more centrally on prominent ridges (Plas Gogerddan), or on valley floors with wide views (Dollwen, Pyllau-isaf, Llangorwen Church). In some instances the strict categorisation of identifiable topographic traits may be misleading; in the network of valleys which connect Plas Gogerddan north to Pant-y-peran, via Pen-y-garn, and west to the sea at Clarach, we see other key monuments in a variety of prominent positions including an elevated hill-shoulder dominating the valley (the Bow Street enclosure and concentric barrow). The five main complexes described in this paper saw ritual activity formalised in the construction of visible monuments, barrows and enclosures. Yet, abundant evidence exists to suggest that unenclosed

– now invisible – burials and settlement activity probably extend for a considerable distance around the recognisable monuments.

The occurrence of these sites in the lowlands of present-day Ceredigion raises inevitable – and pressing – concerns for their future welfare and survival. The Pant-y-peran complex, discovered in 1975, was mapped and published in 1998 (Driver 1998) following an urgent revision of the Llandre Village Plan. Building work had commenced on new housing within the field with no awareness of the pre-existing archaeology but was stopped before any significant damage was done. The Llanilar excavations were partly undertaken in salvage conditions (Briggs 1997), while new aerial photography of cropmarks of the Pyllau-isaf square enclosure in 2006 showed an extension to farm buildings since the site's discovery in 1995 had destroyed part of its south-eastern corner. Further investigation of the marked concentration of ritual and burial activity at a widening of the lower Ystwyth Valley between Pyllau-isaf and Llanilar can only have been hampered by the emplacement of replica flint tools and debitage at Llanilar by a team from Southampton University between 2000 and 2003 (Hosfield and Chambers 2004). This experimental programme using replica Palaeolithic material was undertaken with no recourse to the local or national museums, or regional Sites and Monuments Record, again highlighting the low profile of north Ceredigion's prehistory among the wider archaeological community. A replica ovoid handaxe later discovered by a landowner at Llanilar, one of 49 emplaced, was sent to the National Museum of Wales as a possible Neolithic axe and reported upon. A photo archive of the emplaced axes was belatedly published online in an attempt to identify future discoveries of this modern material, but lithic debitage from in-situ flaking was not so carefully recorded. Together with un-recovered artefacts, the experiment represents a major contamination of the river deposits for future artefact collection and research.

On the grounds of topography and stray finds, one can look to other locations in lowland north Ceredigion and predict the future discovery, or disturbance, of prehistoric monuments. The lowland expanse at Lovesgrove on the Rheidol Valley lies between Llanbadarn Fawr and Penllwyn. A record of megaliths close to Lovesgrove House by Sansbury (1930; Cook 2006), shows considerable promise but the area has long been earmarked for development. There are no cropmarks to guide archaeological evaluation, and how would an unenclosed cremation cemetery be recognised among natural pits on lowland gravels? Other prominent coastal valley junctions like Rhydyfelin south of Aberystwyth, having similar characteristics to known ritual and burial complexes, have seen a recent expansion of housing. Where land is cultivated, the extension of previous campaigns of field walking may be the first way to pre-empt future development with hard artefactual evidence.

Future protection could be fostered through enhanced scheduling, as recommended by Kirk and Williams (2000) for Glandy Cross. Following the recent re-survey of Ceredigion for the Cadw-funded Prehistoric Funerary and Ritual Sites Project

(Cook 2006) a number of lowland sites have been recommended for scheduling which is a welcome development. When plough-levelled sites do not have the demonstrable above-ground remains, or high 'group value' (Cook 2006, 9), to make statutory protection a possibility, an alternative might be to raise community awareness through interpretative signage and other means as Kirk and Williams (2000) suggest.

CONCLUSION

This brief paper has served to place excavated burial and ritual complexes at Llanilar and Plas Gogerddan in a wider context of surviving plough-levelled monument complexes in north Ceredigion. It has demonstrated the need for a fuller regional study undertaking new aerial reconnaissance, surface collection and excavation to properly understand the monuments. A recent study by the author (Driver 2005) of the later prehistoric settlement pattern of north Ceredigion demonstrated how fundamental the lowland river valleys were in providing through-routes for communication linking the coast with the mountain. They were fertile zones in prehistory for farming and agricultural settlement giving rise to 'neighbourhood groups' of smaller hillforts along the Rheidol and the Ystwyth. Work by Timberlake (2001) on the impact of Bronze Age mining in north Ceredigion suggested a network of trackways, or prospector's sampling routes, marked by standing stones and burial monuments linking the coastal plain with the uplands, defining a rich legacy of prehistoric movement. This appears to be a reasonable interpretation of the surviving monument evidence (see also Driver forthcoming). The discovery of the rare gold Banc Tynddol sun-disc (Timberlake *et al.* 2002), of chalcolithic or Early Bronze Age date, from a burial at the foot of Copa Hill in the bottom of the upper Ystwyth Valley (repeating the settings of burials at Penllwyn and Llanilar), has to be interpreted in the context of the Bronze Age mining activity a few hundred metres away (Timberlake 2003). It appears to suggest unusual wealth and social complexity in these Ceredigion hills, being only the third find of Bronze Age gold from the whole of Wales. It may be that the concentration of later prehistoric ritual activity in the north Ceredigion lowlands *is* unusual, with prehistoric communities flourishing on an economy boosted by a legacy of mining in the local hills. Alternatively, they may have exploited a position beneficial to long-distance trade between the west coast of Wales, across a relatively narrow belt of high ground to the communities of the Welsh Borderlands and the Cheshire and Shropshire plains. Better protection of the monument resource we have, coupled with future targeted fieldwork to research it, will shed further light on the hidden archaeology of these Welsh valleys.

ACKNOWLEDGEMENTS

I would like to thank Stephen Briggs for informal discussion relating to this paper, and the landowners of various sites, particularly Elfed and Kathy Price at Dollwen, for willingly allowing access. Dr Nikki Cook kindly forwarded a copy of her report for me to consult. My thanks to the Secretary and Commissioners of the Royal Commission for allowing me to complete part of this paper in official time. I would like to record my personal thanks to Andrew Fleming for his unfailing guidance and wisdom over the years, chiefly through the course of my PhD, and I hope I have demonstrated that the potential for new work on the prehistory of north Ceredigion is far from exhausted.

BIBLIOGRAPHY

Bick, D. & Wyn Davies, P., 1994 *Lewis Morris and the Cardiganshire Mines.* Aberystwyth: The National Library of Wales.

Briggs, C.S., 1994 The Bronze Age. In Davies, J.L. & Kirby, D.P. (eds), 124-218.

Briggs, C.S. (ed.), 1997 A Neolithic and Early Bronze Age settlement and burial complex at Llanilar, Ceredigion. *Archaeologia Cambrensis* 146, 13-59.

Bruck, J. (ed.), 2001 *Bronze Age Landscapes – Tradition and Transformation.* Oxford: Oxbow.

Cook, N., 2006 *Prehistoric Funerary and Ritual Sites Project, Ceredigion 2004-2006.* Unpublished Archaeoleg Cambria Archaeology Report, No. 2006/32, Project Record Nos 50943 and 55922.

Davies, J.L. & Kirby, D.P. (eds), 1994 *Cardiganshire County History. Volume 1, from the earliest times to the coming of the Normans.* Cardiff: University of Wales Press.

Driver, T., 1998 Llandre, Geneu r Glyn (SN 626 862). *Archaeology in Wales* 38, 94-5.

Driver, T., 2002 Plas Gogerddan, Trefeurig (SN 6225 8400). *Archaeology in Wales* 42, 98.

Driver, T., 2005 *The Hillforts of North Ceredigion: architecture, landscape setting and cultural contexts.* Unpublished PhD thesis, The University of Wales, Lampeter.

Driver, T., 2006 A good year for cropmarks in Wales. *CBA Wales Newsletter* 32.

Driver, T., forthcoming Hillforts and human movement: unlocking the Iron Age landscapes of mid-Wales. In Fleming, A. & Hingley, R. (eds).

Driver, T. & Charnock, R., 1999 Plas Gogerddan, Aberystwyth (SN 623 837). *Archaeology in Wales* 39, 78.

Driver, T. & Charnock, R., 2001 Prehistoric flint finds from Plas Gogerddan, near Aberystwyth, Ceredigion. *Studia Celtica* 35, 341-50.

Fleming, A. & Hingley, R. (eds), forthcoming *The Making of the British Landscape: fifty years after Hoskins, prehistoric and Roman periods.* Macclesfield: Windgather Press.

Gibson, A., 1994 Excavations at the Sarn-y-bryn-caled cursus complex, Welshpool, Powys, and the timber circles of Great Britain and Ireland. *Proceedings of the Prehistoric Society* 60, 143-223.

Grimes, W.F., 1939 *Guide to the Collection Illustrating the Prehistory of Wales.* Cardiff: National Museum of Wales and the Press Board of the University of Wales.

Hosfield, R.T. & Chambers, J.C., 2004 Experimental Archaeology on the Afon Ystwyth, Wales, UK. *Antiquity* vol. 78, No. 299 [www.antiquity.ac.uk/ProjGall/chambers/index.html, accessed 5 April 2007]

Houlder, C.H., 1994 The Stone Age. In Davies, J.L. & Kirby, D.P. (eds), 107-23.

Kirk, T. & Williams, G., 2000 Glandy Cross: A later prehistoric monumental complex in Carmarthenshire, Wales. *Proceedings of the Prehistoric Society* 66, 257-95.

Murphy, K., 1992 Plas Gogerddan, Dyfed: a multi-period burial and ritual site. *Archaeological Journal* 149, 1-38.

Murphy. K. Wilson, H., Mytum, H. & Carver, R., 2004 Rectangular cropmarked enclosures in south Ceredigion. *Archaeology in Wales* 44, 117-20.

Sansbury, A.R., 1930 Recent finds in Cardiganshire. *Transactions of the Cardiganshire Antiquarian Society* 7, 72-4.

St Joseph, J.K.S., 1975 Glanfraid (SN 634 878) and Llandre and Aberceiro. *Archaeology in Wales* 15, 69.

Timberlake, S., 2001 Mining and prospection for metals in Early Bronze Age Britain – making claims within the archaeological landscape. In Bruck, J. (ed.), 179-92.

Timberlake, S., 2003 *Excavations on Copa Hill, Cwmystwyth (1986-1999)*. Oxford: BAR.

Timberlake, S., Gwilt, A. & Davis, M., 2002 Cwmystwyth, Banc Tynddol (SN 8090 7484). *Archaeology in Wales* 42, 97-8.

Warrilow, W., Owen, G. & Britnell, W., 1986 Eight Ring-ditches at Four Crosses, Llandysilio, Powys. *Proceedings of the Prehistoric Society* 52, 53-87.

Williams, J.G., 1867 Ancient encampments near Aberystwyth. *Archaeologia Cambrensis* 13 (third series), 284-91.

5

MONUMENTS AS LANDSCAPE: PLACE, PERSPECTIVE AND PERFORMANCE PRACTICE

Mary Ann Owoc

INTRODUCTION

Anyone fortunate enough to have been in the field with a landscape archaeologist like Andrew Fleming will perhaps remember their first experiences with chagrin. Indistinguishable from mounds of heather, clumps of gorse, and granite boulders, the traces of upland prehistory initially elude the novice. In settings such as these, monuments, and other traces of the past have become part of the fabric of the natural landscape – altered for millennia by water, wind, and peat growth, and then enshrouded by shorter cycles of blossom and thorn. In such environments, the land has claimed the past – monuments are natural landscape. To sharper and more disciplined eyes and bodies however, shaped by years of trudging through the rain and mist of an unforgiving English upland and peering across sweeps of moorland, patterns emerge out of the chaos. The past slowly reveals itself as one is taught how to see by example and practice; to discern and recognise the line of a wall, the pattern of a field system, and the low rise of a cairn. The untangling of monument from landscape is a scientific practice; informed by repetition, structured engagement, disciplinary knowledge, and technologies like mapping and recording. To some degree this is a necessary activity, part of the way in which we name, appropriate, and make the past meaningful. At some point however, it becomes necessary to return the monument to its landscape, or alternatively, find a way to discern and narrate the nature of the entanglement between past environments and built form so that we may understand each better.

Time spent in a preserved prehistoric landscape, and a closer inspection of its preserved architectural forms lead one to suspect that earlier travellers, builders, shepherds, and pilgrims did not distinguish 'monument from moorland' in the same manner in which we do. Indeed, one might argue that they did not 'separate' them at all. How might such an intimate, dialectical relationship be understood? Archaeologists have recently attempted to answer this question in a number of ways. The one that I wish to discuss here was addressed by Richard Bradley (2000) in his overview of the archaeology of natural places, and it forms the title to this contribution: monument *as* landscape (see also Richards 1996). A short story, coupled with a few observations may suffice to introduce this notion, which I will further illustrate with several examples drawn from the archaeological record of the south-western British Bronze Age.

One particularly foggy morning on Samson's North Hill in the Isles of Scilly, I was out looking for monuments. Time was valuable, and the morning's plan of assessing the features of the island's entrance graves could not be put off. As I meandered down a line of prehistoric walling, a row of irregular shapes emerged from the mist. My field guide indicated that the monument I sought was probably among them, but for a time, I could not discern the cairn from the row of granite outcrops, or carns, at the edge of the hill. The entrance grave was weathered, and long disturbed, its large granite members somewhat overgrown by grass and heather (*17*). It soon became apparent however, that the similarity between cairn and carn was not simply a case of Samson claiming back its lost materials. A closer examination of many of the entrance graves on Scilly's higher promontories find them claiming key real estate adjacent to, or just below the prominent granite carns which are dominant features of the Scillonian skyline, and highly inter-visible between Islands. The structural forms of the monuments in general replicate that of the natural weathered granite outcrops, and microscopic comparison of certain architectural stones from several selected sites and their nearby granite outcrops suggest quarrying from these locations (Dunn 2005). Further, the choices builders made in selecting certain structural members or capstones appear to have arisen from a sensitivity towards textural variations evident in the granite of local outcrops, as well as the patterning of particular colour variations in the rock and their relationship to natural quartz veins, revealed and influenced by millennia of weathering. Given these observations, it seems clear that the monument on the end of North Hill was nearly indistinguishable from its neighbours because it was *built* to be so. The entrance grave is at once the same and different from the adjacent outcrops, and its careful construction among them highlights this tensioned relationship.

What might other relationships (for indeed, there are many) between the built forms of later prehistory and their local landscapes have signified to their creators and viewers? Was their construction and siting merely a function of available building materials, or is there more to discover, and are such interpretations possible for archaeologists? Mere observational similarities will not suffice to answer such questions. I suggest that coming to terms with monuments as landscape involves both an embodied and theoretical appreciation of place, perspective, and performative practice. In what follows, I would like to illustrate the manner in which monuments and landscapes in the south-western British Bronze Age were intimately associated with one another through timely, social acts of construction and perception.

17 Cairn or Carn? The weathered entrance grave (second from right) on Samson North Hill, Isles of Scilly resembles its neighbours. *Photograph by Mary Ann Owoc*

PERSPECTIVE

As mentioned above, perspective of the past is not limited to past actors alone. The archaeological perspective of the past creates relationships and distinctions, constructs objects, and ultimately creates meaning and significance. Appreciating monument as landscape is a function of a perspective of the archaeological record that starts from the particular, the historical, and the experiential (but is not limited to these points of view). This perspective is phenomenological in that it focuses upon the nuances of human experience in the world and asks how that experience conditions or makes possible particular sorts of readings/understandings of it. It is concerned with and informed by orientation, and inhabitation (Foltz 2000), and relies in part on commonalities in the human experience of the world. It is also hermeneutic, in that the resulting narrative arises from the place where the theoretical/conceptual horizon and language of the trained experienced observer and the particular form of the archaeological record in the landscape meet. It is thus akin to what Victor Baker calls 'earth-directed science' (2000: 3-4), involving disciplined observation, physical experience, and imaginative envisioning (Frodeman 2003). It is a perspective that is therefore neither overly subjective or falsely empiricist. The result of such a viewpoint is not a search for order, but instead a scientific celebration of variability and historical context out of which broader patterns may subsequently be discerned.

The creation of built forms, and the dispositions of bodies in the spaces they create, enables the creation of perspective. Such perspective directs the gaze of the viewer, and also situates them in a place from which to observe, to orient themselves in physical and social relationship to persons and things, and to appreciate other such relations. Discerning perspectival frameworks and their consequences makes it easier to appreciate how people in the past might have seen the landscape and imagined themselves in it. Work on this subject (e.g. Thomas 1991; Parker Pearson and Ramilsonina 1998; Richards 1996) for British Neolithic monuments has extended our understanding of the relationship between cosmology and landscape for this period.

Let us consider for a moment a group of excavated sites that were built on a northern ridge of Davidstow Moor, at the northern edge of the Bodmin Moor granite mass. Forming part of a larger open group of monuments, this landscape of funerary and ceremonial sites reproduced an enduring, evolving tradition of perspective and practice that was materialised and worked on in variable form over the course of at least 600 years between the twenty-second and sixthteenth centuries BC (Christie 1988; Owoc 2004). While this tradition is apparent elsewhere in the region, and varies temporally as well as from area to area based upon available materials, local tradition, knowledge, etc., its manner of creation and reproduction is distinct for this group of monuments. Notable amongst these sites (though not common to all) are attempts by the builders to create dominant solstitial orientations at or near midwinter sunrise (MWSR) and midsummer sunset (MSSS) azimuths (via ditch causeways, enclosure entrances, feature alignments, and other activities). Additionally, particular attention to naturally occurring yellow or white clay subsoil in the area characterises some part of the construction sequence at most of the excavated sites in the group. The subsoil was highlighted in several ways. The most common of these involved the creation of yellow enclosures achieved either through the removal of a narrow circular strip of turf (which created a yellow subsoil clay ring enclosing a platform) or, through the construction of turf and subsoil banks or mound revetments, in which the position of the two materials was reversed. Pit fills and mound components on several sites also contained stratified deposits of charcoal and/or turf and white clay subsoil.

The presence, variability and development of astronomical traditions that focus on solstitial alignments in Britain has been addressed extensively in comprehensive overviews and more particular reports focused on individual sites or regional groups of mouments (e.g. Bradley 2000b; Burl 1981; 1983; Chippindale 1983; Heggie 1981; Ruggles 1999; Ruggles and Whittle 1981). Along with a number of regions outside central southern Britain, particularly in the north and west, earlier building traditions emphasising solstitial alignments appear to have been continued into the later Neolithic/Early Bronze Age in south-western Britain, albeit with some modification. Builders referenced the midsummer, midwinter and equinoctial sunrises and sunsets, as well as northerly and southerly directions. Questions concerning the significance of such azimuths for various communities, and how that significance was demonstrated, must be answered by taking a closer look at individual sites and local building and ritual traditions.

For instance, at Davidstow I (which contained only a minimal deposit of cremated bone amidst a number of charcoal filled pits, deposits, burning and eating episodes), the rising midwinter sun (MWSR) would have appeared on the horizon at the entrance to a stake circle builders initially created on the site. Some 10 degrees to the north of this point, the burning of a large stake inside a small enclosure adjacent to the ring opening, anticipated this event. The MWSR location was also the focus for fires at two other sites. The builders also marked the points of the midwinter and midsummer sunsets at Davidstow I with additional stakes. Further, the circle and the activities within it were demarcated from the surrounding area by a narrow circular band of stripped turf, revealing the bright yellow subsoil as a yellow ring surrounding the site for part of its history. At the site of Davidstow V (18), activities at the site served to create an opposition between an area adjacent to the south-eastern edge of a flat mound near the midwinter sunrise, (where posts were erected and burned, charcoal was deposited, and pits were excavated and backfilled with charcoal or ceramics) and, the north-western crest of the monument at its opposite side, where a row of granite stones had been erected centred on the alignment marking the setting of the midwinter sun on the horizon. The mound at Davidstow V was embellished by the addition of an outer ring of yellow subsoil. Four other sites in the Davidstow group were built as earthen enclosures incorporating a distinctive yellow bank, which had been fabricated by placing an outer cap of subsoil over an initial turf ring base, thus reversing the natural relationship of these materials in the landscape. At Davidstow Moor III and II, this bank was enclosed by a ditch, which exposed the subsoil as a ring around the site, and provided the constructional materials for the bank. Site III was subsequently visited by mourners who deposited some selected cremated remains of one individual, accompanied by a horn ladle into a pit at the centre of the site. Access to the interior circle at Site III was initially available via a wide causeway on its eastern side. Much later in the history of the site, builders restricted this with the addition of a blocking bank, forcing entrance and egress from the central burial area to occur through a narrow gap between the two banks near the alignment of the MWSR on the horizon. This point was also the focus of a deposit of yellow/orange/red clay, further elaborating it. This area had been trampled, indicating much movement between the inside and outside of the ring bank, perhaps by family members who deposited the remains and covered them with a small mound.

The above examples illustrate that perspective on Davidstow Moor was achieved through devices which enabled participants to see the world in particular sorts of ways. The focus upon the rising and setting of the midwinter and midsummer sun created a spatial and axial perspective of the landscape, and a focus on the horizon that was also grounded in the temporal actions of the participants on the site at these times. Thus the onset of light and darkness, and the beginning and ending of the solar calendar were stressed. Further, the orientations were given additional meaningful significance by being associated with contrasting materials, elements or artifacts (fire,

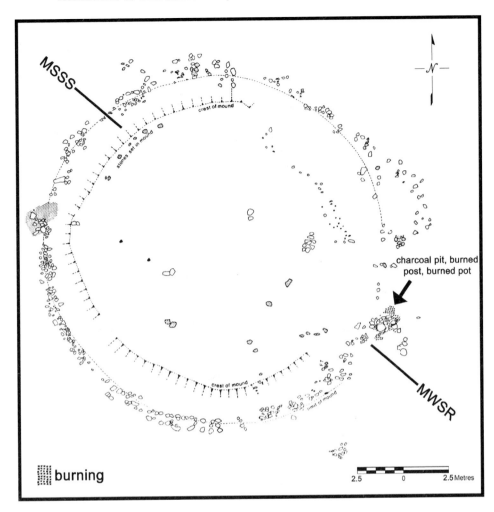

18 Davidstow Moor Site V. *From Christie 1988; reproduced here with permission from The Cornwall Archaeological Society*

wood, charcoal, ceramic, stone). The mounds, wooden and earth/subsoil rings, and revetments demarcated zones of activity in which actions did or did not take place, and with which persons and fragments of the dead were, or were not associated. The intimate relationship and vertical boundary between the world that lay above the ground and the one that lay below it was further elaborated through the labour of the builders on the mounds, and during their construction of the rings and ring banks. In these, (and in the pits) contrasting colours, and the highlighting of natural and reversed stratigraphic positions between the two components directed attention towards their opposed qualities of light/darkness and above/below positions, and the transition between them – themes that were also stressed through other perceptual devices on the sites. As monuments became real and imagined landscapes throughout the centuries on Davidstow Moor through the embodied labour and perception of their builders and visitors, enduring cosmological traditions framing particular understandings of the world and the place and movement of the living, the dead and the sun within it were reinvented and reproduced.

PLACE

As the famous landscape geographer Yi Fu Tuan (1977) noted long ago, *places*, or locales, are created through the life paths of individuals and groups. Over time they become invested with meaning and significance for persons through repeated activities, experiential perspective, movement, memory and storytelling. Further, places define and frame space. As Bradley (2000a) has noted, natural places that served as long term foci for particular activities like deposits, or constructions often have qualities that distinguish them from other locations. Our sensitivity, in the present, to the nature of these qualities is important for understanding what significance such places may have held for past communities, and how that significance influenced their activities. Consider the site of Crig-a-Mennis (Christie 1960), a stratified mound of earth and stone situated along a low ridge in central Cornwall, which was built sometime during the first several hundred years of the second millennium BC. The choices governing the positioning of the monuments of this period have been the subject of considerable speculation, and attention has naturally focused on unique or dramatic settings. Unlike some of its contemporaries in the upland south-west however, Crig-a-Mennis was not built on or near any visibly dramatic, or unusual stone outcrops which might have attracted the attention of generations of prehistoric populations. It was in fact the landscape *below* the surface that afforded the feature of interest. Crig-a-Mennis was built directly on a geological boundary between soft pink sandstone and a harder greenish slate, such that the overlying sediments and soils on the monument's north-west and south sides were different. In stripping part of the site to construct a series of sequential mounds/caps (which covered a series of pits, fires, deposits of charcoal, and the urned and unurned cremated bone fragments of perhaps two individuals) the builders reserved the material overlying each portion of the site for the major mound components, beginning with the softer sandy topsoil overlying the sandstone, and following with the soils overlying the shale portion of the site. Subsequent mound layers also evidence the builders' concern with depth, hardness, and light as a sandy subsoil cap to the mound was followed by the addition of a shale rubble cap, a revetment wall of shale and quartz, and a white quartz final cap, which reversed the natural stratigraphy surrounding the site but maintained its natural symmetry (*19*).

The mound layers, as well as associated charcoal scatters and several features, were created during serial visits to the site following the principal cremations and charcoal

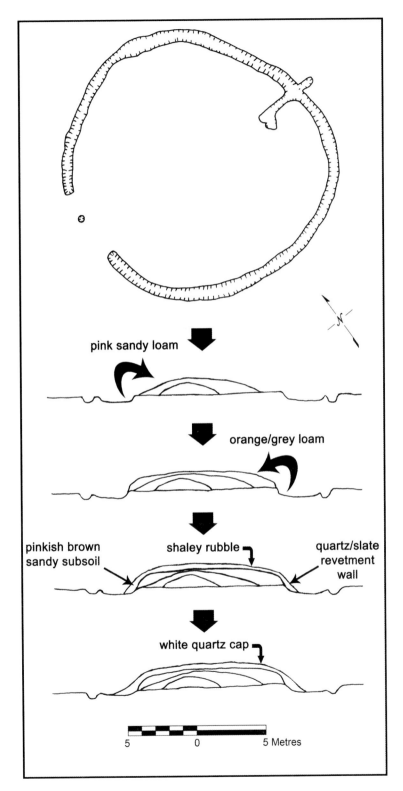

pink sandy loam

orange/grey loam

pinkish brown
sandy subsoil

shaley rubble

quartz/slate
revetment
wall

white quartz cap

5   0   5 Metres

19 Schematic
of mound
construction at
Crig-a-Mennis
using variously
textured and
coloured
materials

deposits, as mourners fulfilled their rite of passage at the location. Additionally, for part of its history, the site existed as an area enclosed by a causewayed ditch, which structured movement into and out of the interior around its southern portion, along the equinoctial axis between an eastern ramp into/out of the ditch and a western causeway. Like the mounds, the ditch orientation and the manner in which it directed movement at the site (referencing the rise, set and movement of the sun across the southern horizon), served to link activities there with the cosmos and the particular nature of the buried landscape (Owoc 2006). The visitor's obligatory and timely labour of construction during the passage rite of secondary kin disposal at Crig-a-Mennis recreated the landscape through enactment, drawing special attention to its particular spatial, stratigraphic and material qualities. Grounded through action in a set of material and visual symbols, the funerary ritual thus enabled practical and meaningful links to be made between the rite of passage for the deceased and community, the landscape, and the timeless repetitive cycles of the natural world. The liminal setting for the monument on a geological margin would have furthered the themes of boundary and transition so evident in other portions of the ritual at Crig-a-Mennis, and on other sites of this period.

PERFORMATIVE PRACTICE

Part of the way in which archaeologists make sense of their data it to categorise it. The range of constructional variability and funerary practice visible among the many ceremonial mounds and enclosures of later Neolithic/Bronze Age has been subjected to numerous attempts to fit it into some form of typological order. In such exercises reality has been forced to conform to expectations, hence the nuanced relationships between monument and landscape, based as they are on choices grounded in perception, embodied experience, and social labour, are difficult for archaeologists to immediately grasp. An alternative to adopting a generalising, de-contextualised approach at the outset is to consider the sites as outcomes of sequential deliberate acts or discrete practices that were informed by tradition, but also influenced by strategic decisions based upon local, contingent circumstances. This allows for every site to be different, but simultaneously enables a sensitivity to the sorts of long-term traditions of thought and behaviour that produce commonalities between them. Further, it enables the viewer in the present to focus on discrete acts that, when considered in context and over time, present a pattern of behaviour that illustrates the embodied and perceptual orientation of actors towards their landscapes, their material culture and each other.

Monuments do not build themselves. The sum total of discrete practices on sites like the ones described above comprises a monumental life history consisting of ordered gestural and kinesthetic *acts* that served to transform persons into social subjects, and natural substances into culturally meaningful materials. Such acts were also strategic, in that through their formality and setting, they established particular distinctions between realms of practice and in the process, drew attention to the important things taking place at these sites. Many of the actions involved in monument construction that are discussed in this contribution also occurred as part of the routine, everyday settings of later Neolithic/Early Bronze Age life (e.g. lighting fires, digging pits, cooking/burning, arranging and weaving posts into a wall, watching the opening and close of the day). Strategic *ritualisation* on these sites, and in domestic settings (Bell 1992, further addressed in Barrett 1991; Bradley 2005; and Owoc 2001) created a tensioned relationship between the two realms, and a same but different quality that 'alerted' (Lewis 1980) participants and viewers to the importance of the monumental context and acts.

With the above remarks in mind we might now consider the site of Trelen 2, in western Cornwall (Smith 1984). In the earlier second millennium BC, mourners inserted a series of wooden posts into the land surface surrounding a central pit, creating a stake circle. As these sorts of circles go, it compares somewhat unfavorably with others like it, and if it had made it into Paul Ashbee's (1957) overview of these things it would have been described as a rather irregular Category A2 circle – end of story. From a practice perspective however, its shape, manner of construction, and place in the sequence of construction tell us something. The circle followed a much earlier stake line on the site which was aligned directly on the MWSR–MSSS axis, and the later fabricators of the site maintained, or renewed this orientation with the addition of two posts to the circle. Further, its irregular form was thought by the excavator to have resulted from *several lines of people* holding stakes, or perhaps lengths of hurdling who *joined together* to create the circular enclosure. They then withdrew these posts and covered the central deposit with a large conical turf mound. The human fabrication of the circle, and its orientation and place in the life history of the monument are instructive, and reveal to us how the principal elements of the monument might have been made meaningful by the actions of the participants themselves. The stake circle was, in point of fact, a circle of kin and community whose unified labour was materialised in circular form, perhaps highlighting and reproducing their social relationships, responsibilities and commitments. Their eventual withdrawal of the stakes and the replacement of the circle by the mound in the ongoing development of the site parallels other instances across the south-west in which wooden elements were removed and replaced or covered by stone or other materials (e.g. Ashbee 1958; Christie 1960, 1988; Miles 1975; Miles and Miles 1971; Pollard 1967). At Trelen 2, the particular temporal-stratigraphic ordering of these landscape elements, and the maintenance of the original orientation would have served to highlight the transient qualities of wood and persons, and beginnings and endings, while also situating the larger community both physically and temporally within the more timeless cycle of the solar year. Moreover, the emphasis on transition for the community and perhaps their deceased kin, was also highlighted through their renewal of and position along the MWSR–MSSS axis. The construction of Trelen 2 then, enabled intimate connections and potential metaphors to be established between the community, their viewscape, time, and the elements of the natural world reworked as material culture.

CONCLUSION

I have suggested here that by being sensitive to place, perspective, and performative practice, we permit the ceremonial sites of later prehistory to tell us a great deal about how their builders constructed the relationship between monument and landscape. For communities in south-west Britain, at the death of friends and family, and at the most important times in the seasonal year, the fabric of earth, stone, living things, and the cosmos were humanly woven into experienced tapestries of light and darkness, texture, colour, orientation, kin and community. These monumental tapestries reworked the inhabited landscape through acts of performative practice that cemented and created social relationships, and temporally, spatially, and meaningfully integrated the living and the dead with the natural world.

ADDENDUM

The analyses of the creation and materialisation of cosmological traditions and social relations briefly outlined here represents but one of the ways in which an archaeology of monuments in the landscape can be written. Other kinds of stories about the relations between these two pivotal themes in contemporary archaeology can be found in this volume. Most however, arise from the particular kind of approach to archaeological practice outlined above, and all were influenced at some point along the way by one person.

Intimacy with the land, vision, and the courage to creatively yet rigorously explore what alternative stories of human landscape experience exist in the traces of the past characterise the many contributions Andrew Fleming has made to the discipline. The movement 'from blindness to insight' (Frodeman 2003: 110) evidenced in his work on Dartmoor and Swaledale represents the sort of landscape-directed science that archaeologists aspire to produce. Those examples, and his ongoing curiosity about the broader social significance of Bronze Age ceremonial monuments enabled and inspired this author's work on these sites many years ago, and continues to do so today.

BIBLIOGRAPHY

Ashbee, P., 1957 Stake and post circles in British round barrows. *Archaeological Journal* 114, 1–8.

Ashbee, P., 1958 The excavation of Tregullan Barrow, Treneglos Parish, Cornwall. *The Antiquaries Journal* 38, 174–93.

Baker, V.R., 2000 Conversing with the Earth: the geological approach to understanding. In Frodeman, R. (ed.), 2–10.

Barrett, J., 1991 Towards an archaeology of ritual. In Garwood, P., Jennings, D., Skeates, R. & Toms, J. (eds), 1–9.

Bell, C., 1992 *Ritual Theory, Ritual Practice*. Oxford: Oxford University Press.

Boivin, N. & Owoc, M.A. (eds), 2004 *Soils, Stones and Symbols: cultural perceptions of the mineral world*. London: UCL Press.

Bradley, R., 1998 *The Significance of Monuments: on the shaping of human experience in Neolithic and Bronze Age Europe*. London: Routledge.

Bradley, R., 2000a *An Archaeology of Natural Places*. London: Routledge.

Bradley, R., 2000b *The Good Stones: new investigations of the Clava Cairns*. Edinburgh: Society of Antiquaries of Scotland.

Bradley, R., 2005 *Ritual and Domestic Life in Prehistoric Europe*. London: Routledge.

Burl, A., 1981 'By the light of the cinerary moon': chambered tombs and the astronomy of death. In Ruggles, C. & Whittle, A. (eds), 243–74.

Burl, A., 1983 *Prehistoric Astronomy and Ritual*. Princes Risborough: Shire.

Chippindale, C., 1983 *Stonehenge Complete*. London: Thames and Hudson.

Christie, P., 1960 Crig-a-Mennis; A Bronze Age barrow at Liskey, Perranzabuloe, Cornwall. *Proceedings of the Prehistoric Society* 33, 76–97.

Christie, P., 1988 A barrow cemetery on Davidstow Moor, Cornwall: wartime excavations by C.K. Croft Andrew 1939–1944. *Cornish Archaeology* 24, 27–169.

Dunn, J., 2005 *A Comparative Analysis of Lithic Materials Utilized in the Construction of Chambered Cairns on the Isles of Scilly, UK*. Unpublished BA thesis, Mercyhurst College.

Foltz, B.V., 2000 Inhabitation and orientation: science beyond disenchantment. In Frodeman, R. (ed.), 25–35.

Frodeman, R. (ed.), 2000 *Earth Matters: the earth sciences, philosophy, and the claims of community*. Upper Saddle River: Prentice Hall.

Frodeman, R., 2003 *Geo-Logic: breaking ground between philosophy and the earth sciences*. Albany: State University of New York Press.

Garwood, P., Jennings, D., Skeates, R. & Toms, J. (eds), 1991 *Sacred and Profane*. Oxford: Oxford University Committee for Archaeology Monograph.

Heggie, D.C., 1981 *Megalithic Science: ancient mathematics and astronomy in Northwest Europe*. London: Thames and Hudson.

Lewis, G., 1980 *Day of Shining Red: an essay in understanding ritual*. Cambridge: Cambridge University Press.

Miles, H., 1975 Barrows on the St. Austell granite. *Cornish Archaeology* 14, 5–81.

Miles, H. & Miles, T.J., 1971 Excavations on Longstone Downs, St. Stephen in Brannel and St. Mewan. *Cornish Archaeology*, 10, 5–28.

Owoc, M.A., 2001 Bronze Age cosmologies: the construction of time and space in South-Western funerary/ritual monuments. In Smith, A.T. & Brookes, A. (eds), 27–38.

Owoc, M.A., 2004 A phenomenology of the buried landscape: soil as material culture in the Bronze Age of South-West Britain. In Boivin, N. & Owoc, M.A. (eds), 107–21.

Owoc, M.A., 2006 Beyond geoarchaeology: pragmatist explorations of alternative viewscapes in the British Bronze Age and beyond. In Robertson, E.C., Seibert, J.D., Fernandez, D.C., & Zender, M.U. (eds), 3–14.

Parker Pearson, M. & Ramilsonina, 1998 Stonehenge for the ancestors: the stones pass on the message. *Antiquity* 72, 308–26.

Pollard, S.H.M., 1967 Seven prehistoric sites near Honiton, Devon, Part I, a Beaker flint ring and three flint cairns. *Proceedings of the Devon Archaeological Society* 25, 19-39.

Richards, C., 1996 Monuments as landscape: creating the centre of the world in Orkney. *World Archaeology* 28, 190-208.

Robertson, E.C., Seibert, J.D., Fernandez, D.C., & Zender, M.U., (eds) 2006 *Space and Spatial Analysis in Archaeology*. Calgary: University of Calgary Press.

Ruggles, C., 1999 *Astronomy in Prehistoric Britain and Ireland*. New Haven: Yale University Press.

Ruggles C. & Whittle, A., (eds) 1981 *Astronomy and Society in Britain during the Period 4000-1500 BC*. Oxford: BAR.

Smith, A.T. & Brookes, A. (eds), 2001 *Holy Ground: theoretical issues relating to the landscaped and material culture of ritual space*. Oxford: BAR.

Smith, G., 1984 Excavations on Goonhilly Downs, The Lizard. *Cornish Archaeology* 23, 3-24.

Thomas, J., 1991 *Rethinking the Neolithic*. Cambridge: Cambridge University Press.

Tuan, Y-F., 1977 *Space and Place: the perspective of experience*. Minneapolis: University of Minnesota Press.

6

STEPPING ONTO THE COMMONS: SOUTH-WESTERN STONE ROWS

Peter Herring

LINES OF STONES

Stepping out of the mud and running across the bare rab goes a trail of small stones, a pace apart, some standing, some fallen, fading as they enter furze and grass above the high watermark: a previously unrecorded stone row found while walking around Colliford Lake reservoir, on Bodmin Moor, when the water level was particularly low after the dry summer of 2006. A new discovery – now the Moor's ninth known row – allowing us to walk again in the footsteps of a group of prehistoric people. Cause for brief comment, perhaps, but possibly not the most substantial monument from which to sound a tribute to someone who has transformed south-western prehistoric archaeology. The row's discovery, survey and interpretation do, however, throw light on several aspects of the south-western uplands, past and present, that have long intrigued Andrew Fleming.

Thirty-two stones form the 66m-long straight line of the Searle's Down stone row (named after the rounded hill on whose eastern flank it lies). Its downhill SSE end probably continues into the reservoir; any stones here drowned not only in water, but also in soft black peaty silt, washed down from upslope soil. The row would have lain in rough pasture to the east of nineteenth-century intake fields associated with the several Searle's Down farms. Its line does not conform to the rectilinear pattern of those fields, and is not, therefore, an unfinished element of their system. Field evidence confirms that the rough pasture has never been intensively farmed, although there has been prospecting, streamworking and openworking for tin in the near vicinity. Away from the tinning, any prehistoric remains can be expected to survive well. There appears to be no terminal feature, no larger stone or cairn, at the uphill NNW end of the row, at the crest of the steeper part of the hill.

Reservoir wave action has scoured soil away from most stones so that only 15 are still on edge, their long axes following the row's line, as do those in all Bodmin Moor stone rows. Gaps between closest parts of adjacent stones range from 0.6m to 0.9m in the better preserved stretches; there were probably originally a further 34 to 39 stones in the length of row recorded here (i.e. 66 to 71 in all). Around six stones were lost to an un-dated hollow-way near the NNW end. The location of one lost stone, recently pulled out, is betrayed by a fresh 0.14m-deep hole, and others seem to have also been wholly removed, perhaps by modern stone-splashers.

For elements of a monument, the stones are tiny. None of the toppled ones, whose greatest dimensions can be measured, is longer than 0.5m, and no standing stone rises more than 0.2m (eight inches) above the rabby subsoil into which they are set. Seven are less than 0.1m high, and the average height is a mere 0.107m (four inches); if we factor in an inch or two for washed-away topsoil then we must imagine the stones barely breaking the surface. They are also irregular in shape and inconsistent in quality, most being coarse-grained granite, but three fine-grained. Searle's Down is, then, one of Bodmin Moor's more modest rows, which are themselves generally less substantial and dramatic than the better-known Dartmoor sites, but similar in scale to some on Exmoor, whose stones can again be as low as 0.1m (see Johnson and Rose 1994; Riley and Wilson-North 2001).

Nicholas Johnson noted in 1994 that six of the seven rows then known on Bodmin Moor had southern terminals: four as the row's tallest stone; two as transversely set slabs (Johnson and Rose 1994; Bender *et al.* 1995). Further examination of the reservoir foreshore established that the Searle's Down row also has a southern terminal, a 0.55m high orthostat. Our row is perfectly on line with this stone, but as the intervening 230m is under water it is not possible to verify that stones extended all the way to it. The suggested total length (296m) fits well with the range of Bodmin Moor rows (59-560m) and the Colvannick and East Moor rows on Bodmin Moor and the Nine Maidens row on St Breock Downs all have sizeable gaps between the main stretch of the row and the terminal stone (Johnson and Rose 1994).

Frances Griffith (1984) excavated three round cairns on the low spur here in 1977-8 in advance of the reservoir. The orthostat, now fallen, was barely 1m north-west of the largest and lowest-lying cairn's outer edge and up-throw from the holes for this stone and a second, 4.5m to its east, was apparently in place for only a very short time before being covered by earth 'mounding', part of the cairn's perimeter. A small cairn, 5m in diameter, 10m SE of the orthostat, and more or less on line with two other closely spaced small cairns (CRIVB and CRIVC) to its SW, was enclosed by an outer ring cairn (CRIVA) shortly after its construction. The orthostat, which predated this outer ring but not necessarily the inner cairn, and the row which it ends, may account for why the outer ring is not concentric with the 'inner cairn'. There seems to have been a need for the outer circuit to have been pulled to the north-west to be just a step away from the row.

The site's stratigraphy and soils convinced Frances that all elements of the cairn were created, and the orthostats were erected, at essentially the same time – there was no significant period of inactivity. This is important as radiocarbon dating of charcoal samples from beneath the inner cairn came out at 1560 ± 80 BC (Griffith 1984), recalibrated to 2040-1620 cal. BC (Jones 2005). As the charcoal is oak, it is safest to simply state that cairn and orthostat are from the early second millennium BC (Andy M. Jones, pers. comm.). Nevertheless this is still the tightest dating evidence for a stone row in south-west Britain.

LINES IN THE LANDSCAPE

Little is known of stone row function, although most would agree with John Barnatt (1982, 94) that 'as it clearly was not practical, some form of ceremonial use must be proposed'. Emmett demolished any astronomical associations: few rows are straight (and so do not point directly at anything) and there is no preferred orientation. Indeed, Emmett laid emphasis on their, 'apparently casual' design (1979, 97).

So how might such slight monuments have been used, and in what sorts of social contexts? Barnatt was not the first to consider that they, 'could have been designed to be followed' (1982, 94; see Fox 1973), and he wondered whether they may have also served as a 'symbolic barrier', perhaps with different land use to be expected on each side (Barnatt 1982, 94).

Andrew Fleming noticed that ceremonial complexes including stone rows are fairly regularly spaced around Dartmoor (with the exception of the NW quarter), suggesting first that they were created by 'different, contemporary human groups, each working within the framework of beliefs and rituals associated with stone rows to create its own distinctive sacred place' and secondly that 'most of the fringe zone of the Moor had been claimed, in some sense, by about 2500 BC' (Fleming 1988, 97-8). The date might now be placed a little later, but the spaced-out and moor-edge pattern of rows is repeated in the sparser distributions on Exmoor and Bodmin Moor (Riley and Wilson-North 2001; Johnson and Rose 1994).

After considering the design of Bodmin Moor rows, Chris Tilley felt that 'their main purpose would seem to have been mnemonic, to confirm where one was, the margins or centre of a sacred area, and that this area of ritualised geographic space (bog, stream, Tor or area of higher land) was linked to another, providing a tangible cognitive map of Bodmin Moor' (Tilley 1995, 34). At three rows Tilley noted 'perspective effects' as one walks along them: views of significant features of the moorland landscape, such as the summit tors of the two great hills, Roughtor and Brown Willy, poking over the shoulder of intervening downland, either open up or are closed off as the row is moved along. Such effects, though subtle, are simple and effective devices. It is not surprising to see them in other historical contexts, such as in contrived approaches to medieval castles (Herring 2003), and, of course, in the eighteenth-century English landscape parks. Lancelot 'Capability' Brown and his followers made full use of the 'burst', a sudden opening up of a significant view – the house, a lake, a church tower – when moving along a carefully placed drive or ride (Phibbs 1996).

Many prehistoric Cornish monuments appear to have been designed and positioned in a similar way. The earlier landscape architects may have been using controlled revelations, bursts, as means of introducing initiates to deeper knowledge of the community's world, its ancestral world, perhaps, but also the world in which the young person would spend the rest of their life. A crucial feature of a burst is that your breath is only properly taken away at your first exposure to it. Once you know what will happen you may still admire the conceit when revisiting the monument, but the effect is then more about remembering the pleasure, deepening the understanding, and reinforcing the commitment to the community's world.

It is difficult to present the power of bursts, like other experiential observations, in standard archaeological literature. Grammatical constructs give the game away too soon and graphic representations and photographs freeze and flatten revelations that depend on movement and surprise. To even-handedly appraise the validity of such observations, and apply the level of critique that Fleming (1999) has himself brought to bear on Tilley's work in Wales, there is no alternative to getting out and walking the sites oneself. It can be said that for the Bodmin Moor stone rows, each of the visual effects Tilley describes does seem to work. Indeed it is possible, with the privileged knowledge of the Moor's topography gained from 25 years work on it, to strengthen Tilley's arguments for this quality of the rows.

For example, at Buttern Hill, not only does Brown Willy disappear from view as the row is walked along from north to south (Tilley 1995), but a significant burst is experienced precisely when the tallest southern stone, the row's terminal, is reached. At that moment the early Neolithic quoit on the western slope of Leskernick Hill, pops into view on the horizon, having been previously masked by Buttern Hill's flank. The quoit is only skylined from certain directions, making the Buttern row burst more convincing and is also incorporated into designed landscapes involving other early second millennium monuments (Herring 1997). That the effect only works for people of average adult height (around 1.6m) might even suggest that the set-up was indeed intended for revealing key features of the world (Brown Willy; the ancestral quoit) during an adolescent's rites of passage ceremony.

Two further bursts, at Tolborough Tor and Searle's Down, like that at the Leskernick row (Tilley 1995), both involve revelation of the Moor's second-highest hill, Roughtor; the multi-peaked site of an apparently early Neolithic tor enclosure, a later Neolithic bank cairn, and the focus of landscape design for numerous cairns, stone circles and other later prehistoric ceremonial monuments (20) (Herring forthcoming; Herring and Kirkham forthcoming).

Roughtor

Brown Willy

Catshole long cairn

20 Part of the dramatic visual 'burst' of tor-topped hills seen once the summit cairn on Tolborough Tor is climbed. Roughtor's southern tor pokes over Brown Willy's shoulder and appears to merge with its descending line of tors

The first row identified on Bodmin Moor was a line of five low uprights on the high south-eastern slope of Tolborough Tor, 'the tail-end of a stone row erected for an unknown purpose' (Malim 1936, 25). Nick Johnson and Pete Rose surveyed it and thought a sixth upright, on line with the others and perched on the eastern side of the summit tor cairn, was also part of the row, suggesting that it post-dated the cairn (Johnson and Rose 1994). The most south-easterly stone, next to a small tor skylined on the crest of the hill when approaching from the Moor's great dividing valley, the Fowey, signposted the row to those who knew it, enabling them to lead those who didn't along the correct route up the hill's long and steep south-eastern slope. When the crest was reached the cairn itself would block views to the north-west and only when the short row was walked along, and the cairn itself was mounted, did one of the most spectacular bursts on Bodmin Moor open up. After travelling through the middle Moor's rounded downlands, the initiate suddenly saw the great tors of Brown

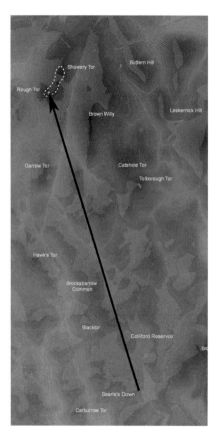

21 The line of sight to Roughtor from the NW end of the Searle's Down row

Willy, Catshole, Butterstor and Garrow, but they probably had to have the southern rockpiles of Roughtor itself pointed out to them, discreetly poking above Brown Willy's stony skyline.

At Searle's Down the two related bursts are less dramatic. The orthostat and three cairns are placed where Roughtor, a distant presence on the northern skyline, disappears from view when approached from the south-west, from off the Moor. If the row were then walked along the initiate would not see Roughtor again until precisely where the row ends, on the crest of Searle's Down, when the tor rises above Menniridden Downs once more. This is corroborated by GIS modelling of a line-of-sight analysis based on a 5m resolution Digital Terrain Model of Cornwall (Bryn Tapper pers. comm.). This effect helps explain why the row is orientated as it is. If it had continued north-east, along the line of the three cairns, Roughtor would not re-emerge for over a kilometre (north of Stuffle); the 296m-long line taken by the row is the shortest available to the row's builders that would allow the second burst to work, an economy that increases the probability that the site was really meant to work in this way (*21*). This reconstruction also allows us to suggest a sequence for the group of monuments at Searle's Down and Colliford: (1) the three small cairns; (2)

the stone row and orthostat; (3) the outer cairn of CRIVA, the walk along the row commencing by stepping off the outer edge of the cairn.

OF STONE AND WOOD

The Searle's Down stone row would not have been discovered if vegetation cover had not been removed by waves. Large parts of Bodmin Moor are scrubbing up due to recent reductions in grazing levels, intended to improve the rough ground's biodiversity. The period of well-grazed acid grasslands, when all earthworks were visible, and when seven stone rows were found in less than as many years, appears to be over. Low banks are largely lost now, and it is becoming increasingly difficult to locate well-known sites on Bodmin Moor; for example at East Moor, one of the more substantial rows (stones averaging 1.0m high) is effectively lost to dense stands of European furze that have developed in the last 10 years. Loss to view of important monuments is compounded by root and rhizome damage to below-ground remains, and increased erosion caused by the remaining cattle and ponies tracking along narrow passages through the scrub.

While concerned about recent developments, we nevertheless appreciate that the low levels of vegetation that enabled the discovery of Bodmin Moor's stone rows should also be modelled for the time when they were created. They would have been just as lost then in anything other than low heath or cropped grass.

The suggestion that rows and other late third and early second millennia BC monuments were created in clearings in oak woodland (e.g. Quinnell 1994) depends partly on the only pollen evidence possibly associated with a Dartmoor row; that from near the atypical Cholwichtown Waste site which is at the second lowest altitude (243m) of the 71 Dartmoor rows assessed by Emmett (1979), and had unusually large stones (to 1.9m high), able to be seen in relatively dense vegetation. Although Emmett was unsure whether the pollen evidence could really be used to reconstruct the environment in which the Cholwichtown row was built, it suited his scepticism of all things aligned or designed for him to agree with Lady Fox that stone rows occupied 'opened swathes in an oak forest, rather than marching across open moor' (Fox 1964, 65). Environmental evidence is invaluable when considering the open-ness of vegetation cover, but constructive dialogue with palaeo-environmentalists should also include confident presentation of the implications for an understanding of the vegetation of different forms of landscape design (see Chapman and Gearey 2000). Pollen from soils buried by the Colliford cairns indicates that when the Searle's Down row was erected the immediate area was open grassland that 'had developed into a heather-dominated community'; oak and hazel were of minor importance (Caseldine 1984, 110). Other palaeo-environmental evidence for the later third and early second millennia BC also suggests an increasingly open landscape on Bodmin Moor, with trees largely confined to sheltered valley bottoms (Gearey and Charman 1996; Gearey *et al.* 2000; Jones and Tinsley 2000-1). The bursts to Roughtor, from Leskernick, Tolborough and Searle's Down of course suggest that the intervening downs, higher and in the centre of the Moor, were also clear of woodland or scrub.

Maintenance of cleared areas on the central downs of Dartmoor, Exmoor and Bodmin Moor could only have been achieved through fairly intensive grazing with large herds and flocks, animal numbers in the tens of thousands (Herring forthcoming). As well as digesting the obvious implications for our understanding of early farming economies (comparable to Pryor 2006), we have to appreciate that the Moors had been subjected to startling transformations; woodlands which limited long views, except from summit tors, had been replaced by undivided grasslands in which one could move and see in all directions. We are accustomed to such freedom, but it seems reasonable to imagine that for those who created this newly open world, the ability to see downland rolling into downland, with distant tors poking over the backs of closer ones, would have been a source of wonder and pleasure. It is not surprising that they worked with this quality when designing their landscapes.

COMING OF THE COMMONS

It seems unlikely that the extensive but intensively used pastures, effectively commons, were either created or managed haphazardly. They were probably subject to controls on livestock numbers and against trespassers familiar to those with rights on modern commons. If two functions of community gatherings at early Neolithic tor enclosures and quoits and later stone circles were formal co-ordination of the establishment and use of commons, and the settling of disputes between people (Herring forthcoming), then these ancestral monuments would retain significance for later commoners.

We have seen that on Dartmoor, Exmoor and Bodmin Moor stone rows tend to be either on or near the edges of areas of higher ground, probably open commons by the Early Bronze Age. They are also relatively close to valleys (probably still wooded) along which people heading for the downs probably came. Stone rows, if partly designed for moving along by groups emerging with their livestock from these wooded valleys onto the downlands in the late spring time, when the rough grasses become palatable, would work in several ways:

- As Chris Tilley's mnemonics, they reminded people of their rights on the Moor, the areas where their hefted flocks and herds customarily grazed and watered, and the other places where they met and worked with the other communities with whom they shared the Moor.

- As ceremonial sites, associated with standing stones, cairns, and significant tors like Roughtor, they enabled young adults to be formally introduced via bursts to the communal geographies of their adult world.
- As monuments they celebrated several things: the transformation of the dark wooded world; the herds and flocks that helped achieve this and which were their companions, wealth and food; and the increasingly complex communities of which they were part. Those rows, like Searle's Down, with tiny stones, may well have been especially admired, being only visible because the grass was so closely grazed, thus making the low grassland itself an essential part of the monument.

Of course, Andrew Fleming pre-empted some of this when writing nearly 20 years ago: 'We must ... take seriously the possibility that these stone rows, and the cairns and standing stones associated with them, were placed in areas transitional between zones of different land use, for example on the edge of an upland common' (Fleming 1988, 45). Andrew and I are therefore suggesting that the basic land use patterns on the south-western uplands, that would be more formally fixed 500 years later by the reaves and co-axial field systems, were in place by the early years of the second millennium BC.

ACKNOWLEDGEMENTS

Billy Herring assisted in surveying the Searle's Down row. Bryn Tapper helped with the GIS analysis. I am one of many south-western landscape historians inspired by Andrew Fleming's sharpness in the field. He showed how survey could and should be analytical and critical: record faithfully, but always be alert for the anomaly that throws the most revealing light on the features and patterns being plotted and described. I believe Andrew's major contribution to prehistoric archaeology in the South West was drawing out as clear an exposition of prehistoric multi-layered rural social structure as any yet presented (Fleming 1988), a structure that holds up well as a framework for more particularist post-processualist musings. He did this by recording, analysing and probing the patterns of Dartmoor's Middle Bronze Age reaves, the great significance of whose date, extent and design he was the first to recognise.

BIBLIOGRAPHY

Barnatt, J., 1982 *Prehistoric Cornwall, The Ceremonial Monuments*. Wellingborough: Turnstone Press.
Bender, B., Hamilton, S., & Tilley, C., 1995 Leskernick: the biography of an excavation. *Cornish Archaeology* 34, 58-73.
Chadwick, A. (ed.), forthcoming *Recent Approaches to the Archaeology of Land Allotment*. Oxford: Archaeopress.

Chapman, H.P. & Gearey, B.R., 2000 Palaeoecology and the perception of prehistoric landscapes: some comments on visual approaches to phenomenology. *Antiquity* 74, 316-9.

Charman, D.J., Newnham, R.M. & Croot, D.G. (eds.), 1996 *Devon and East Cornwall Field Guide.* London: Quaternary Research Association.

Emmett, D.D., 1979 Stone rows: the traditional view reconsidered. *Proceedings of the Devon Archaeological Society* 37, 94-114.

Fleming, A., 1988 *The Dartmoor Reaves, Investigating Prehistoric Land Divisions.* London: Batsford.

Fleming, A., 1999 Phenomenology and the megaliths of Wales: a dreaming too far? *Oxford Journal of Archaeology* 18, 119-25.

Fox, A., 1964 *South-West England.* London: Thames and Hudson.

Fox, A., 1973 *South-West England 3500 BC – AD 600.* Newton Abbot: David and Charles.

Gearey, B. & Charman, D., 1996 Rough Tor, Bodmin Moor: testing some archaeological hypotheses with landscape palaeoecology. In Charman D.J., Newnham, R.M. & Croot, D.G. (eds.), 101-19.

Gearey, B.R, Sharman, D.J. & Kent, M., 2000 Palaeoecological evidence for the prehistoric settlement of Bodmin Moor, Cornwall, south-west England: Part II – land-use changes from the Neolithic to the present. *Journal of Archaeological Science* 27, 493-508.

Griffith, F., 1984 Archaeological Investigations at Colliford Reservoir, Bodmin Moor, 1977-78. *Cornish Archaeology* 23, 49-140.

Herring, P., 1997 Early prehistoric sites at Leskernick, Altarnun. *Cornish Archaeology* 36, 176-85.

Herring, P., 2003 Cornish medieval deer parks. In Wilson-North, R. (ed.), 34-50.

Herring, P., forthcoming Commons, fields and communities in prehistoric Cornwall. In Chadwick, A. (ed.).

Herring, P. & Kirkham, G., forthcoming, A bank cairn on Roughtor. *Cornish Archaeology.*

Johnson, N. & Rose, P., 1994 *Bodmin Moor, an Archaeological Survey; Volume 1: The Human Landscape to c.1800.* London: English Heritage and the Royal Commission on the Historical Monuments of England.

Jones, A.M., 2005 *Cornish Bronze Age Ceremonial Landscapes c.2500-1500 BC.* Oxford: Archaeopress.

Jones, A.M. & Tinsley, H.M., 2000-1 Recording ancient environments at De Lank, St. Breward, Cornwall. *Cornish Archaeology* 39-40, 146-60.

Malim, J.W., 1936 *The Bodmin Moors.* London: Methuen.

Maltby, E. & Caseldine, C.J., 1984 Environmental reconstruction at Colliford. In Griffith, F., 92-117.

Phibbs, J., 1996 *The Assassination of Capability Brown.* Cirencester: Debois Landscape Survey Group.

Pryor, F., 2006 *Farmers in Prehistoric Britain.* Second edition. Stroud: Tempus.

Quinnell, H., 1994 New perspectives on upland monuments – Dartmoor in earlier prehistory. *Proceedings of the Devon Archaeological Society* 52, 49-62.

Riley, H. & Wilson-North, R., 2001 *The Field Archaeology of Exmoor.* Swindon: English Heritage.

Tilley, C., 1995 Rocks as resources: landscapes and power. *Cornish Archaeology* 34, 5-57.

Wilson-North, R. (ed.), 2003 *The Lie of the Land.* Exeter: The Mint Press.

7

TOMBS FOR THE LIVING: THREE DECADES LATER, STILL A QUESTION OF VISION AND DESIGN IN NEOLITHIC/ CHALCOLITHIC PORTUGAL

Ivone Canavilhas

INTRODUCTION

Megalithic monuments attract and capture our attention, giving free reign to the imagination. Built to endure, they recall past histories and memories, convey sensations of wonder and awe, and arouse curiosity. Though monument forms varied over time and space, their use as burial spaces and places for ritual worship followed formalised schemes adapted to the regional, social, cultural and natural geographies of the different communities.

In the early 1970s Andrew Fleming (1972; 1973) wrote two radical papers concerning the study of megalithic monuments, 'Vision and Design' and 'Tombs for the Living', which departed from previous interpretations and provided the foundations of subsequent approaches to the study of megaliths. Fleming argued against the diffusion of cultural attributes as an explanation for morphological similarity, regarding monumental design to be of central importance, reflecting responses to the functional requirements of ritual organisation. He saw the design of chambered cairns in terms of problem-solving wherein the socially imposed need for components such as receptacles for ancestral remains, ceremonial areas and/or foci and control over access was fulfilled by local design solutions, dependent upon the availability and procurement of appropriate material resources.

Fleming also argued that the tombs' conspicuous nature was intended to attract and focus communal reflection, throughout periods of ritual activity and during the seasonal routine as a constant presence in the landscape. He noted their potential as material foci for territorial identity. The tombs were considered to operate within a 'signalling' system intended to reinforce existing leadership patterns. Fleming pointed out the limitations of typologies, showing it was difficult to discover how far a typological series approaches a chronological sequence; moreover, a typology could not explain why artefacts, including monuments, change. For him 'new and original types of ceremonial monuments have usually arisen not as a result of the diffusion of foreign models nor of local degeneration, but in response to local design requirements' (Fleming 1972, 71). Fleming suggested that the critical variable for the different type of monuments was design, since even ceremonial monuments have to perform clearly-defined functions; local design could be a solution to problems imposed by social structure among other things. In 'Tombs for the Living', Fleming argued against the rigid standpoint, accepted for a long time, which stated that these monuments functioned solely as burial chambers. He saw monuments as products of design, thus it is obvious that only one of their functions was to provide a container for the dead; another was to look as impressive as possible to the living communities. Tombs were sited with regard to their position on the skyline and in order that they might be seen by other groups. A considerable degree of control and deliberation must be postulated. Fleming, in bridging the gap between the two opposing theories of the time, diffusion of foreign models or local degeneration, can be seen as antecedent to later ideas about the choreography of monuments and the importance of the landscape in the study of these monuments.

MEGALITHS IN PORTUGAL

Megalithic monuments are amongst the most prominent remains left by past populations in Portugal. Throughout Europe they comprise a heterogeneous group of constructions; hence, monuments of highly different character may be described as 'megalithic tombs'. However, one shared characteristic is monumentality, a concept which creates useful distinctions from earlier burial forms and the demarcation of a confined space for the dead. The origins of megalithic monuments have been discussed in Portugal along the same lines as in other parts of Europe.

The megalithic phenomenon in Portugal can be characterised as the materialisation through a distinctive funerary architecture of a complex set of beliefs and attitudes starting in the Neolithic and lasting through the Bronze Age. Thus megaliths evolved in different regions in distinctively different ways. The evolution of funerary practices between the fourth and the end of the second millennium BC was not linear or constant, neither are these monuments distributed evenly throughout Portugal; frequent in the interior of south and central Portugal, their incidence declines in the coastal areas of the south-west, though are found in larger numbers in the north-west.

Similarly, various types of megalithic monuments are not confined to particular regions as some geographical differences exist. In the central and southern regions the majority of monuments have a polygonal chamber and passage, *sepulcros alentejanos* (e.g. Anta Grande do Zambujeiro, Alentejo), in the south-west there is a clear predominance of *tholoi* – corbel vaulted chambers and *hypogea* – rock cut tombs (e.g. *Tholos* Praia das Maçãs, Estremadura), which are non-existent in the northern part of Portugal where the *mamoas* – small circular/polygonal chambers (e.g. Mamoa 2 Meninas do Castro, Entre Douro e Minho) are the most common monuments.

Other typical elements of architectural diversity in the use of space visible both inside and outside the tombs are characteristic of the different areas. For example, inside the chambers, rock art and side niches distinguish the north and south, with the latter found only in the south. Although widely distributed throughout Portugal the majority of decorated megalithic tombs, mostly passage graves, occur in northern and central Portugal. The main concentration of decorated sites is bounded in the south by the Serra da Estrela, the 'schist plaque' northern boundary. The schist plaques, common in the south, are rare in the north (with the exception of Vale de Fachas, Beira Alta). Long stalled passages are more common in the south than the north. Recent excavations have uncovered a variety of structures such as forecourts and facades associated with ritual activity, especially in the north.

It is possible that one of the factors which contributed to this diversity was associated with the different time frames of the tombs. Based on evidence recovered in Beira Alta it seems that tombs were continually built and sealed after a short time, while in the south tombs remained open for longer and were often later re-used. Possibly this diversity can be explained through the different conceptions of time encapsulated in these tombs as well as their relationship with the landscape. I will explore this possibility in a case study of Alcalar 7.

ALCALAR 7: A THOLOS IN THE MEGALITHIC NECROPOLIS OF ALCALAR (ALGARVE)

The cemetery of Alcalar has been explored and studied since 1880 by different Portuguese scholars: Nunes da Glória (1880), Estácio da Veiga (1880-9), Pereira Jardim (1900), Santos Rocha (1906-11) and José Formosinho (1933). Most recently extensive work was undertaken by Rui Parreira and later Elena Morán. The necropolis of Alcalar consists of at least 22 tombs: one passage grave, 14 *tholoi*, six cists and one hypogeum.

Two major construction techniques are identified in Alcalar: orthostatic construction, where the structural strength of the wall is contained in a few, relatively large, upright standing stones or orthostats. These orthostats may protrude into the chamber and delimit space into compartments or they may be flush with the chamber wall. Orthostats may be the only components of the chamber wall or the intervening space may be linked with sections of horizontally laid stones forming a conventional dry stone wall between neighbouring orthostats. The second technique is to build the chamber with horizontally laid slabs throughout. These chambers are of complex

22 Ceremonial niche. *Courtesy of Parreira and Morán*

shape and large area. For the same reason that walling of the chambers was required to be of strong construction, roofing needed to be capable of withstanding great pressure. The method commonly adopted was corbelling. This method of construction leads to chambers high in comparison to width, since each successive course may only overlap by a small proportion of its depth.

Alcalar 7 is a *tholos* with corbel-vaulted chamber and schist wall passage. According to Estácio da Veiga (1891) the chamber had two side niches, one pointing NE the other SSW. Recent excavation uncovered another niche not considered a burial niche but a ritual one where ceremonies using fire were performed (*22*).

One of the peculiarities of this tomb is the schist walls, in that not only the chamber had dry-stone walling but for the first time the monoliths of the passage were replaced by rows of small schist slabs. The passage, *c.*9.5m long, was subdivided into three spaces which follow the forecourt, starting at the entrance of the tomb:

- Three steps lead the way to the square forecourt – *c*.0.88m each side to the door of the passage.
- The beginning of the passage as far as the second door is *c*.3.20m long x *c*.0.88m wide.
- The passage follows for another *c*.2.40m to the third door.
- The rest of the passage up to the entrance of the chamber is 1.55m long.

The entire passage is only 1.20m high and was covered by capstones placed on top of the lateral masonry walls. The passage orientation is E–SE and the chamber W–NW. Outside the tomb on the path close to the facade lie two red sandstone *menhirs*.

The modern excavation of Alcalar 7 revealed the monument in its entirety and complexity. According to Morán (2001) the tomb sequence would have been as follows:

- The first phase in construction was the preparation of the ground where the tomb was going to be built – this action denotes a careful choice of the specific location for the tomb. The ground was marked and consecrated through fire as attested by the hearth found underneath the structure.
- The opening of a large pit at the geometrical centre of the mound intended to be the location of the chamber and side niches.
- The bottom of the pit was paved with limestone slabs which form the chamber floor; the edge of the pit was lined with dry walling (schist slabs), the lowest courses of the chamber wall.
- On the top, at the levelled layer height, earth was laid for an even surface used to set down a peripheral wall to the tomb, revetting the cairn, and the back support of the chamber.
- The inside of the area delineated by the exterior wall was filled with small limestone blocks (no earth was used).
- On the west niche a ritual ceremony using fire occurred.
- After the niche's ceiling collapsed, the niche was walled up (still in prehistoric time) and its face rebuilt from the interior with a narrower wall.
- The interior of the tomb was blocked with a sealing structure.
- The closed monument maintained external ritual spaces. The facade overlies the sealing devices, illustrating a continuity of use. Abandoned as a burial space it was still used as a ritual space.
- Re-use during the Roman period.
- Re-utilisation of the chamber during the Muslim period.
- Archaeological excavation led by Estácio da Veiga in 1882.
- Use of the chamber as a rain water cistern for cattle.

23 Alcalar 7 (Mexilhoeira Grande, Algarve)

The monument comprises a white limestone cairn covering the *tholos*, sealed by a blocking structure covering the exterior mouth of the passage (*23, 24*). The modern excavation evidence of Alcalar 7 shows a lengthy history of the tomb and acts of maintenance, modification and even transformation, reaffirming its importance as a ceremonial centre. The various acts of modification illustrate the increasing importance attached to the control of space and the regulation of movement, perhaps only understood and manipulated by an elite of initiates, not known to the entire community.

Until recently, in conventional accounts both monumentality and architecture were seen as important only in connection with the process of construction. Little attention was given to the intended use of the building, the activities undertaken within it, the paths of the people moving through it, the significance of particular landscapes and places or the principles of order and ideas of cosmology embodied and inscribed within the tomb's form.

When studying the particular architecture of Alcalar 7, the facade, forecourt and vestibule show a good example of some elements inherent to the concepts of vision and design. These elements were common in those monuments where visibility was both enhanced and involved concealment from the community outside. In the construction of this tomb and in its detailed features, access and screening were a predominant element.

The deliberate architectural arrangements of forecourt and facade, in terms of size, shape and profile, clearly structure the way this tomb should be approached and perceived, and physically orchestrated bodily movement and attention paid to

24 Alcalar 7, detail of
entrance

particular spatial areas of the tomb. There is a clear delimitation of spaces in the tomb;
door slabs were found, the space was fragmented, broken down and concealed using
pillar orthostats. It is clear that different rituals occurred inside the tomb, only known
to a few, as the choreography of space was also intimately linked to differential access
to knowledge. Thus different members of the community would have engaged with
the monuments at different levels of intensity; people's different modes of participation
in prescribed formulae of speech, action and movement likely acted as a means for
the establishment and reproduction of various social wisdoms and authorities. The
monument's exterior space provided a primary focus for legitimisation of authority
and knowledge claims, indeed for possible challenges to the existing order, precisely
because of its public nature.

The passage is a transitional space from inside to outside designed to convey this experience to the body and also involved movement from light to darkness. The corbelling of the chamber shapes and limits architectural possibilities but also offers scope for niches and differentiated spaces within the chamber.

The architecture at Alcalar 7 was intended to have theatrical bodily effects. Thus the tomb can be seen as a performative space, a transformer of experience as evidenced by:

- Forcing changes in physical/bodily posture: being able to stand straight upright or having to crawl.
- Changes in volume: contrast between the wider open spaces of the chamber and narrower confinement of the passage.
- Successive darkening of space and the changing effects of light. The experiences created in the interior transformed the daily experience evoking a sense of the infinite and eternal.
- The manipulation of perspective, internal distances often cannot be accurately discerned or judged, the portal doorways both frame and hide what is beyond.
- The creation of special visual effects through light (natural or fire) and specific architectural elements such as the side niches.

This monument can be seen as a theatre for communal action, where different plays were staged and perceived in differing ways by community members, depending on their degree of understanding and ritual knowledge.

The interior of the chamber would only be accessible to a few. Other areas would be open to all, the most public being the forecourt areas immediately in front of the entrance or passage. Evidence implies the majority of people were excluded from the tombs, this possibly being the domain of a 'specialist priestly elite' holding knowledge and power. Thus space and movement were carefully orchestrated as different messages were inscribed in the monuments.

The tomb sits in the central area of a ridge crest overlooking the alluvial valley. This is the most prominent point in the vicinity as well as an area with relatively wide views, suggesting that the tomb's builders carefully chose and manipulated this space to enhance the tomb structure and the ritual areas outside the tomb. The individual's perception of the locale is directed by the architecture of the tomb, whose positioning directly orchestrates movement as one ascends the gentle slope up to the entrance before descending into what might have been perceived as the 'womb of the world'.

CONCLUSION

Much has been written about megaliths and while it can be said that megaliths were built to last, they were also constructed to make people aware of them independently of their different types of monumentality and function. The significance of megalithic tombs embraces not only complex ideas reflected in their architectural features and design but their use, patterns of location and most importantly the relationship between monuments, the landscape and other monuments.

The spatial and architectural arrangement of the tombs orchestrated bodily movement within and around them and included elements of visibility and concealment which could be used as a means of social control over the living and the dead. The monuments had power and were perhaps symbolic of the social order and group identity within this society; monuments were the focus of a variety of ritual practices during which they were continually visited and revisited; monuments embodied ideas about the world and were adapted and changed as these ideas themselves changed.

Tombs show cohesion in architecture irrespective of the choices of architecture, mortuary practice or artefact deposition and ritual. Thus it is possible to suggest that each individual monument was built and used following choices and agendas set by the community, or specific members of the community, whilst acting upon and through their understanding of the world and their place within it. This included beliefs surrounding the negotiation and understanding of death and perhaps legitimisation of resource control. This idea involved the building of monuments, with spaces to house the dead, a passage to access the inner chamber and a forecourt in which ritual activity could take place, all delineated by a large round mound, permanently inscribing itself and becoming one with the landscape.

The power and significance of tombs can be assessed in their capacity to link and relate the social and cosmological domains, lived life, ceremonial practices and cosmologies, principles of social and ritual order. In building tombs, people made fundamental statements regarding themselves and their place in the world. Much of the mortuary rites performed at the monuments is unknown but all the evidence suggests that mortuary practice was a complex procedure involving a number of stages, before the bones got to the tombs, after they were there and finally when the tombs were sealed and no further access could be gained.

The interpretation of megalithic monuments must include a perception and understanding of their location, orientation and relationship with the surrounding landscape as integral parts of their architecture, which refer and link to the wider landscape, and help us gain an insight into prehistoric people's views of their world. Monuments are profoundly embedded in their landscape, copying or enhancing their topographical positions. They might be seen as continuations of the land on which they were built and seem to respond to landscape features, both in form and location; this response is accentuated by use of local materials. This could be interpreted as a desire to modify nature within certain limits. As well as transforming the landscape, efforts were made to conceal these impressive constructions. Specific movement through the landscape can be considered centrally important to the maintenance of the relationship people have with their environment, the reaffirmation of metaphorical bonds between people and landscape situates the individual within a cosmic order. The landscape was used as a medium for engineering specific social goals and was an integral part of these monuments.

Andrew Fleming was the first to note that megalithic monuments were not only tombs or ossuaries to house the bones of the dead, but that they were also places of meeting, transformation and celebration, built to engrave the landscape and store memory. Though the forms of monuments varied over time and space, their use as graves and stages for ritual plays followed a formalised scheme, adapted to the regional social, cultural and natural geographies which, as we have seen with the example of Alcalar 7, can be better understood when looking at their positioning in their local landscape.

BIBLIOGRAPHY

Fleming, A., 1972 Vision and Design: approaches to ceremonial monument typology. *Man* (ns) 7, 57-73.

Fleming, A., 1973 Tombs for the Living. *Man* (ns) 8, 177-93.

Kalb, P., 1989 O Megalitismo e a Neolitização no Oeste da Penisula Iberica. *Arqueologia*, 22, 33-48.

Morán, E., 2001 Conjunto Megalítico de Alcalar (Portimão) – Alcalar 7 – Campanha 11 (1999-2000) – Relatório dos trabalhos de terreno e balanço final dos resultados da intervenção do IPPC/IPPAR no monumento. Unpublished report IPA, Lisboa.

Parreira, R., 1997 Alcalar. O Território, os lugares habitados e as criptas mortuárias dos 4° e 3° milénios A.C. *Noventa Séculos entra a Serra e o Mar.* Lisboa, IPPAR. 1: 191-206.

Parreira, R. & Morán, E., 1998 Conjunto Megalítico de Alcalar (Portimão).Monumento n°7 – Campanha 9 (1997). Relatório dos trabalhos de terreno. Unpublised report IPA, Lisboa.

Parreira, R. & Morán, E. 1999 Conjunto Megalítico de Alcalar (Portimão) Monumento n°7 – Campanha 10 (1998). Relatório dos Trabalhos de terreno. Unpublished report IPA, Lisboa.

Parreira, R. & Serpa, F., 1995 Novos dados sobre o povoamento da região de Alcalar (Portimão) no IV e III milénios a.C. 1 *Congresso de Arqueologia Penisular, Porto, Trabalhos de Antropologia e Etnografia.*

Veiga, S. E. d., 1886, Antiguidades monumentaes do Algarve. *Tempos Prehistoricos. Paleoethonologia* I, 213-42.

Veiga, S. E. d., 1887, Antiguidades monumentaes do Algarve. *Tempos Prehistoricos. Paleoethonologia* II, 328-40.

Veiga, S. E. d., 1889, Antiguidades monumentaes do Algarve. *Tempos Prehistoricos. Paleoethonologia* II, 78-249.

Veiga, S. E. d., 1891 Antiguidades monumentaes do Algarve. *Tempos Prehistoricos. Paleoethonologia* IV, 230-7.

8

PARALLEL LIVES:
LANDSCAPE ARCHAEOLOGY
IN BRITAIN AND FRANCE

John Collis

In Britain we consider landscape archaeology to be a normal part of the archaeological study of the past, but it is not until one works elsewhere on the continent that one realises that, while it is not unique to the British Isles (e.g. in Scandinavia and the Netherlands), it is exceptionally developed here, and also there are some countries where it is virtually non-existent (e.g. in Spain and France). In this chapter I shall explore briefly why this should be, and then look at a case study in France to suggest that the approach has considerable potential elsewhere.

THE BRITISH TRADITION

The BBC television series *A Picture of Britain* and the accompanying exhibition at Tate Britain documented the rise of an appreciation of the landscape, natural and man-made, which developed in the late eighteenth century and which has continued both as something to define the character of the regions of Britain but also to form a fundamental element of 'Britishness', for instance in its use in the work of artists such as John Nash and especially Frank Newbould whose pictures were used as national propaganda during the Second World War (Dimbleby 2005). But this was by no means peculiar in a European context, indeed the initiators of the tradition can be found in Italian and especially Dutch painters in the seventeenth and eighteenth centuries, or even further back in the work of the Brueghels in the sixteenth century. Nor was there a special concern in Britain for the historic landscape; Girtin's, Turner's and Constable's romantic views of Stonehenge (Smiles 1994) are matched by Tischbein's views of megalithic tombs in the landscape (Schnapp 1993; Sklenář 1983). But the detailed recording and analysis of historic landscapes, especially the rural landscape, is something which has only faint echoes on the continent.

In Britain it has a long history, even if we ignore the earlier work of antiquarians such as Stukeley. One of the first was Colt Hoare (1822), who in *Ancient Wiltshire* recorded prehistoric linear earthworks, and, later in the century, excavators such as Mortimer (1905) on the Yorkshire Wolds were also recording similar features. The early interest in earthworks, like Havercroft's *Earthwork of England* (1908) and Williams-Freeman's *An Introduction to Field Archaeology as illustrated by Hampshire* (1915) still treated sites in isolation, but in the latter case we know he had interests in the wider landscape in his comment to O.G.S. Crawford that to understand the ancient fields of Hampshire one needed to become a bird, what effectively Crawford did when he took to the air, resulting in his joint publication with Alexander Keiller, *Wessex from the Air* (1928). The prehistoric date of some field systems had already been recognised by the Curwens (1923), and they coined the term 'Celtic fields' to describe them. Throughout the 1930s and 1940s various fieldworkers planned and published examples of prehistoric boundary and field systems, such as Hawkes' study of the 'ranch boundaries' of northern Hampshire and southern Wiltshire (Hawkes 1939), but typically this was done in the context of an excavation, in the case of Hawkes exploring the relationship of the linear boundaries to the hillfort of Quarley Hill, or of Grimes in his wartime excavations on Charmy Down, Somerset (Grimes 1960). In other cases it was in the context of surface planning of visible ancient settlements, like Ralegh Radford's (1952) study of Foales Arrishes on Dartmoor.

It was not until the 1950s that landscape archaeology as we know it really developed, and it came from two major sources, firstly from a school of social and economic historians posing questions about the nature of the medieval village – its origin, nature, functioning and especially the abandonment of many of them in the late medieval period, sites which were a major feature of the landscape, especially in Yorkshire and the Midlands (Beresford 1954). The result was an upsurge of local interest in the 'humps and bumps' of the villages themselves which were not only visible on the ground, but which produced spectacular aerial photographs, but also the surrounding field systems, the ridge and furrow which survived extensively over large areas of central England. It linked in with classic works such as that of the Orwins (1938) on the open field systems of the medieval period; we all learnt at school about the 'infield' and 'outfield' and the field and crop rotation used by the medieval peasant. I have also argued that the revolution in excavation techniques, with the adoption of open area excavation in the 1960s lies in the same movement especially in the excavation of the deserted medieval village of Wharram Percy (Collis 2002b, 2004a; Beresford and Hurst 1990). The other seminal work to come out of this historical school was W.G. Hoskins' *The Making of the English Landscape* which more than any other work captured the imagination of the British public (Hoskins 1955, Johnson 2005), and gave a multi-period view of the overall development of the landscape. Both Beresford and Hoskins were inspiring teachers not only in the developing university schools of Local History Studies, but especially in Extra-Mural classes and local archaeology groups, and fieldwork linked with the study of written archives became a popular activity of amateur groups.

The second major input into landscape studies as we know it now – multi-period, multi-layered interpretations of the landscape – derives especially from the work of the Royal Commission on Historical Monuments (RCHM) which had been recording individual monuments, especially standing buildings, since it was established in 1908, but it was mainly from the 1950s that this remit was extended to include the wider landscape in which these monuments were found, and especially the agricultural landscape of fields and pasture, indeed, to a study of the field systems in their own right. This development was especially associated with the Salisbury Office and their survey of Dorset, and with one individual in particular, H.C. (Collin) Bowen. He encouraged the use of aerial photographs, indeed he did much to encourage local amateurs such as John Boyden, and was instrumental in the appointment of John Hampton whose task was to go beyond the photographing of spectacular individual sites, to recording landscapes where the evidence was more sparse and fragmented; this work formed the foundation for the aerial photography collections now housed by the National Monument Record in Swindon. But this work was followed up by extensive ground survey, though Bowen's work and those of his collaborators usually appeared anonymously in the Commission volumes, one major exception being the study of Bokerley Dyke (1990). He supported young researchers in his office such as Peter Fowler, Jeff Radley, Christopher Taylor and Desmond Bonney, as well as other local fieldworkers, myself included.

The chronological range of the RCHM remit forced staff who were dealing with the landscape to become specialists in an area rather than a period, a contrast with what one finds on the continent where my experience with colleagues is that they have a deep understanding of their own specialist periods, i.e. the Iron Age or perhaps prehistory, but this rarely extends into, say, the medieval period. This too was the attitude of Andrew Fleming and myself when we started work on Dartmoor, with our training as Cambridge prehistorians. We might deign to look at a medieval longhouse in passing, but I remember Andrew's rather dismissive comments about parallel reaves which initially we thought to be of medieval date. In my case it was perhaps more reprehensible as I had been brought up in urban excavation, and in the 1960s had worked with Martin Biddle in Winchester where he had been pioneering the concept of the city as a multi-period organic phenomenon which had to be studied in its chronological entirety rather than concentrating on the Roman phases, as commonly happened in the 1950s and 1960s. I had even been forced to defend the time I had spent excavating medieval and post-medieval levels in Exeter in 1971 rather than plunging headlong after the 'important' Roman deposits – I now regret not spending more time on some of the nineteenth-century features! On Dartmoor we learnt from first principles the error of our ways: from a initial dismissal of later activities which destroyed our fascinating prehistoric features; to a recognition that the prehistory could only be understood by studying the later phases in which earlier boundaries might have become fossilised and reused, or the problem of dating specific features like the ploughing on Holne Moor (prehistoric or later); and finally accepting that the later features were fascinating to study in their own right, e.g. Fleming's study of the medieval colonisation of Holne Moor (Fleming and Ralph 1982).

The year 1976 was remarkable for two simultaneous events; a conference on Early Land Allotment held at Bristol (Bowen and Fowler 1978) and Southampton beating Manchester United in the cup final. I was the luckless chairman for the almost deserted afternoon session which coincided with the game, and speakers had to be summoned from the television room to give their papers (it was Peter Fasham who announced to the conference on his arrival at the podium the scoring of the goal which won the game; my memory is that Andrew Fleming was the only participant supporting Manchester). Though it concentrated on prehistoric field systems, the conference was important in bringing together in one volume much fieldwork which had been going on in the previous decade, and showing how widespread such earlier field systems were, and so it was a good counterbalance to the impression left by Hoskins who had only included a few brief pages on early pre-medieval systems (though in other volumes he had given greater attention to prehistoric landscapes). The Bristol conference perhaps surprised us all in demonstrating the extent to which prehistoric field systems still survive in the modern landscape, and more recent work has only continued to underline this, for instance the extensive occurrence of clearance cairns and small-scale enclosures on sites such as Gardom's Edge, or the extensive 'cord-rig' of the Cheviots. But in the 1980s there was an increasing emphasis on the study of multi-period landscapes, encouraged again by workers in the Extra-Mural field, like Trevor Rowley and Mick Aston.

Within the universities too, Landscape Archaeology became an accepted field of research, especially of the rural landscape and villages – the urban landscape has remained almost a reserve to historical geographers, e.g. Conzen's (1969) study of Alnwick. Two main trends encouraged the new approach: firstly the breakdown of the traditional division of courses by period. As subject areas such as Archaeological Theory and scientific approaches to archaeology developed, they cut across the chronological divisions which had largely dominated up to that time. As departments expanded (by continental standards British archaeology departments are huge) they invaded the subject areas of neighbouring disciplines such as Zoology, Botany or Metallurgy. Though people appointed to lectureships were still usually expected to have period specialisms, increasingly they were appointed primarily for their specialist skills – fieldwork, theory, archaeozoology, ceramics, environmental reconstruction, what I have termed the 'Open System' and which I have contrasted with the 'Closed System', found in countries like Germany where each discipline has tended to stay within its traditional boundaries (Collis 1995, 2002a). This reflected similar developments within the profession as a whole, and, to provide for the increasing demands in specialist skills, suddenly in the 1980s 'Taught Masters Courses' took off, and are now a major aspect of university teaching, perhaps more important than the undergraduate degree as the entry point into the profession.

Landscape Archaeology was part of this development, and Andrew Fleming was one, perhaps *the* pioneer, in setting up a Masters course in the subject. Sheffield was certainly one of the leaders in this process, and field training deliberately took on a multi-period aspect; several of us were involved in field walking, something which has taken off in various countries such as France, Spain and Italy, but I consider this as only one component of Landscape Archaeology, with aerial photography and landscape analysis forming the other major elements. The field archaeology courses in Sheffield included not only Andrew's work on Dartmoor and, later, Swaledale, but also the Roystone Grange Project headed by Richard Hodges (e.g. 2006), and at a later date, the Gardom's Edge project run by Mark Edmonds, Andrew's successor in Sheffield, with staff from the Peak Park (Bill Bevan and John Barnatt), all projects which were at the cutting edge of new approaches (we should note that the employment of archaeologists on the staff of national and regional parks is largely a British and American phenomenon with few counterparts in continental Europe). Though Sheffield was not alone in these university developments in Landscape Archaeology – Reading with Richard Bradley and East Anglia with Tom Williamson are two other obvious examples.

My own involvement with Dartmoor was short-lived. Perhaps here I should take the opportunity to correct or add to important points in Andrew Fleming's narrative of how we discovered the reaves; I am sure we did not eat our sandwiches at the Cholwichtown Enclosure (Lee Moor), but at Penn Moor, after our recognition of the reaves' antiquity, and though I may have been the first to say 'They must be Bronze Age', both of us recognised instantly the significance of what we were looking at; it was a phone call to Ann Hamlin that introduced us to the word 'reave' (Fleming and Collis 1973; Fleming 1988). Subsequently I did most of the survey of the Shaugh Moor and Wotter systems (Collis 1978, 1984) and my plan was incorporated into the main publications (Wainwright *et al.* 1979). Then, with Dave Gilbertson, as part of student training (Collis and Gilbertson 1983, 1985; Collis *et al.* 1984), I took on the survey of Crownhill Down in advance of the unfulfilled threat of destruction due to mining, and took on the controversial role of advising the mining company at the Public Inquiry.

But as someone who has always considered himself more of an excavator than a landscape archaeologist, I felt I could contribute more by working primarily in France, and later in Italy and Spain. However, sites needed to be placed in their wider context, and both Fleming and I were involved with the Montarrenti Project with Riccardo Francovich which had a major landscape component from its inception; but neither in France or Spain were there indigenous traditions for survey. In none of these countries was there a developed school of aerial photography, and even in France, despite Roger Agache's spectacular results in Picardy, it was not established until the 1990s, while in Italy, until recently, aerial photography was banned, and in Spain it is even now under military control. Though Italy was very much involved in the development of field walking techniques, initially this was primarily due to the British School at Rome and American universities. Both in Italy (Montarrenti) and in Spain (in the field walking project in the Ambles Valley at Avila with Gonzalo Ruiz Zapatero), we were dealing with local colleagues who were eager to train their students in what were unfamiliar techniques. In France the first major field walker was Nigel Mills, initially in the south of France, but subsequently with Olivier Buchsenschutz in the Berry and myself in the Auvergne (Mills 1985, 1986). In the mid-1980s there was a specific push to develop field walking in France with a major national conference held in Paris (Ferdière and Zadora-Rio 1986), and it is now a standard part of the French methodology, with a number of areas such as the Auvergne and Provence having been intensively investigated.

Clearly, as in the case of aerial photography, there were institutional and legal restrictions to development, and similar problems occurred, for instance, in the former communist countries. Field walking too was affected by the legal access (or lack of) to the land. However, these were not the only reasons; a major one was the sort of questions being asked, and this came out clearly at the Paris conference, between those simply involved in Culture Resource Management (e.g. finding and protecting sites or digging them before they were destroyed) versus a more academic problem-oriented approach, derived largely from models taken from the 'New Geography' of the 1960s. These were ideas which have been slow to impact on many parts of Europe, but which are presently enjoying a revival as more sophisticated approaches to analysis become possible, e.g. with computerised approaches such as GIS.

However, landscape archaeology, in terms of the study of the physical surface remains, in the form of bumps and hollows, has still largely failed to develop on the continent. In part this is a matter of preservation, as I shall argue in France, where intensive agriculture especially on the richer soils on the loess, sands and gravels has destroyed all physical remains, and in upland areas where preservation might have been expected to have been better as in Britain, much has been lost in the intensive exploitation and land-hunger of the eighteenth and nineteenth centuries. But it is also connected with regional and national traditions. In the Mediterranean countries the rich survival of monuments from the Classical and medieval periods has left a strong tradition for architectural and art historical approaches, while artefact-rich central Europe is more concerned with material culture and the typological study of artefacts.

THE FRENCH TRADITION IN LANDSCAPE ANALYSIS

It was only in the last decade or so of the twentieth century that much interest was shown in France in historical analysis of the landscape; in the study of

Montaillou, for instance, one looks in vain for a detailed study of the landscape in which the events unfolded, even a plan of the modern village, despite a chapter headed 'Environment and authority' (Le Roy Ladurie 1980). One approach that has emerged emanates from attempts to identify the centuriation around Roman Orange in the modern landscape (Chouquer and Favory 1991), and this has led to attempts to identify similar centuriation in landscapes where there is no epigraphic or historical evidence, for instance in the Cantal (Phalip 1993), and these interpretations have become more wisely disseminated in French specialist literature, for instance in the *Carte Archéologique de la Gaule* (e.g. Provost and Vallat 1996). The concept has been extended to trying to identify other types of planned landscapes (Chouquer 1996a, 1996b, 1997), especially in the Auvergne, around Clermont-Ferrand and Lezoux (Provost and Mennessier-Jouannet 1994), on the analogy of the planned landscapes identified in Britain such as the Dartmoor reaves. Where multi-period analyses of ancient landscapes are being attempted, they often have rather to rely on archaeological and environmental data rather than surviving features in the landscape, (e.g. the analysis of the development of settlement around Nîmes by Séjalon *et al.* 2007).

The main methodology developed in France is to use modern maps and look for regular alignments within the modern field systems. Where such regularities exist, it is suggested that the fields were laid out at a particular moment in time; around Clermont-Ferrand, for instance, three different groups of alignments have been identified. Around medieval villages it has been noted that such regularities tend not to exist, and it is suggested that the implantation of these villages has disrupted a pre-existing pattern. Seen from a British perspective, we would naturally reverse the sequence, seeing the medieval villages or settlements as the starting point for enclosure, with the more regular systems dating to the post-medieval period as part of the process of enclosure, e.g. in the case of Roystone Grange (Hodges 2006). In fact, where any checks have been made on the date of the supposed Iron Age field systems, they have proved to be post-medieval (V. Guichard, pers. comm.).

The problem with the French approach is that it is too reliant upon present-day maps, rather than trying to look in depth at earlier documentary and cartographical evidence. It starts with a presumption that there are large-scale layouts of landscapes; boundaries are chosen selectively and those that do not confirm are ignored. The other problem, previously mentioned, is that the French landscape was much more heavily used than Britain's in the eighteenth and nineteenth century. For instance, around Clermont-Ferrand, the rectilinear field system on Gergovie was laid out at the end of the eighteenth century at a period of land-hunger, and similar areas with poor quality soils in highland areas were also being enclosed at this time often with the construction of elaborate terrace systems, effectively destroying any earlier traces. It was not until the last century that this intensive use started to diminish. A recent exhibition of photographs of the village of Blesle in the Cantal shows clearly the

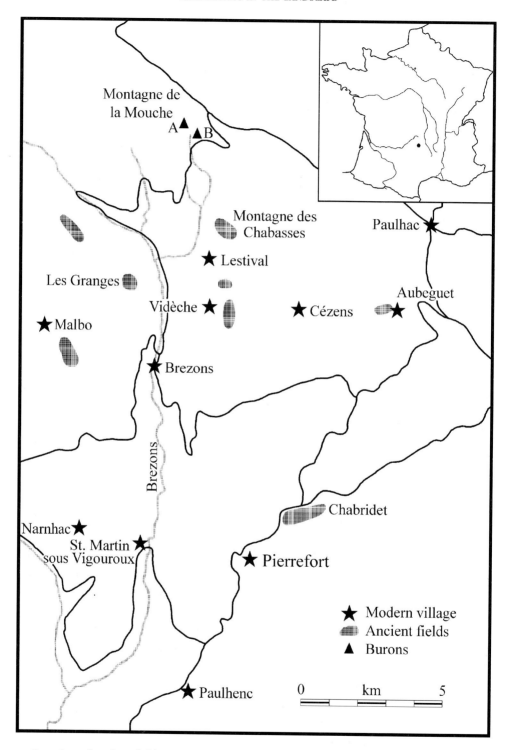

25 Location of ancient field systems and burons studied in the Canton of Pierrefort

process of abandonment. In photographs of the late nineteenth century the terraced fields on the hillside adjacent to the village all seem to be in cultivation, but successive photographs up to the modern day show the gradual development of initially scrub, and finally trees on the terraces, starting with the highest, and today only the lowest fields are still in use. In the valley of the Brezons (*25*), which is the focus of this article, many of the fields shown on the Napoleonic cadastral plans (in this area dated to the 1820s), and even some of the farms and hamlets, are now under heavy woodland. At its worst, this failure to understand the landscape and field systems can lead to misinterpretations of field monuments such as hillforts (Collis 2005), for instance, on the site of the Côtes-de-Clermont, where post-medieval field terraces have been interpreted as the defences of an Iron Age oppidum (Eychart 1961; 1969; 1994; Texier 1999), and on the adjacent hill of Chanturgues as a Roman fort with barrack blocks (Eychart 1975; 1987; Texier 1999). Similarly in Spain, the published plan of the hillfort of Sanchorreja near Ávila includes terraced fields of more recent date (Collis 2004b).

HIGHLAND AND LOWLAND IN THE AUVERGNE

The Auvergne is essentially a highland area encompassing much of the Massif Central, but it does include some rich agricultural areas, notably the limagnes along the River Allier, including the Grande Limagne, with its black soils, one of the richest agricultural areas of France despite lying at about 400m. In the Late Iron Age the south-western part of the Grande Limagne to the east of Clermont-Ferrand is the core of the territory of the major Gallic tribe of the Arverni, with a major nucleated settlement in the plain around the modern airport at Aulnat, subsequently replaced by a number of oppida: Corent, Gondole and Gergovie. Outside of this zone, Late Iron Age finds tend to be sporadic, and largely confined to the smaller limagnes or the river valleys. What, if anything, was happening on the higher ground above 1000m is obscure. From the Neolithic there are a small number of megalithic tombs, and from the Early Bronze Age there are round barrows. The majority of barrows however seem to date to the Early Iron Age, especially Hallstatt C; in some areas, they are grouped into cemeteries of up to 500 mounds (Provost and Vallat 1996; Milcent and Delrieu 2007).

There is then a gap of some 1500 years during which there is little evidence of what was happening in the upland areas. Roman sites and finds are rare, but by the early modern period this was an area of transhumance, exploiting the rich pastures especially for the production of cheeses, in the area of the Cantal for the Salers cheese, which has a more subtle taste than the Cantal cheese which is produced on the lower pastures and in the winter months. Only cheeses produced on the high pastures between 15 May, when the cattle were taken up to the summer pastures, and 15 October when they were brought back down and allowed the appellation of 'Salers'. Quite when this system came into existence is unclear. Gabriel and

Pierre-François Fournier (1983) have bought together the documentary evidence, such as court cases over the ownership of cheeses, and certainly by the fifteenth century we encounter the first mention of 'mazucs' (subterranean houses) and other constructions including sties for the pigs which, accompanied by the cattle, were to be fattened up on the residues of the cheese making. However, there are strong hints that buildings were already being constructed by the mid-thirteenth century.

The major study of the burons (i.e. summer dwellings in the uplands) is that of Jean-Claude Roc of the Musée de la Haute Auvergne at St Flour, though this is mainly from an anthropological point of view. He made a record of the last functioning buron at La Croix Blanche (Roc 1989) and also made a video of its last year of cheese making in 1985, which can be seen at the reconstructed buron of Laveissiére at Le Lioran. Roc has also produced a gazetteer of burons in the Haute Auvergne illustrated with spectacular photographs (Roc 1992), and he has made a typology of the burons. For the later phases from the eighteenth century onwards dating is assured

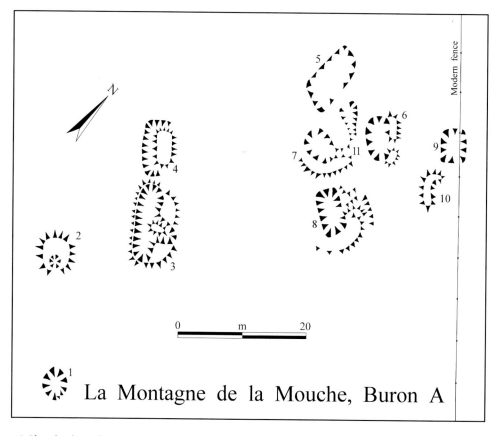

26 Sketch plan of a buron at Montagne de la Mouche A (X 637.5EY 200.3N). 1, 10: shallow depressions; 2: circular platform; 3: banked linear depression; 4-9: probable mazucs; 11: hollowed pathway

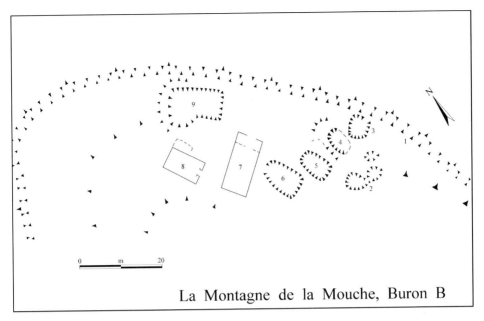

La Montagne de la Mouche, Buron B

27 Sketch plan of a buron at Montagne de la Mouche B (X 638E Y 200.7N). 1: ditch or leat; 2-6, 9: mazucs; 7, 8: collapsed burons

by the inscribed lintels which appear on many of the burons. He has suggested that the early mazucs are represented by rectangular pits which are visible on the sites of many of the more recent sites. However, beyond this, no archaeological work has been done; there are no plans of sites other than of modern layouts, and certainly no excavations, and we know very little about the date of the mazucs, what they actually look like when excavated (are they only underground stores for cheeses?), and how early they start. Further, what other structures can we expect on the sites? We also need to initiate a regional comparison between the structures of burons. The sites in the Haute Auvergne are very distinctive with their large stone buildings and milking parlours, and the continuity of use of the same site (many of later sites also have mazucs), but they are all single isolated structures (*26, 27*). In contrast the early burons in the Puy-de-Dôme, as typified by the huge concentration of sites around Lac Servière are linked together in a long line with entrances to each pit coming from the same direction; from the air they give the appearance of a comb. My fleeting acquaintance with the burons between these two areas, in the Cézallier, suggests they are different again: the buildings are smaller than in the Cantal, and they also seem to lack the mazucs.

I have also identified possible ancient field systems and cairn clearance in these areas especially at Lestival and Chabridet (*28*) (and other researchers have also noted them (Luc Tixier, pers. com.)) associated with barrow cemeteries. On the hillfort of St Victor at Massiac in the Cantal there is an area of cairns and field clearance in the

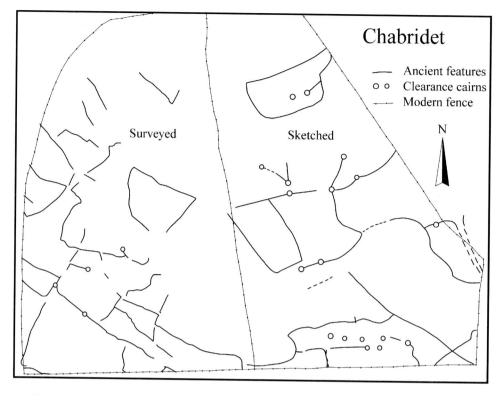

28 Plan of the field systems in fields 2 and 3 at Chabridet (EDM survey by Rupert Featherby and Steve Marsden)

south-east corner of the prehistoric defended site (Collis 2000). I also noted a series of lynchets when visiting the site just north of Allenches where Fabien Delrieu was excavating a tumulus. There was no visible link between the terraces and the nearby buron, and there is just a possibility that one of the tumuli is actually constructed on one of the lynchets; it requires a detailed survey. Recent radiocarbon dates for some of these small cairns may indicate a Roman or medieval date, and there are hints at extensive ploughing in some areas, perhaps of Roman date (Pierre-Yves Milcent and Fabien Delrieu, pers.comm.). Hopefully these are questions which will be tackled by the new research group which has just been set up in the Université Blaise Pascal at Clermont-Ferrand by Frédéric Trément.

CONCLUSION

This brief survey of Landscape Archaeology in Britain and the near-continent illustrates the potential of applying the distinctively British approach to a French context. The uplands of the Auvergne and the Massif Central more generally have huge potential for elucidating a long-term history of the landscape similar to those already developed for Dartmoor and the Peak District in England. The summer sheilings or burons especially are a research topic with great potential, especially if this work can be linked with environmental studies such as pollen analysis.

ACKNOWLEDGEMENTS

Our thanks to Michel Couillaud who made all the arrangements necessary for our work at Pierrefort, and to Sophie Couillaud for feeding and accommodating us so well at their home in the chateau at Lescure. The work was financed by the Association 'Les Chemins de l'Europe Cantal Aveyron', and the Service Regional de l'Archéologie d'Auvergne. Equipment and expertise was loaned by the University of Sheffield and the Association pour la Recherche sur l'Âge du Fer en Auvergne (ARAFA).

BIBLIOGRAPHY

Allcroft, A.H., 1908 *Earthwork of England*. London: MacMillan & Co.

Beresford, M., 1954 *The Lost Villages of England*. London: The Lutterworth Press.

Beresford, M. & Hurst, J.G., 1990 *Wharram Percy: deserted medieval village*. London: English Heritage/Batsford.

Bowen, H.C., 1961 *Ancient Fields*. London: British Association for the Advancement of Science.

Bowen, H.C., 1990 *The Archaeology of Bokerley Dyke*. London: Her Majesty's Stationery Office.

Bowen, H.C. & Fowler P.J. (eds), 1978 *Early Land Allotment in the British Isles*. Oxford: BAR.

Carver, G. (ed.), 2004 *Excavation Techniques in Europe: excavation in a new millennium*. Oxford: BAR.

Chouquer, G. & Favory, F., 1991 *Les Paysages de l'Antiquité*. Paris: Errance.

Chouquer, G. (ed.), 1996a *L'Étude des Paysages: essais sur leur formes et leur histoire. I. Études sur les parcellaires*. Paris: Errance.

Chouquer, G. (ed.), 1996b *L'Étude des Paysages: essais sur leur formes et leur histoire II. Archéologie des parcellaires*. Paris: Errance.

Chouquer, G. (ed.), 1997. *L'Étude des Paysages: essais sur leur formes et leur histoire III. L'analyse des systèmes spatiaux*. Paris: Errance.

Collis, J.R., 1978 Fields and settlements on Shaugh Moor, Dartmoor. In Bowen, H.C. & Fowler, P.J. (eds), 23-8.

Collis, J.R., 1984 Field systems and boundaries on Shaugh Moor and at Wotter, Dartmoor. *Devon Archaeological Society* 41, 47-61.

Collis J.R., 1995 Celts, power and politics: whither Czech archaeology? In Kuna, M. & Venclová, N. (eds), 82-92.

Collis, J.R., 2000 *The Hill-Fort Study Group: visit to Burgundy and the Auvergne, April 15th-19th 2000*. Oxford: Hill-Fort Study Group.

Collis, J.R., 2002a L'avenir de la recherche archéologique française sur l'âge du Fer. In Maranski, D. & Guichard, V. (eds), 353-63.

Collis, J.R., 2002b *Digging up the Past*. Stroud: Sutton.

Collis J.R., 2004a Paradigms and excavation. In Carver, G. (ed.), 31-43.

Collis J.R., 2004b *Hill-Fort Study Group, visit to Ávila, Spain, April 20th-23rd 2004: Guide.* Oxford: Hill-Fort Study Group.

Collis J.R., 2006 Enclosure in an open landscape: Iron Age Wessex and modern Amblés Valley. In Harding, A., Venclová, N. & Sievers, S. (eds), 155-62.

Collis, J.R. & Gilbertson, D., 1983 Mapping three millennia of settlement and land use on Crownhill Down, South West Dartmoor. *Field Studies* 5, 555-67.

Collis, J.R. & Gilbertson, D., 1985 Linear banks on Crownhill Down, Dartmoor. *Landscape History* 5, 57-65.

Collis, J.R., Gilbertson, D.D., Hayes, P.P. & Samson, C.S., 1984 The prehistoric and medieval field archaeology of Crownhill Down, Dartmoor, England. *Journal of Field Archaeology* 11, 1-12.

Colt Hoare, R., 1822 *Ancient History of North and South Wiltshire II.* London: W. Miller.

Conzen, M.R.G., 1969 *Alnwick, Northumberland: a study in town plan analysis.* London: Institute of British Geographers.

Crawford, O.G.S. & Keiller, A., 1928 *Wessex from the Air.* Oxford: Clarendon.

Curwen, E. & Curwen, E.C., 1923 Sussex lynchets and their associated field-ways. *Sussex Archaeological Collections* 64, 1-65.

Dimbleby, D., 2005 *A Picture of Britain.* London: Tate Publishing.

Eychart, P., 1961 *L'Oppidum des Côtes, Augustonemetum, Gergovie.* Clermont-Ferrand: Editions Volcans.

Eychart, P., 1969 *Préhistoire et Origines de Clermont-Ferrand.* Clermont-Ferrand: Editions Volcans.

Eychart, P., 1975 *Chanturgue: camp de César devant Gergovie.* Clermont-Ferrand: Editions Volcans.

Eychart, P., 1987 *La Bataille de Gergovie (Printemps 52 av. J.C.): les faits archéologiques, les sites, le faux historique.* Créer: Nonette.

Eychart, P., 1994 *La Destruction d'une Site majeure: Gergovie.* Brioude.

Ferdière, A. & Zadora-Rio, E. (eds), 1986 *La Prospection Archéologique: paysage et peuplement.* Documents d'Archéologie Française 3.

Fleming, A., 1988 *The Dartmoor Reaves: investigating prehistoric land divisions.* London: Batsford.

Fleming A. & Collis, J.R., 1973 A prehistoric reave system at Cholwich Town, Dartmoor. *Devon Archaeological Society* 31, 1-21.

Fleming, A. and Ralph, N., 1982. Medieval settlement and land use on Holne Moor, Dartmoor: the landscape evidence. *Medieval Archaeology* 26, 101-37.

Fournier, G. & Fournier, P.-F., 1983 La vie pastorale dans les montagnes du Centre de la France: recherches historiques et archéologiques. *Bulletin Historique et Scientifique de l'Auvergne* 91, 199.

Grimes, W.F., 1960 *Excavations on Defence Sites 1939-1945 I: mainly Neolithic - Bronze Age.* London: Her Majesty's Stationery Office.

Harding, A., Venclová, N. & Sievers, S. (eds), 2006 *Enclosing the Past: inside and outside in prehistory.* Sheffield: J.R. Collis.

Hawkes, C.F.C., 1939 The excavations at Quarley Hill, 1938. *Proceedings of the Hampshire Field Club and Archaeological Society* 14, 136-94.

Hodges, R., 2006 *Roystone Grange: 6000 years of a Peakland landscape.* Stroud: Tempus.

Hoskins, W.G., 1955 *The Making of the English Landscape.* London: Hodder & Stoughton.

Johnson, M., 2005 Intricate themes and magic harmonies. *British Archaeology* 82, May/June, 16-9.

Kuna, M. & Venclová, N. (eds), 1995 *Whither Archaeology? Papers in honour of Evžen Neustupný.* Prague: Institute of Archaeology.

Le Roy Ladurie, E., 1980 *Montaillou: Cathars and Catholics in a French village 1294-1324.* Harmondsworth: Penguin.

Macready, S. & Thompson, F.H. (eds), 1985 *Archaeological Fieldwork in Britain and Abroad.* London: Society of Antiquaries.

Maranski, D. & Guichard, V. (eds), 2002 *Les Âges du Fer en Nivernais, Bourbonais et Berry oriental. Regards Européens sur les Âges du Fer en France. Actes du XVIIe Colloque de l'Association française pour l'Etude de l'Âge du Fer, Nevers – mai 1993.* Bibracte 6.

Mennessier-Jouannet, C.& Deberge, Y. (eds), 2007 *L'Archéologie de l'Âge du Fer en Auvergne. Actes du XXVIIe colloque international de l'Association française pour l'Étude de l'Âge du Fer (Thème régional)*. Lattes. Association pour le Développement de l'Archéologie en Languedoc-Rousillon.

Milcent, P.-Y. & Delrieu, F., 2007 Tertres et archéologie funéraire en Haute Auvergne dans le contexte du premier âge du Fer en Gaule méridionale (VIIIe–Ve s. av. J.-C. In Mennessier-Jouannet, C. & Deberge, Y. (eds), 2007.

Mills, N., 1985 Iron Age settlement and society in Europe: contributions from field surveys in central France. In Macready, S. & Thompson, F.H. (eds), 74-100.

Mills, N., 1986 Recherches sur l'habitat et la société au cours de l'Âge du Fer en Auvergne (France). In Ferdière, A. & Zadora-Rio, E. (eds), 121-8.

Mortimer, J.R., 1905 *Forty Years' Researches in British and Saxon Burial Mounds of East Yorkshire*. London: A. Brown & Sons.

Orwin, C.S. & Orwin, C.S., 1938 *The Open Fields*. Oxford: Clarendon.

Phalip, B., 1993 Les vestiges de centuriations antiques des plateaux cantaliens du nord. *Revue de Haute-Auvergne* 55, 41-75.

Provost, M. & Mennessier-Jouannet, C., 1994 *Carte Archéologique de la Gaule: 63/2: Le Puy-de-Dôme*. Paris: Fondation Maison des Sciences de l'Homme.

Provost, M. & Vallat, P., 1996 *Carte Archéologique de la Gaule: 16: Cantal*. Paris: Fondation Maison des Sciences de l'Homme.

Radford, C.A.R., 1952 Prehistoric settlement on Dartmoor and the Cornish Moors. *Proceedings of the Prehistoric Society* 18, 55-84.

Schnapp, A., 1993 *The Discovery of the Past*. New York: Harry N. Adams.

Sklenář, K., 1983 *Archaeology in Central Europe: the first 500 Years*. Leicester: Leicester University Press.

Smiles, S., 1994 *The Image of Antiquity: ancient Britain and the romantic imagination*. New Haven: Yale University Press.

Texier, Y., 1999 *La Question de Gergovie: essai sur un problème de localisation*. Bruxelles: Collection Latomus, 251.

Roc, J.-C., 1989 *Le Buron de la Croix Blanc*. Brioude: Editions Watel.

Roc, J.-C., 1992 *Burons de Haute Auvergne: architecture et environnement, sept siècles d'histoire*. Brioude: Editions Watel.

Séjalon, P., Bel. V., Breuil, J.-Y. & Pomarèdes H., 2007 Définition et organisation du terroir protohistorique de Nîmes, Gard (fin VIe-Ier s. av. J.-C.). Unpublished paper given at the XXXXIe Colloque International de l'Association française pour l'Etude de l'Âge du Fer, Chauvigny, May 2007.

Williams-Freeman, J.P., 1915 *An Introduction to Field Archaeology as Illustrated by Hampshire*. London: Macmillan.

9

THE CHRONOLOGY OF CO-AXIAL FIELD SYSTEMS

Richard Bradley and Michael Fulford

INTRODUCTION: FIELD SURVEY AND EXCAVATION

Survey and excavation are very different activities and are often undertaken by different people. They draw on distinctive skills and each provides its own perspective on the past. Field survey records the relationship between features visible on the surface; excavation explores the sequence of deposits underneath it. Thus one method studies several phases of activity simultaneously. Excavation investigates the past a layer at a time.

Both approaches should be complementary, but that is not always the case. There are excavated monuments whose earthworks have been studied long after excavation has taken place, and most field surveys propose an interpretation that is never tested by another method. Andrew Fleming has avoided both these pitfalls, for his fieldwork has involved a combination of the two techniques. Still more important, they have been undertaken in the right order, so that excavation has been directed towards clearly formulated questions. That is true of his work on Dartmoor (Fleming 1988) and of his project in Swaledale (Fleming 1998). As it happens, both were concerned with the chronology of field systems. That also provides the subject of our paper.

Survey is one of the main methods of classifying monuments, and the categories that result play a role in the management of the ancient landscape. At the same time such schemes can be much too rigid, so that superficially similar earthworks may have been built in more than one period. Fleming made this point in an article published in 1987, 'Co-axial field systems: some questions of space and time'. It illustrated the range of contexts in which this phenomenon appeared. The distribution of co-axial fields extended from East Anglia to the west of Ireland, just as their chronology ran from the Neolithic to the Roman period.

The present paper focuses on just one area, Salisbury Plain, but considers a region in which co-axial field systems were used during two different phases. It also discusses the problems of distinguishing between the remains of those separate periods.

THE CO-AXIAL FIELD SYSTEMS OF SALISBURY PLAIN

The field systems of Salisbury Plain did not feature in Fleming's 1987 article, for they had yet to be recorded in any detail. There had been small-scale projects, like Crawford's analysis of air photographs (Crawford 1953), Hawkes's account of land boundaries in the Bourne Valley (Hawkes 1939), or Appelbaum's study of Figheldean Down (Appelbaum 1957), but the systematic mapping of the surviving earthworks promised by the Ordnance Survey (Crawford 1937) was never issued. As a result, fieldwork was delayed until changes in troop deployment led to a series of surveys of the Military Training Area during the 1980s and 90s. The first was a study of the prehistoric land boundaries (Bradley, Entwistle and Raymond 1994). There followed a second programme of excavation concerned with the Iron Age and Roman settlement of this area (Fulford *et al.* 2006), and in parallel with both these projects the surviving earthworks were recorded by the then Royal Commission on the Historical Monuments of England (McOmish, Field and Brown 2002). Now that this work has been published it is possible to compare the results.

The Linear Ditches Project was based on excavation and ended before the earthwork survey was complete. The study of Iron Age and Roman settlement built on the results of both projects. All three paid special attention to the co-axial field systems on the Plain, but, somewhat surprisingly, they produced quite different results. Earthwork survey suggested that extensive field systems were already well established when ditched land boundaries cut across them in the Late Bronze Age. Excavation, however, was confined to those areas where the earthworks had been damaged by ploughing or by military activity, and here there was stratigraphic evidence that the field systems extended across the prehistoric boundary ditches. More recent excavation of well-preserved lynchets suggests that they were associated with Late Iron Age and Roman activity.

Thus the fieldwork of the 1980s and '90s suggested three interpretations which were difficult to reconcile:

- The linear ditches were built during the Late Bronze Age and some of them continued in use into the Iron Age.
- Where earthworks survived above ground, certain of the linear ditches cut across co-axial fields in a way that would have put them out of use. It followed that those fields must have originated in the Late Bronze Age or earlier.

- Where the earthworks had been reduced to soil marks there was not much evidence that linear earthworks cut through earlier fields. Rather, it seemed as if co-axial field systems had taken little account of these features, and in some cases their banks and ditches had been levelled. The fields themselves were of Late Iron Age/Roman origin.

THE DIFFICULTY OF DATING LYNCHETS

At about the same time similar problems were recognised during fieldwork on the Berkshire Downs. Again it appeared that linear ditches had cut across co-axial field systems, putting them out of use. On excavation, however, most of the ditches proved to be of Late Bronze Age or Early Iron Age date (Ford 1982a and b), whilst the majority of the lynchets were Roman (Gaffney and Tingle 1989; Bowden, Ford and Mees 1993).

Was such a reappraisal justified? Perhaps there is a clue in the publication of this project. Although Roman sherds were found in excavating field boundaries on the Berkshire chalk, they were associated with an unusual quantity of worked flint, suggesting that older deposits had been disturbed (Bowden, Ford and Mees 1993). The significance of this observation is apparent from more recent excavation on Salisbury Plain, where it is clear that each successive ploughing reworked the deposits that were there before (Fulford *et al.* 2006). Prehistoric pottery does not survive well on the surface of a cultivated field, whereas flint is almost indestructible. Only the most durable sherds would remain in the material of the lynchets and they need not reflect the entire period of cultivation.

In fact lynchets have a distinctive character. Eroding ploughsoil seems to have built up against quite insubstantial barriers until they developed into considerable features. Once created, they were not easy to eradicate; that is why they were later chosen as parish boundaries. For that reason the same plots of ground may have been cultivated at quite different times, for it was difficult to modify their outlines. Some of the co-axial fields created and abandoned in the Bronze Age could have been re-used when new systems were being established on the downland.

A REVISED SEQUENCE FOR SALISBURY PLAIN

That is certainly suggested by renewed fieldwork on Salisbury Plain (McOmish, Field and Brown 2002; Fulford *et al.* 2006). Rather than envisaging one phase of co-axial fields and another of ditched land boundaries, it suggests a more complex sequence which draws on other kinds of evidence. Now it can be divided into four main phases:

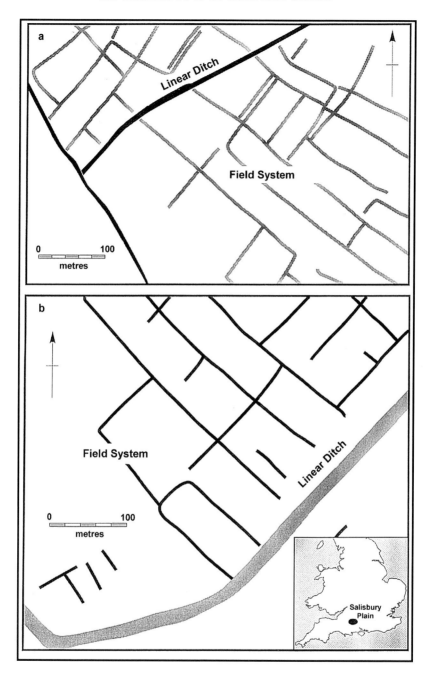

29 Linear earthworks and co-axial field systems at two sites on Salisbury Plain. In each case the earlier features are shown stippled and the later ones are in bold outline: (a) Bronze Age linear ditches cutting through the earthworks of a co-axial field system on Dunch Hill. Information from McOmish, Field and Brown (2002); (b) Co-axial fields dating from the Roman period running up to a prehistoric linear ditch on Weather Hill. Information from Fulford, Powell, Entwistle and Raymond (2006). *Drawing by Margaret Mathews*

Phase 1

There seem to be a number of co-axial field systems aligned on Early Bronze Age round barrows. Individual fields are sometimes associated with small earthwork enclosures which produce sherds of Middle and Late Bronze Age pottery. Groups of secondary burials are associated with some of the older barrows, and new, much smaller mounds may have been built at this time.

Phase 2

During the Late Bronze Age a series of ditched territories was established. Like the later parishes in the same area, these extended from the main rivers onto the high ground of the interfluves. They were often long, narrow strips of land, each of which would have provided suitable areas for grazing and cultivation. These land blocks were associated with large open settlements that included round houses (Andrews 2006). Beyond the limits of the enclosed area there were major flint sources which seem to have been exploited during this period. There were also burnt mounds and the site of a metalwork hoard. In most cases the newly created boundaries cut across the older field systems, apparently putting them out of use, but in some instances they respected existing divisions (*29*).

Phase 3

In the Early and Middle Iron Age a number of these boundaries were levelled and others were rebuilt. In certain cases the network of land divisions was extended. Deposits of human and animal remains, similar to those associated with settlements, were buried in the ditches. Open settlements were fewer and a new range of enclosed occupation sites was established. Major hillforts were constructed on the boundaries established by the linear ditches and, in particular, in places where several territories converged. Although there is considerable evidence of crop production, there is little to suggest that new field systems were created during this phase.

Phase 4

In the Late Iron Age and Early Roman periods (the distinction is not always apparent from the excavated pottery) the linear ditches went out of use and they were sometimes levelled by the plough. Co-axial fields were established across larger areas and many open and enclosed settlements were established. This represents a major transformation of the landscape of Salisbury Plain and may be associated with unexcavated sites, including villas, located in the main river valleys.

EXCAVATION AND FIELD SURVEY

It is significant that these relationships were established by different kinds of fieldwork. The very existence of an early phase of co-axial fields depends on their survival as standing earthworks which had been cut by linear ditches. Had these features been destroyed by the plough, as happens in most of the field systems recorded as soil marks, there would be little or no evidence for the early phase of cultivation. In the absence of a well-preserved buried soil, it would seem as if the linear earthworks represented the earliest period of land enclosure. That was the view taken during the Linear Ditches Project (Bradley, Entwistle and Raymond 1994), and it was only the subsequent publication of the Royal Commission's survey of the surviving earthworks that rectified the error (McOmish, Field and Brown 2002). Excavation would be poorly equipped to achieve this unless it took place where surface remains were well preserved.

Where excavation did provide vital results was in establishing the character of a second series of co-axial fields on Salisbury Plain. This happened for two reasons. Even where the banks of linear earthworks had been levelled by the plough, the fillings of the ditches preserved an important sequence. This identified a deposit of ploughsoil in its upper levels. Taken in combination with molluscan analysis, it indicated a major period of cultivation impinging on the earthwork. Secondly, excavation of standing lynchets shed considerable light on their distinctive structure. Not only did it help to date some of these earthworks, it showed the extent to which the sediments had been reworked. This raises the possibility that the remains of an earlier phase, or phases, of cultivation could have been largely eradicated.

It is only the combination of these two different methods that has allowed the history of this landscape to be written. Without the detailed survey undertaken by the Royal Commission it would have been difficult to identify – still less to date – the first co-axial field systems on Salisbury Plan. Without excavation, it might have been equally difficult to show how the linear ditches which took their place were levelled during a second phase of intensive cultivation. Similarly, it was only through excavation of well preserved earthworks that the complexities of lynchet formation in the study area were appreciated.

DATING CO-AXIAL FIELD SYSTEMS

Andrew Fleming will recognise this lengthy process of discovery, for he has followed a similar course in his own research. He may also be intrigued by the dating evidence from Salisbury Plain, for it suggests that here the co-axial field systems were established during two distinct phases: the Middle and/or Late Bronze Age, and the Late Iron Age/Roman period. In his 1987 article he set out the dating evidence for other field systems of this kind. Although the Dartmoor reaves were among the earliest, at least four of the sixteen groups that he discussed were probably used during the Later Bronze Age. Another five were Late Iron Age or Roman. Others may have been Neolithic or early medieval, but it is striking how few examples predated the Later

Bronze Age or were assigned to the centuries in between that period and the end of the Iron Age. Does the evidence from Salisbury Plain conform to a wider pattern?

Much has happened in the 20 years since Fleming's paper appeared, but the main development has undoubtedly been the growth of developer-funded archaeology which now constitutes the main kind of fieldwork carried out in Britain and Ireland. This new work has several distinctive features. It is often geographically extensive, so that entire landscapes can be revealed rather than the small samples that were available for study before. It also extends outside the areas in which excavation has normally taken place, with the result that there are many more excavations in lowland landscapes than in the upland areas where earthworks are better preserved. Still more important, because the new fieldwork takes place as part of the planning process it has also extended into regions of the country which had rarely been investigated in the past. Both the present authors have made use of this new source of information, Michael Fulford (1992) in a review of the Iron Age and Roman use of the river gravels and Richard Bradley (2007) in a study of the prehistory of Britain and Ireland.

The results of developer-funded fieldwork have shed light on all four phases identified in the archaeology of Salisbury Plain. The first is the creation of the earliest co-axial field systems. The Neolithic credentials of the fields in the west of Ireland have been confirmed by radiocarbon dating, but few new examples have come to light and their distribution still seems to be confined to the Atlantic coastline (Bradley 2007). On the other hand, the Early Bronze Age fields first identified in Andrew Fleming's work on Dartmoor now have counterparts in lowland areas, most particularly on the river gravels at Bestwall Quarry near Wareham where a co-axial system of similar age has been identified by excavation (Ladle and Woodward in press). This site is especially important as it is located to the south of the Wessex chalk where so much work had taken place before. Otherwise it is to the Middle and Late Bronze Ages that most co-axial systems belong. Yates (2001) has argued that many of them were associated with stock raising in major river valleys. They are often associated with groups of round houses, raised storage structures, ponds and even wells, but the overall distribution of these enclosed landscapes is limited to lowland England and does not extend much further north than the Welland Valley or far westwards into the Midlands (Bradley and Yates in press). Beyond those areas similar settlements can be found, but they are not accompanied by regular land divisions.

A still more striking feature is that there is little evidence for the creation of ditched fields of this kind after the Late Bronze Age/Early Iron Age transition. Although it has been suggested that older plots remained in use, divided from one another by long-established hedges (Carew et al. 2006), the associated settlements often changed their locations or even disappeared. Instead it seems as if longer linear boundaries not unlike those on Salisbury Plain were built throughout an area extending from the Midlands, East Anglia and the Welsh Marches to the Scottish border and beyond. They took several forms, from single or multiple ditches to lengthy pit alignments, and their chronology has been difficult to establish. Even so, the earliest examples were probably constructed during the Late Bronze Age and the latest examples in the middle of the Iron Age (Bradley and Yates in press). Like those on the Wessex chalk, they can enclose large territories, often running up to a river, and may contain one or more major settlements. They seem to have replaced the co-axial field systems of the Bronze Age and perhaps provide evidence for a new tenurial system. One possibility is that small areas of land were allocated to different members of the community and redistributed at regular intervals. Those plots did not have any substantial boundaries. In the same way, the evidence from Iron Age hillforts suggests that the storage of food may have been centrally controlled.

A major change took place during the later years of the Iron Age, and in some areas it may have happened at the same time as the abandonment of those hillforts. There was less emphasis on fortified enclosures, and individual settlements certainly increased in size. More important, it may have been in this phase that a second series of co-axial fields was established. They had a much wider distribution than their Bronze Age precursors and are a particular feature of the North Midlands and North-East England where Bronze Age co-axial field systems have not been found. The best known examples of this type are the 'brickwork' systems discussed by Fleming in 1987. It is still too soon to say quite how these areas were used, nor is the dating evidence altogether satisfactory, but there seems little doubt that a major transformation of the lowland landscape was taking place. It seems to have begun during the later years of the Iron Age but it certainly established the structure of the Romano-British rural landscape. Again the complex sequence worked out on Salisbury Plain can be paralleled in many other areas. In lowland England co-axial field systems of Late Iron Age/Roman date are often superimposed on those of the Later Bronze Age.

We have emphasised the protracted process of defining and dating the field systems of the Wessex chalk, as illustrated by the remarkable landscape of Salisbury Plain. That involved a combination of excavation and surface survey which would not be possible in many other areas. When this work took place, its initial results were unexpected and it was difficult to tell whether they might be of more general application. The same was true when Andrew Fleming first recognised the distinctive character of the Dartmoor reaves. Now it is possible to see that these findings were only the first stage in a prolonged investigation. The 'questions of time and space' which he asked in 1987 still require an answer, but now there are indications of the lines of enquiry to pursue.

ACKNOWLEDGEMENTS

We are grateful to Margaret Mathews for drawing figure 1 and to Roy Entwistle and Frances Raymond with whom we worked on Salisbury Plain. Andrew Fleming inaugurated a programme of research that has run for two decades and still produces surprising results. It is a hard act to follow.

BIBLIOGRAPHY

Andrews, P., 2006 A Middle to Late Bronze Age settlement at Dunch Hill, Tidworth. *Wiltshire Studies* 99, 51-78.

Appelbaum, S., 1957 The agriculture of the British Early Iron Age as exemplified at Figheldean Down, Wiltshire. *Proceedings of the Prehistoric Society* 20, 103-14.

Bowden, M., Ford, S. & Mees, G., 1993 The date of the ancient fields on the Berkshire Downs. *Berkshire Archaeological Journal* 74, 109-33.

Bradley, R., 2007 *The Prehistory of Britain and Ireland.* Cambridge: Cambridge University Press.

Bradley, R., Entwistle, R. & Raymond, F., 1994 *Prehistoric Land Divisions on Salisbury Plain.* London: English Heritage.

Bradley, R. & Yates, D. in press After Celtic Fields. The social organisation of Iron Age agriculture. In Haselgrove, C. & Pope, R. (eds), *The Earlier Iron Age in Britain and the Near Continent.* Oxford: Oxbow.

Brück, J. (ed.), 2001 *Bronze Age Landscapes – Tradition and Transformation.* Oxford: Oxbow.

Carew, T., Bishop, B., Meddens, F. & Ridgeway, V., 2006 *Unlocking the Landscape. Archaeological Excavations at Ashford Prison, Middlesex.* London: Pre-Construct Archaeology.

Crawford, O.G.S., 1937 *Ordnance Survey 1:25,000 Salisbury Plain, Old Sarum Sheet.* Southampton: Ordnance Survey.

Crawford, O.G.S., 1953 *Archaeology in the Field.* London: Phoenix House.

Fleming, A., 1987 Coaxial field systems – some questions of time and space. *Antiquity* 61, 188-203.

Fleming, A., 1988 *The Dartmoor Reaves: Investigating Prehistoric Land Divisions.* London: Batsford.

Fleming, A., 1998 *Swaledale. Valley of the Wild River.* Edinburgh: Edinburgh University Press.

Ford, S., 1982a Fieldwork and excavation on the Berkshire Grims Ditch. *Oxoniensia* 47, 13-36.

Ford, S. 1982b Linear earthworks on the Berkshire Downs. *Berkshire Archaeological Journal* 71, 1-20.

Fulford, M., 1992 Iron Age to Roman: a period of radical change on the gravels. In Fulford, M. & Nichols, E. (eds), 23-38.

Fulford, M. & Nichols, E. (eds), 1992 *Developing Landscapes of Lowland Britain.* London: Society of Antiquaries.

Fulford, M., Powell, A., Entwistle, R. & Raymond, F., 2006 *Iron Age and Romano-British Settlements and Landscape of Salisbury Plain.* Salisbury: Wessex Archaeology.

Gaffney, V. & Tingle, M., 1989 *The Maddle Farm Project.* Oxford: BAR.

Hawkes, C., 1939 The excavations at Quarley Hill, 1938. *Proceedings of the Hampshire Field Club* 14, 136-94.

Ladle, L. & Woodward, A. in press *Excavations at Bestwall Quarry, Wareham 1992-2005, Volume 1.* Dorchester: Dorset Natural History and Archaeological Society.

McOmish, D., Field, D. and Brown, G., 2002 *The Field Archaeology of the Salisbury Plain Training Area.* Swindon: English Heritage.

Yates, D., 2001 Bronze Age agricultural intensification in the Thames Valley and Estuary. In Brück, J. (ed.), 65-82.

10

CO-AXIAL LANDSCAPES: TIME AND TOPOGRAPHY

Tom Williamson

INTRODUCTION

It was Andrew Fleming who, in the 1970s, first coined the term 'co-axial' to describe field systems which had boundaries running for a greater distance, and more continuously, in one direction than in another, so that in plan they resemble slightly wavy brickwork. Such arrangements formed a significant proportion of the cohesive prehistoric field systems already known, in the form of earthworks or cropmarks, from various areas of Britain. But none were as extensive, or as impressive, as the Bronze Age reaves of Dartmoor to which Fleming first applied the term.

Co-axial field systems have been identified in a number of chronological contexts, ranging from the Neolithic to the later Iron Age and Roman periods (see Bradley and Fulford this volume). More controversially, in a number of areas of England the patterns of upstanding field boundaries, or those of open-field furlongs shown on pre-enclosure maps, take broadly analogous forms, implying that these developed from similar systems of prehistoric land division. It is these 'relict co-axials' which form the subject of this chapter.

The notion that prehistoric or Roman patterns of land division could have survived into the medieval and modern landscape was first mooted by Rodwell and Drury in the late 1970s. Both men worked in Essex, an anciently-enclosed county with little evidence for either extensive medieval open fields or for large-scale post-medieval enclosure (Drury 1978; Rodwell 1978; 1980; Drury and Rodwell 1978). Most historians and geographers assumed that the field and road patterns of the county were of Anglo-Saxon or medieval date, but Drury and Rodwell suggested they had, at least in part, much earlier origins. Their arguments were partly based on the apparent existence of organised, planned landscapes covering areas far more extensive than the vills or manors of the Middle Ages, and thus presumably created in an earlier period, when forms of territorial organisation had been more extensive; also partly on the evidence of horizontal stratigraphy. In a number of places, that is, Roman roads appeared to slice through the field patterns extant, or shown on early maps, in such a way that (following the normal rules of horizontal stratigraphy) the fields appeared earlier, and thus presumably of prehistoric date.

Rodwell and Drury did not employ the term 'co-axial', although a number of the landscape patterns which they discussed, as in the area around Thurrock on the Thames gravels, would now be classified in this way. Subsequent investigations of 'relict landscapes', however, did identify many as being of co-axial form. Most examples were in the east of England: in parts of Norfolk and Suffolk (Williamson 1987; 1993; 1997; Davison 1990; Hesse 1992; 1998), in western and in south-eastern Cambridgeshire (Oosthuizen 1998; 2003; Harrison 2002), on the dipslope of the Chiltern Hills in Hertfordshire (Williamson 2000) and on the London clay uplands in the south-east of that county (Bryant, Perry and Williamson 2005). But such landscapes are certainly not restricted to the east: extensive examples are thus known from the Arrow Valley of Shropshire, around Hergest and Lyonshall (White 2003). It is worth noting, perhaps, that the identification of relict co-axials was in fact pioneered by Fleming himself, in his observation that many of the major axes of the Dartmoor parallel reave systems were directly continued, beyond the edge of the moor, as 'medieval' field walls (Fleming 1988, 30). Indeed, he described how on the eastern edge of the Moor, around Kestor and in the Bittaford-Ivybridge area, 'most of the evidence' for the reave systems 'comes from the regular orientation of modern field boundaries' (Fleming 1988, 28-9).

The similarity between the various 'relict' co-axial landscapes, and some of the larger co-axial field systems surviving in truly 'archaeological' form – and especially the Dartmoor reaves – is striking, not only visually but also in terms of their relationship with natural land forms. The major axes of the reaves thus run from lower ground, up onto the high interior of the moor: yet while in broad terms their layout is thus related to topography, in detail they tend to be 'terrain oblivious', in that they ignore not only minor features of the topography but also major obstacles, such as the Dart Gorge. Co-axial field patterns in the modern landscape display similar tendencies, generally running at right angles to major rivers, directly from valley floors up onto higher ground, ignoring en route local subtleties of topography. On the claylands of south Norfolk for example, in the area around Scole and Dickleburgh, a co-axial landscape covering more than some 80sq km, and which appears to be stratigraphically earlier than the Roman Pye Road, is based on sub-parallel lanes and boundaries which run at right angles to the River Waveney, up the sides of the valley and far out onto the level boulder clay plateau to the north, terminating at a transverse element which was variously, along its length, a watershed trackway, a parish boundary and a hundred boundary (30). Similar landscapes, exhibiting a similar relationship with the rivers Waveney and Chet, were noted by the late Alan Davison

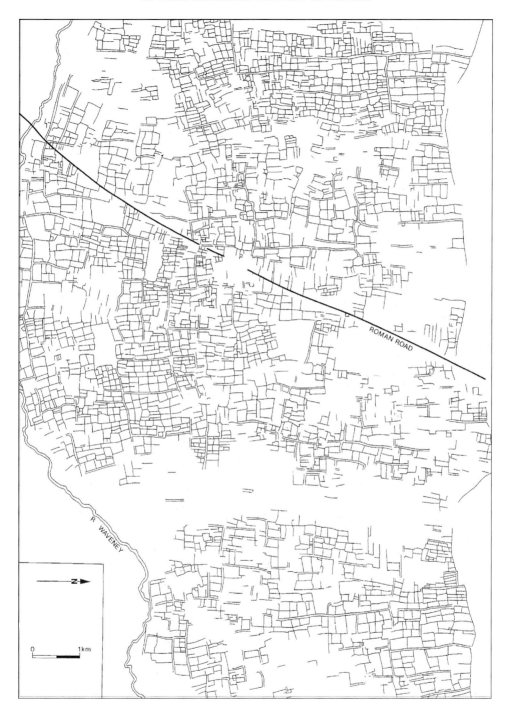

30 The so-called 'Scole-Dickleburgh field system', an extensive co-axial landscape based on the Waveney valley in south Norfolk. *After Williamson 1998*

(1990) in south-east Norfolk (Williamson 1987; 1993; 1998). In both cases, the major axes appear unaffected by minor valleys running at oblique angles to the dominant 'grain', although in this more muted terrain such disregard for topography is rather less visually dramatic than it is on Dartmoor.

A number of important questions are raised by these relict co-axial landscapes, and two in particular will be framed and addressed, although not fully answered, here. The first concerns whether these arrangements of medieval and modern boundaries are indeed versions of the 'archaeological' landscapes to which they appear so similar. Are they, in other words, *really* organised field systems of prehistoric or Roman date which have survived, albeit perhaps in altered form, into the medieval and modern periods? And if so, what explains their somewhat patchy distribution in England?

THE DATE AND CHARACTER OF 'RELICT CO-AXIALS'

The idea of relict landscapes in general, and of relict co-axials in particular, has not gone entirely unchallenged by archaeologists, and it is true that the original claims for and interpretations of these landscapes were often exaggerated and at times naïve (e.g. Williamson 1987). In particular, the implicit or explicit suggestion in some early work that such landscapes are largely or entirely survivals from the pre-medieval period is now difficult to sustain (although it has become dangerously embedded in some parts of the archaeological establishment, and especially in some 'landscape characterisation' exercises). The most important critique remains that by Steven Rippon (1991), who re-examined a number of Rodwell's Essex examples and, in the light of limited excavation and, in particular, cropmark evidence, demonstrated that while some of their elements were potentially very early in date, others were not. On the other hand, the more sweepingly sceptical attacks on the 'relict landscapes' idea – attacks based on a resolute belief that the survival in the modern landscape of prehistoric systems of land division is simply impossible, and that co-axial patterns are either illusory, or created through the subjective selection of landscape elements (e.g., Hinton 1997; Martin 1999) – are equally open to criticism (Williamson 1998).

This is because the evidence from a number of excavations strongly suggests that some elements, at least, of these landscapes are of prehistoric or Roman date. In north west Norfolk, for example, an area in which pre-enclosure maps indicate that the layout of the open fields was dominated by co-axial furlong patterns, excavations by Sarah Percival at Burnham Sutton in 1998 produced clear evidence not only for the survival and continued development of a late prehistoric co-axial field system through to the late Saxon period, but also apparently for the subsequent insertion within this of bundles of open-field strips (Percival and Williamson 2005). In the Broxbourne and Wormley area of south-east Hertfordshire an extensive co-axial field system runs out of the Lea Valley, and onto the heavy soils of the London clay plateau above it (Bryant, Perry and Williamson 2005) (*31*). An excavation within Cheshunt Park, more or less in the centre of this area, revealed field ditches conforming in orientation to the surrounding landscape. These contained first- and second-century pottery in their basal infill, and had apparently been filled-in during the construction or expansion of a small Roman settlement (Ely and Edwards 2003, 15). On the other side of Hertfordshire, just to the north of Watford, similar evidence was recovered during the excavations carried out at the Grove in 2000. The site – over four hectares of which were systematically stripped prior to the construction of a golf course – lies within an eighteenth-century landscape park in the valley of the River Gade, one of the rivers cutting at right angles through the dipslope of the Chiltern Hills. The landscape of the area is dominated by a series of extensive co-axial field systems, which run – in typical fashion – at right angles to the principal rivers, up the valley sides and far onto the level interfluves between, terminating at long trackways which run very close to the precise line of watersheds (*32*) (Williamson 2000). All field boundaries had been erased within the excavated area by the creation, in the 1760s, of the landscape park, but the excavation revealed (along with a wide range of other features) a number of ditches which were clearly parts of the surrounding co-axial boundary pattern. Several contained, in their basal fills, sherds of unabraded Iron Age pottery (le Quesne pers. comm.): the line of one is directly continued, beyond the boundary of the park, as an upstanding boundary, to the northern edge of Whippendell Wood.

On the other side of England, in Shropshire, it was noted during a landscape characterisation exercise that one of the extensive co-axial field systems in the Arrow Valley was visibly 'slighted' by the Rowe Ditch, a linear earthwork of presumed late Roman or early post-Roman date, in the vicinity of Leen Farm in Pembridge. It was speculated that perhaps the field pattern predated Rowe Ditch and the scale and orientation of the field pattern had been inherited and only slightly modified over the centuries. This idea was further supported by an aerial photograph taken in 1999 of what appear to be internal divisions detected as faint cropmarks within the larger modern-day fields that now characterise the landscape (White 2003).

A number of excavations were duly carried out in order to 'establish the date of these cropmark boundaries, the general orientation of which appears to survive more widely within the current landscape. The excavated examples contained large quantities of Romano-British pottery and the excavators concluded that 'perhaps the organisation of the field pattern today is derived from the organisation of the landscape nearly 2000 years ago' (White 2003, 45). But other cropmarks investigated in the vicinity, laid out on the same orientation, produced evidence for Iron Age occupation, suggesting a still earlier origin for the pattern (White 2003).

Yet while such investigations seem to confirm the prehistoric or Roman origins of many co-axial relict landscapes, they do not prove either that such landscapes are *in their entirety* of this kind of antiquity, or that they survived into the medieval

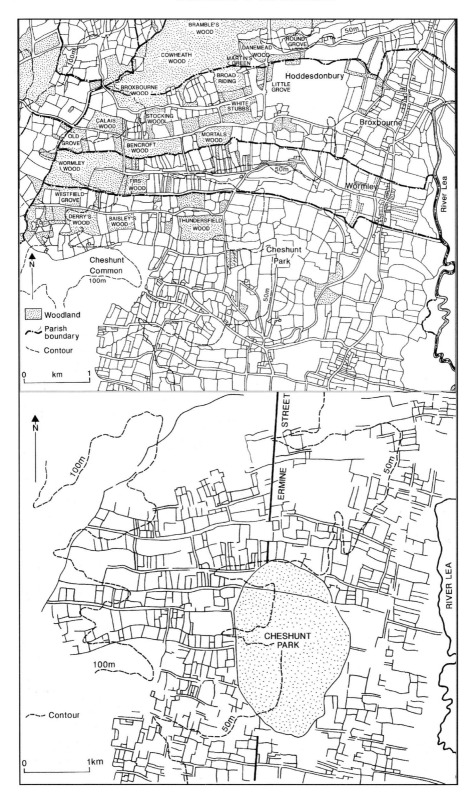

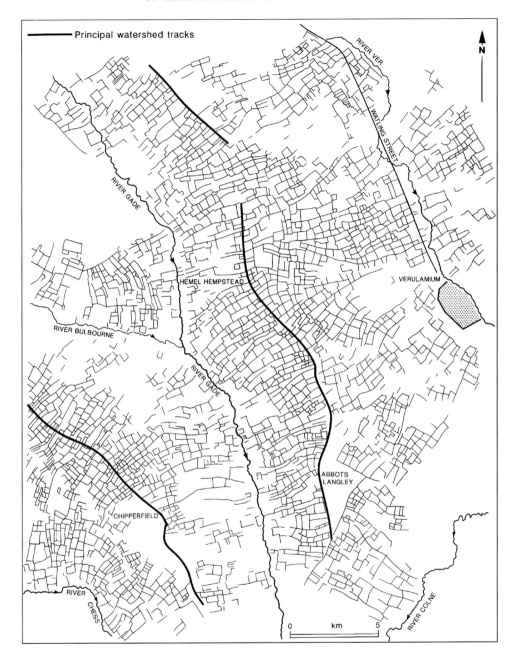

Above: 32 Co-axial landscapes on the Chiltern dip slope in west Hertfordshire. The co-axial boundaries, based on the major valleys draining the dip slope, terminate at long watershed tracks (marked by heavy lines)

Opposite: 31 A co-axial landscape in the Broxbourne and Wormley area of south-east Hertfordshire: top, the layout of roads and boundaries appearing on the earliest available maps; below, the pattern enhanced by the selective removal of features

and modern periods entirely unchanged. It is noticeable that in some cases – most notably at Leen Farm – the orientation of the archaeologically 'dated' features, while very close to, is nevertheless very slightly different from that of the neighbouring, upstanding boundaries; while at Burnham Sutton in Norfolk the original Iron Age fields had already been considerably modified – some boundaries added, some removed – before their incorporation into a medieval open field system (Percival and Williamson 2005). Rather than seeing relict co-axials simply as surviving prehistoric field systems, in other words, we should think of them as landscapes which may have prehistoric origins, but which have been developing continuously ever since. This in turn raises the question of how closely the present appearance of these landscapes relates to their original layout, and what proportion of the extant elements directly perpetuate prehistoric ones. In some cases – as at Burnham Sutton, or at Cheshunt within the Wormley system – excavations suggest that fairly minor field boundaries within areas of co-axial landscapes have prehistoric origins, implying in turn that much of the fine grain of the surrounding countryside could, potentially, be of the same antiquity. Similarly, the topographic evidence for Roman roads slighting individual fields within co-axial landscapes – as at Yaxley in north Suffolk (Williamson 1987) – suggests that these sometimes originated, at least in part, as networks of small enclosures. But even in the case of Wormley, field investigations strongly imply that much of the existing landscape results from the infilling, over time, of an originally much sparser pattern of land division. This is densely-wooded country, characterised by a number of extensive, semi-natural hornbeam woods. The main longitudinal axes of the co-axial landscape continue through these woods, in earthwork form, but few other boundaries are here evident: the areas defined by earthwork banks and hollow ways within and on the perimeter of the wooded areas are in general significantly larger than the fields conforming to the pattern lying *outside* them. This suggests that, on the higher ground at least, where the soils are heavier, the present co-axial 'field system' is the consequence of the later infilling of what was originally a much sparser pattern of parallel boundaries.

Of particular importance in all this is the fact that most if not all co-axial landscapes share a feature which sharply distinguishes them from the majority of co-axial field systems surviving in more conventional archaeological form. A high proportion of the linear axes of the former consist of roads or tracks, features which do not, for the most part, feature prominently in the latter, whose principal longitudinal elements mainly take the form of simple boundaries. It is possible that this distinction is more apparent than real, and a function of the later development of the landscapes in question. On Dartmoor, for example, it is noteworthy how, in the area around Bittaford and Ivybridge, where the outline of the parallel reaves has been preserved within the modern landscape, roads often form major elements of the system, yet are absent where the reaves continue as earthworks and tumbled walls onto the open moor to the north. Here, and possibly elsewhere, tracks may have developed some time after the original system of land division, alongside substantial linear boundaries which could not easily be crossed, or moved. Slight kinks, where a road or track is deflected a few metres to right or left but otherwise continues on the same alignment, are sometimes a feature of relict co-axials and perhaps indicate places where a major boundary was breached, and a road ceased to follow one side of it, crossing over to the other. This said, in many cases roads run continuously from one end of a system to another, or do so with only minor discontinuities, in such a way that it is hard to believe that they were not integral parts of these landscapes: although, without question, not all of the major longitudinal elements in them seem to have originally taken this form.

THE GEOGRAPHICAL CONTEXT OF CO-AXIAL LANDSCAPES

Relict co-axials thus differ from their 'archaeological' cousins in that roads and tracks seem to be more prominent elements. They do not appear, moreover, to be in any simple and direct manner 'living' examples of these archaeological field systems, but rather landscapes which have developed along co-axial lines over long periods of time. In part, such a pattern of development may simply be due to the influence of an early, originally rather much sparser, framework of parallel tracks and boundaries, as suggested in the case of the Wormley/Broxbourne 'system'. But in addition, it is probable that in all periods the evolution of such landscapes was influenced by the same, strong environmental factors.

One indication of this, not previously commented upon, is the fact that many co-axial landscapes are found in precisely the same areas as parishes laid out in the form of long, parallel strips. This correspondence is especially clear in north-west Norfolk, in south Norfolk, in south-east Hertfordshire and in south-east Cambridgeshire (Harrison 2002; Williamson 2000). As a number of writers have observed, such parochial arrangements developed where natural resources are arranged as a series of parallel bands: parishes were laid out at right angles to these, running for example from valley meadows, across a chalk escarpment, up to a drift-covered plateau (Rackham 1986). This ensured that each medieval community had access to a range of resources, and where parishes or townships were closely packed, each was correspondingly narrow and strip-like. The frequent coincidence of such medieval tenurial arrangements, and co-axial landscapes, does not mean that both have the same cause, and certainly does not imply that the two were coeval. On the contrary: in the case of south Cambridgeshire, for example, Harrison was able to demonstrate that the strip parishes were imposed upon an earlier arrangement of co-axial features, so that their boundaries follow for a while, leave, and then rejoin prominent linear elements, especially roads, which run for long distances from the edge of the Fens, up the chalk escarpment of the East Anglian Heights, and onto the boulder clay plateau above (Harrison 2002). The recurrent association does, however, suggest that both were a response to similar environmental circumstances.

A closer examination of their environmental context provides a possible explanation. Most co-axial landscapes, and many strip parishes, run at right angles to a major river floodplain or other wetland area (such as a low-lying fen or coastal marsh) which has an edge that is relatively straight, or gently curving, rather than displaying a series of marked bends (as with a convoluted river valley). Such landscapes occur, more importantly, in places where the areas separating these wetlands – such as the interfluves between major river valleys – are extensive, usually greater than *c*.8km in width. Where valleys are more closely spaced such landscapes are not in evidence.

FUNCTION, EVOLUTION AND PLANNING

Co-axial landscapes thus probably developed in part as a response to a strong parallel banding of resources and, in particular, from the need to move commodities – wood, timber and stock – at right angles to this, especially where such resources covered an extensive area of ground. The fact that the high ground onto which most co-axials run is occupied by heavy or infertile soils – boulder clay, London clay or clay-with-flints in the case of eastern England – which Domesday or place-name evidence suggests were once heavily wooded, and which still often carry extensive areas of woodland, and that many (although not all) co-axials terminate at extensive tracts of former low-lying wetland, suggests that a key factor in their creation or development was the regular movement of stock from winter grazing in upland wood-pastures, to spring fallows on the arable, and summer grazing on low-lying wetlands. Yet, as we have seen, not all the major elements in such systems are formed by roads, and early transverse boundaries also existed, so the more general need to divide banded resources between communities and individuals must also have been a factor.

Relict co-axial 'field systems' are usually seen as the result of conscious, large-scale planning in the remote past. The implications of the argument presented here is that such an interpretation is too simple. While some of the elements of these landscapes are indeed early, others are later alterations and additions. Moreover, the distinctive form of such landscapes derives not simply from their evolution within an ancient, parallel frame of roads and boundaries, but also from the response of successive later agrarian communities to a particular set of topographic imperatives. Such landscapes, one might almost say, have histories, not dates. But this in turn raises the possibility that any coherence and regularity that these landscapes display is similarly the consequence, not of deliberate planning, but of organic development within a structured natural framework. In other words, their resemblance to planned, large-scale field systems is misleading, and illusory on not one but two counts.

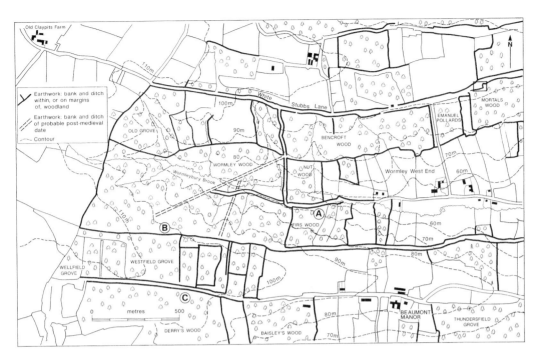

33 Detail of the Broxbourne/Wormley co-axial landscape, showing 'terrain oblivious' features (A) and regularly-spaced axes (B and C)

There are, however, good grounds for believing that most of these landscapes do indeed include an element of planning, especially in the case of the major long-distance elements, those which are most likely to be of prehistoric date. In this context, two recurrent features of co-axial landscapes are worth noting. The first is that while, as already described, their overall layout is related to the broad sweeps of natural landforms, in detail they are 'terrain oblivious'. Major linear features will run directly from river, to watershed, without deviating where minor valleys cut across their path at an acute angle, or as a response to other local topographic imperatives. In the Wormley/Broxbourne system – to take a typical example – axis 'A' begins by running above and to the north of the Wormleybury Brook but, as it progresses westwards, it crosses the stream, near the north-eastern corner of Firs Wood, and climbs gradually up the opposite side of the valley (*33*). Such relationships imply the imposition of a large-scale, preconceived plan onto the local terrain.

The second noteworthy feature is that the layout of the major (and thus potentially early) elements often displays a marked degree of regularity – greater than we might expect from organic development – although this, somewhat curiously, is often localised within the landscape in question, and not evident throughout it. In the case of the Broxbourne/Wormley 'system', for example, the two axes lying to the south of that just described ('B' and 'C') run almost exactly parallel, *c.*250m apart, for a distance of over 2km between Beaumont Manor and Westfield Grove. It is hard to see how such an arrangement could be fortuitous, the result of an organic response to the configuration of natural landforms.

CONCLUSION

This above discussion does not provide a clear or definitive answer to the questions posed at the start of this chapter. It does, however, suggest that relict co-axial landscapes are more complex entities than their original advocates, including myself, first believed. If the arguments advanced here are correct, moreover, they may have implications for some of the co-axial field systems surviving in truly archaeological form. In particular, we should be more concerned to examine these within their topographical and environmental contexts: Fleming of course did with the Dartmoor reaves but not all prehistorians have been so assiduous. We should be alive to the possibility that landscapes which *appear* to be the creation of a single planned event may, in some cases, have a longer and more complex history.

BIBLIOGRAPHY

Bowen, H.C. & Fowler, P.J. (eds) 1978 *Early Land Allotment*. Oxford: BAR.

Bryant, S., Perry, B. & Williamson, T., 2005 A 'relict landscape' in south east Hertfordshire: archaeological and topographic investigations in the Wormley area. *Landscape History* 27, 5-15.

Buckley, D. (ed.) 1980 *The Archaeology of Essex to AD 1500*. CBA Research Report 34. London: Council for British Archaeology.

Davies, J. & Williamson, T. (eds) 1999 *The Iron Age in Northern East Anglia*. Norwich: Centre of East Anglian Studies.

Davison, A., 1990 *The Evolution of Settlement in Three Parishes in South East Norfolk*. East Anglian Archaeology 49. Norwich: Norfolk Museums Service.

Drury, P.J., 1978 *Excavations at Little Waltham 1970-1*. CBA Research Report 26. London: Council for British Archaeology.

Drury, P.J. & Rodwell, W., 1978 Investigations at Asheldham, Essex: an interim report on the church and the historic landscape. *Antiquaries Journal* 51, 133-51.

Drury, P.J. & Rodwell, W., 1980 Late Iron Age and Roman settlement. In Buckley, D. (ed.), 59-75.

Ely, K.D. & Edwards, K., 2003 Cheshunt Park, Hertfordshire. An archaeological evaluation by the Time Team. Unpublished report, Bristol.

Fleming, A., 1988 *The Dartmoor Reaves: Investigating Prehistoric Land Divisions*. London: Batsford.

Harrison, S., 2002 Open fields and earlier landscapes: six parishes in south east Cambridgeshire. *Landscapes* 3, 35-54.

Hesse, M., 1992 Fields, tracks and boundaries in the Creakes, north Norfolk. *Norfolk Archaeology* 41, 305-24.

Hesse, M., 1998 Medieval field systems and land tenure in South Creake, Norfolk. *Norfolk Archaeology* 43, 79-97.

Hinton, D., 1997 The 'Scole-Dickleburgh field system' examined. *Landscape History* 19, 5-13.

Martin, E., 1999 Suffolk in the Iron Age. In Davies, J. & Williamson, T. (eds), 44-99.

Oosthuizen, S., 1998 Prehistoric fields into medieval furlongs? Evidence from Caxton, south Cambridgeshire. *Proceedings of the Cambridgeshire Antiquarian Society* 86, 145–52.

Oosthuizen, S., 2003 The roots of common fields: linking prehistoric and medieval field systems in west Cambridgeshire. *Landscapes* 4, 40–64.

Percival, S. & Williamson, T., 2005 Early fields and medieval furlongs: excavations at Creake Road, Burnham Sutton, Norfolk. *Landscapes* 6, 1–17.

Rackham, O., 1986 *The History of the Countryside*. London: Dent.

Rippon, S., 1991 Early planned landscapes in south-east Essex. *Essex Archaeology and History* 22, 46–60.

Rodwell, W., 1978 Relict landscapes in Essex. In Bowen, H.C. & Fowler, P.J. (eds), 89–98.

White, P., 2003 *The Arrow Valley, Herefordshire: Archaeology, Landscape Change and Conservation*. Herefordshire Studies in Archaeology, Series 2. Hereford: Herefordshire Archaeology.

Williamson, T., 1987 Early co-axial field systems on the East Anglian boulder clays. *Proceedings of the Prehistoric Society* 53, 419–31.

Williamson, T., 1993 *The Origins of Norfolk*. Manchester: Manchester University Press.

Williamson, T., 1998 The 'Scole-Dickleburgh Field System' revisited. *Landscape History* 20, 19–28.

Williamson, T., 2000 *The Origins of Hertfordshire*. Manchester: Manchester University Press.

11

FIRE FROM HEAVEN: DIVINE PROVIDENCE AND IRON AGE HILLFORTS IN EARLY MEDIEVAL BRITAIN

Alex Woolf

§*32*. In [Vortigern's] time Saint Germanus, renowned for his many virtues, came to preach in Britain, and through him many were saved, and very many perished. I shall write of some miracles which God performed through him.

The first of his miracles. There was a certain king, very unjust and tyrannical, whose name was Benlli. The holy man wished to visit him, and hastened to the unjust king that he might preach to him. But when the man of God came to the gate of the *urbs* with his companion, the porter came and greeted them, and they sent him to the king. The king gave them a dour answer, saying, with an oath, "If having come they wait until the end of the year, they shall never gain access to the interior of my *urbs*." While they waited for the porter to announce the tyrant's pronouncement to them the day was ending and evening and night approached, and they did not know where to go. Meanwhile one of the *servi* of the king came out of the interior of the *urbs* and bowed to the man of God, and announced to them all the words of the tyrant. He invited them into his own house and they went with him and were kindly received. And he had no livestock of any sort except one cow with a calf, and he killed the calf and cooked it and set it before them. Saint Germanus commanded that not a bone of it should be broken, and so it was done. On the morrow the calf was found before his mother, healthy, alive and unharmed.

§*33*. Again in the morning they arose and sought audience with the tyrant but while they were waiting and praying next to the gate of the *arx* [fort], behold, a man came running with sweat pouring down from his head to the soles of his feet. He bowed before them and St Germanus said, "Do you believe in the Holy Trinity?" and he replied "I believe!", he was baptised and he kissed him. And he said to him "Go in peace, in this hour you will die and the angels of the God are waiting for you in the air, and you will proceed with them to God, in whom you have believed." Then he joyfully entered the *arx* and was seized and bound by the prefect and led before the tyrant and he was slain. It was the custom with that vile tyrant that those who did not arrive before the rising of the sun, to do service in the *arx*, were executed. And they waited the whole day by the gate of the *civitas* but were not admitted to greet the tyrant.

§34. As was his wont, the aforementioned *servus* remained and Saint Germanus said to him, "Take care that not one man of your men remains this night in the *arx*." And he returned to the *arx* and led out his sons, who were nine in number, and they returned to the aforementioned house with him. And Saint Germanus commanded that they observe a fast with the doors closed and he said, "Be on your guard and, whatever you do, do not look upon the *arx*, but pray ceaselessly and call loudly upon your God." And, shortly after nightfall, fire fell from heaven and burnt the *arx*, and all the men who were with the tyrant, and, to this day, they have not re-appeared; and the *arx* has not been rebuilt to this day.

§35. In the morning, that man who had given them hospitality believed and was baptised along with all his sons and the whole district. His name was Cadell, and he blessed him, saying also, "A king of your seed shall not be wanting" (that is Cadell Dyrnllug) "and you alone shall be king from this day." And so it transpired, and the word of the prophet came to pass, who said "He raiseth up the poor out of the dust and lifteth the needy out of the dunghill; that he may sit with princes and occupy a throne of glory." [1 Samuel 2:8] Just as St Germanus said, he became a king and all his sons became kings, and from their seed all Powys is ruled to this day.

So chapters 32 to 35 of the early ninth-century Cambro-Latin text *Historia Brittonum* describe the rise to power of the dynasty of Cadell Ddyrnllug who ruled much of eastern Wales at the time of writing (my translation; see also, Morris 1980; Rowley 2005). As such it is a fairly typical dynastic origin legend, in which a man of humble birth, or in some stories a returning exile, receives the kingdom for himself and his descendants as a result of displaying better moral judgement than the incumbent king. This particular narrative is set during Late Antiquity, and the Germanus of this tale is to be identified with the bishop of Auxerre, in Gaul, who is known to have visited Britain in AD 429 to combat the Pelagian heresy (Thompson 1984). Elements of such stories may vary to reflect the specifics of the time of composition. In this case, for example, the attribution of nine sons to Cadell, the slave who will be king, may provide a clue as to the extent of Powys at the time this story was written down. By analogy with other such stories it seems likely that a more expanded version of the tale would have identified the sons as the ancestors of the ruling houses of the constituent parts of Powys, its *cantrefi*. At its greatest extent Powys comprised 13 *cantrefi*, stretching from the valley of the Dee to the valley of the Wye, but according to *Historia Brittonum* (chapter 49) the southern portion of this territory, *Rhwng Gwy a Hafren*, 'between Wye and Severn', was ruled in the early ninth century by a dynasty claiming descent not from Cadell but from Gwrtheyrn (Vortigern). These lands, in the basin of the Wye, comprised the four *cantrefi* of Gwrtheyrnion, Elfael, Maelienydd and Buellt (Builth). Removing the *cantrefi* of the Wye basin from Powys we are left with the six *cantrefi* of the Severn Valley (Mochnant, Cyfeiliog, Arwystli, Caereinion, Mechain and Cedewain) and the three of the Dee (Maelor, Swydd y Waun and Penllyn), giving a total of nine, equal to the sum of Cadell's sons.

Within the story of Germanus, Cadell and Benlli cited above seem, however, to be more localised geographical references. Though Benlli himself does not appear in other historical writings nor in any of the many medieval Welsh genealogical tracts, and elsewhere survives only as a folkloric giant (Bartrum 1993), he is memorialised toponymically in the hillfort known as Moel Fenlli (also Foel Fenlli) in the Clwydian Hills (*34*). The modern Offa's Dyke path curves around its ramparts though it lies somewhat to the west of any of the earthworks traditionally associated with the Mercian king. Moel Fenlli is the highest of several hillforts in the Clwydian range, at 511m, and its ramparts enclose an area of about 9.7ha (CPAT nd). Excavations of a limited nature were carried out in 1879 and much of the interpretation of the site is based on plausible analogy with better excavated sites in the neighbourhood such as Moel Hiraddug, Dinorben and Pen y Corddyn (Gale 1991). It seems likely that Moel Fenlli is, like its neighbours, a multiphase construction of the Iron Age, although the nineteenth-century excavations recovered some material of the Roman period dating to perhaps as late as the fourth century. Many hut platforms are still visible in the interior of the fort but, as with all such sites, the interpretation of its status and function is open to debate.

Standing on the watershed of the Clwydian range, Moel Fenlli also stands on an historical boundary. Although fairly central to the modern County of Clwyd, this unit was itself a creation of the 1974 local government reorganisation in England and Wales and prior to this the watershed had, at this point, formed the boundary between Flintshire and Denbighshire. During the Middle Ages its function as a boundary was more clearly defined for the eastern side of the hills, at this point, dividing the *cwmwd* (commote) of Iâl (Yale), in Powys, from the *cantref* of Dyffryn Clwyd, in Gwynedd. Strictly speaking, the hillfort itself lies in the parish of Llanbedr-Dyffryn-Clwyd, to the west, but our narrative from *Historia Brittonum* suggests an ancient connection with Iâl and the east. The parish on this side of the mountain is Llanarmon-yn-Iâl and the church there was the original mother church of the *cwmwd*. The secular centre of the *cwmwd*, the *maerdref*, lay some 300m east of the church, across the river Alyn, at the site known today as Tomen-y-Faerdre (Jones 1991). Llanarmon is the *llan*, or 'church precinct', of Garmon, the vernacular form of the name Germanus. According to Wade-Evans (1910) there were nine churches in Wales dedicated to Saint Garmon, whose feast was celebrated on 31 July. Three of these churches lay in Gwynedd but

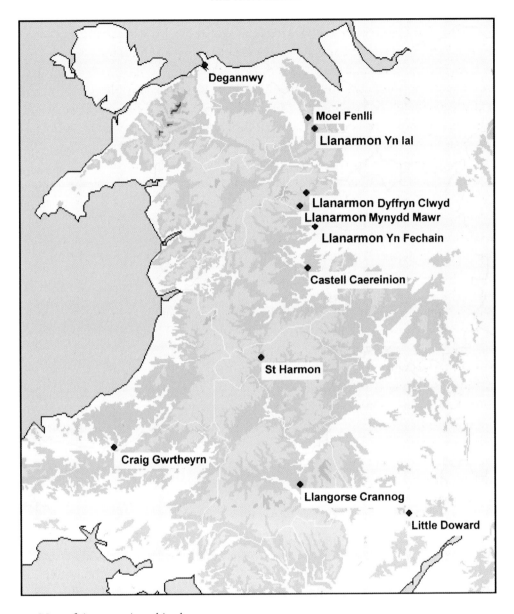

34 Map of sites mentioned in the text

the other six all lay in Powys and of these three lay in northern Powys at Llanarmon-yn-Iâl, Llanarmon Dyffryn Ceiriog and Llanarmon Mynydd Mawr. In mid-Powys lay Llanarmon-yn-Fechain (now Llanfechain) and Castell Caereinion. In the south the chief church of Cantref Gwrtheyrnion, now known as St Harmon, was also dedicated to Garmon. The distribution of these churches in the heartlands of the kings of Powys would seem to confirm the link between the dynasty and the cult of Garmon suggested by the story of Cadell and Benlli. The one Powysian outlier, St Harmon, lies significantly in Gwrtheyrnion, the cantref which bears the dynastic name of the original dynasty of the Wye Valley. Possibly the cult there was an imposition from the north at a time of dynastic change.

Returning to Llanarmon-yn-Iâl, the present gate to the churchyard faces north and frames Moel Fenlli on the horizon five kilometres away. As both a landscape feature and as a monument of human activity, the hill, as seen from the church, remains an impressive sight today. In the early Middle Ages its impact would surely have been even more significant. It seems likely that the story of the destruction of the fortress of king Benlli by fire from heaven at precisely the point at which St Garmon brought Christianity to the region, and by implication when the church of Llanarmon was founded, tells us something about the part which the landscape played in discourses of power in the early Middle Ages and about people's understanding, or perhaps lack of understanding, of processual change. The survival and flourishing of Llanarmon as the central place in Iâl whilst the ancient hillfort became overgrown with heather and gorse is reminiscent of a stanza penned by Oengus mac Oengobann, an Irish contemporary of the author of the *Historia Brittonum*, in the introduction to his *Martyrology*:

> The strong fortress of Tara has perished
> With the death of her princes.
> With its quires of sages,
> Great Armagh lives on.
> (Stokes 1984 [1905]: 24)

In both cases the survival and flourishing of the leading ecclesiastical settlement of the region, Llanarmon for Iâl and Armagh for Ireland, is contrasted with the transient nature of royal association with abandoned prehistoric sites. With regard to the Irish material, Aitchison (1994) has gone so far as to claim that the identification of impressive Iron Age monuments with national and provincial centres of kingship may have been entirely the product of an ecclesiastically driven discourse of this sort. Where *Historia Brittonum* diverges from the Irish examples is in the ascription of the destruction of the pagan *arx* of Benlli by direct divine intervention. It is not merely that worldly power is by its nature transient but that God will destroy it. This element of the narrative reflects the very real discourse of authority between the Church and secular rulers that characterised much of the early Middle Ages, reaching its climax in the Investiture Contest of the eleventh and early twelfth centuries.

On a more mundane level, however, such narratives became available to these discourses precisely because early medieval people lacked a sense of historical process beyond the level of dynastic conflict. Behind modern ideas of periodisation utilised and explored by historians and archaeologists there usually lie concepts of cultural, technological and economic disjunctures. At its simplest this can be seen as the three-age model for prehistory but also in the modern preoccupation with concepts like urbanisation, monetarisation and manorialisation. The unchanging past imagined by medieval writers can be seen throughout texts like *Historia Brittonum* which, for example, describes the period of Roman dominion over Britain (chapters 19-28) as a series of expeditions led by the rulers of Rome to impose temporary submission and tribute. Presumably the model for this was the kind of regional hegemony exercised by contemporary rulers such as the kings of Mercia or Tara who frequently humbled neighbouring kings but rarely annexed their kingdoms.

The nature of elite residence in ninth-century Wales is at present poorly understood. Between the fifth and seventh centuries royal residences do seem to have favoured fortified hilltop sites, though few, if any, were as impressive as Iron Age sites like Moel Fenlli (Arnold 2000). On the basis of archaeological evidence the only certain elite residence from the ninth century is the crannog, or artificial island, in Llangorse Lake, near Brecon, but it is far from clear that this site is representative (Campbell and Lane 1989). This said, under the year 811 the A- and C-texts of *Annales Cambriae* record the burning of Degannwy, following a lightning strike, and the A-text, the older of the two, describes Degannwy as an *arx*, the same word used for Benlli's fortress in *Historia Brittonum* (Dumville 2002). The *arx* of Degannwy seems likely to have been on the same site as the later medieval castle, a rocky outcrop overlooking the mouth of the Conwy. In this annalistic reference we seem to have an account of a hilltop citadel actually being destroyed by fire from heaven at about the time that *Historia Brittonum* was being composed. This episode may have been the inspiration for the story of Benlli but, in any event, it tells us that hilltop strongholds which could be severely damaged by fire were a part of the real world of ninth-century Wales and not just of the imagined past. Unlike the *arx* of Benlli, Degannwy must have been rebuilt since it was destroyed 11 years later by the Mercians (Dumville 2002). The story of Degannwy in this period confirms the hypothesis that the author of *Historia Brittonum* was imagining the past as the present and that he required specific events to explain the abandonment of prehistoric sites rather than having recourse to processual explanations.

That the trope of divine destruction of hillforts in this way was not an original contribution by the author of *Historia Brittonum* is confirmed by the account of the death of Vortigern which he gives in chapter 47:

Truly Saint Germanus used to preach to Vortigern that he should convert to the Lord and that he should cease his unlawful union with his own daughter; wretchedly he fled to Gwrtheyrnion, the region which bears his name, where he might remain hidden with his wives. And Saint Germanus went after him with all the clergy of the Britons, and he prayed on a crag, and remained there for forty days and forty nights, and day and night he used to stand there. And a second time Vortigern shamefully fled, as far as the *arx* of Vortigern, which is in the land of Dyfed, by the River Teifi.

And in his accustomed manner St Germanus went after him, and there with all the clergy, fasted for his cause for three days and as many nights; and on the fourth night, at about the hour of midnight, fire sent from the heavens fell suddenly, the heavenly fire burning the whole fortress; and Vortigern with all his household, and with all his wives, was killed. This is the end of Vortigern as I found it in the Book of the Blessed Germanus; others, however, told it differently. (My translation)

The final sentence here makes it clear that at least some of the material relating to Germanus came from a pre-existing written source. It would be interesting to know whether both fire-from-heaven stories came from this source. It would be atypical for early medieval hagiography to have two such similar accounts and they look very much like too versions of the same story connected to a different local dynasty in each case. The *arx* of Vortigern in this story is usually thought to be Craig Gwrtheyrn, near Llandyssul, a smallish fort standing about 100m above the Teifi. There has been no serious modern archaeological investigation here (Gardner 1932). Geoffrey of Monmouth also tells of Vortigern's death by burning in a hillfort, this time Little Doward by Ganarew, on the Wye. It cannot be coincidence that this site is only five kilometres from Monmouth but whether Geoffrey deliberately relocated the story to his homeland or whether, having grown up there, he knew a local version of the story cannot be determined. It should also be noted that, in line with his general rationalising of the supernatural, Geoffrey had the fire started by human agency (Thorpe 1966).

The episode at Degannwy in 811 demonstrates fire from the heavens could and did destroy royal citadels in early medieval Wales. What the author of *Historia Brittonum* and before him the author of the *Book of the Blessed Germanus* show us is that such events were interpreted as acts of divine justice visited upon immoral rulers. Locating such events at prehistoric hillforts first indicates that not only were all the products of medieval *scriptoria* regarded as in some sense edifying but that those who read the landscape also found a moral in their texts.

BIBLIOGRAPHY

Aitchison, N.B., 1994 *Armagh and the Royal Centres in Early Medieval Ireland: monuments, cosmology and the past.* Woodbridge: Boydell & Brewer.

Arnold, C.J., 2000 Early Medieval Wales, AD 400-1000: an introduction. In Arnold, C.J. & Davies, J.L., 141-97.

Arnold, C.J. & Davies, J.L., 2000 *Roman and Early Medieval Wales.* Stroud: Sutton.

Bartrum, P.C., 1993 *A Welsh Classical Dictionary: people in history and legend up to about AD 1000.* Aberystwyth: National Library of Wales.

Campbell, E. & Lane, A., 1989 Llangorse: a 10th century royal crannog in Wales. *Antiquity* 63, 675-81.

CPAT, nd *A short guide to Moel Fenlli and other Clywidian hill forts.* www.cpat.org.uk/educate/guides/clwydhil/clwydhil.htm, accessed 2007.

Dumville, D.N. (ed. & tr.), 2002 *Annales Cambriae, AD 682-954: texts A-C in parallel*. Cambridge: Department of Anglo-Saxon, Norse and Celtic.

Gale, F., 1991 The Iron Age. In Manley, J., Grenter, S. & Gale, F. (eds), 82-96.

Gardner, W., 1932 Craig Gwrtheyrn Hill Fort, Llanfihangel ar Arth, Carmarthenshire. *Archaeologia Cambrensis* 87, 144-50.

Jones, G., 1991 Medieval Settlement. In Manley, J., Grenter, S. & Gale, F. (eds), 186-202.

Manley, J., Grenter, S. & Gale, F. (ed.), 1991 *The Archaeology of Clwyd*. Clwyd County Council.

Morris, J., 1980 *Nennius: the British History and the Welsh Annals*. Chichester: Phillimore.

Rowley, R., 2005 *Historia Brittonum: The History of the Britons attributed to Nennius*. Felinfach: Llanerch.

Stokes, W., 1984 [1905] *Félire Óengusso Céli Dé. The Martyrology of Oengus the Culdee*. London: Henry Bradshaw Society, reprinted Dublin: Dublin Institute for Advanced Studies.

Thompson, E.A., 1984 *St Germanus of Auxerre and the End of Roman Britain*. Woodbridge: Boydell and Brewer.

Thorpe, L. (tr.), 1966 *Geoffrey of Monmouth: The History of the Kings of Britain*. Harmondsworth: Penguin.

Wade-Evans, A.W., 1910 *Parochiale Wallicanum. Y Cymmrodor* 22, 22-124.

12

UNTANGLING UPLAND LANDSCAPES: 30 YEARS OF ARCHAEOLOGICAL SURVEY IN THE PEAK DISTRICT

John Barnatt

ARCHAEOLOGICAL SURVEY IN THE PEAK DISTRICT

The Peak District, while having its own distinctive regional character, is similar to many other upland areas of Britain, such as those studied intensively by Andrew Fleming on Dartmoor and Swaledale, in that it has rich and complex historic landscape (Fleming 1988, 1998; Barnatt and Smith 2004). In such places survival of extant archaeological earthworks is exceptional. This chapter introduces the variety of these found in the Peak District, giving a flavour of what can be experienced here, and celebrates the value of archaeological landscape survey as a practice.

The multi-period surveys undertaken in the Peak District allow conservation of the archaeological resource to be more effective and better informed. At an early stage a survey strategy was devised that allowed maximum coverage to be achieved. This comprises rapid but detailed sketch plotting, accompanied by catalogues which give descriptions of form, observed stratigraphic relationships, depiction on historic maps and other sources, and interpretation. While metrical precision was sacrificed, the surveys are sufficient to relocate features in the field with ease, and are detailed enough to interpret something of the character of what has been found.

For the most part the many surveys undertaken have never been published; often there are issues of confidentiality. Also, unlike archaeological excavation, there is no professional ethic that demands publication, as nothing is destroyed in the process of the investigation. More importantly, the surveys are in effect work in progress. As a record is made on a farm-by-farm basis this is gradually building up a jigsaw in which many of the pieces are still missing. The work to date has shown that, as with all Historic Environment Records in upland regions, what was known previously was woefully inadequate. Tens of thousands of archaeological features have been recorded for the first time. With sites that are of regional and national importance there are a significant number away from roads and footpaths which had previously slipped through the net. For example, we regularly find one or more prehistoric barrows per year. We also record what many would regard as the 'ordinary', such things as relict field boundaries, field barns, quarries and disused routeways. Here there has been an exponential increase in our knowledge, where over 95 per cent of features had no previous formal record. The value of the 'ordinary' should not be undervalued for this makes an invaluable contribution to defining local distinctiveness. This 'complete' record allows the development of the historic landscape through time to be assessed. It is only when something of the activities of people in recent centuries are better understood that earlier features can be addressed at a landscape scale, once such factors as differential survival rates from place to place are put into the equation. Conversely, the record of the 'ordinary' in itself presents opportunities for research into the agricultural and industrial character of the region over the last 1000 years. For me, as a researcher, this has widened my perspectives and offered broad scope for new and exciting study. What follows are four case studies that illustrate something of the range of variety and the problems and opportunities involved in untangling and interpreting landscapes where so much survives.

The North Lees Estate

This survey, undertaken in 1991 (Barnatt 1991), covers an area of moorland and farmland north of Hathersage, situated below the impressive and often-visited five kilometre-long cliff of Stanage Edge. It presents a classic example of the multi-period features that are extant within a small area of Peak District landscape (35). There is a broad range of elements telling of settlement, agriculture, industry and communications. Highlights include prehistoric settlements and cultivation plots on a high shelf, with associated barrows. On the valley slopes below there is more recent settlement, including the small but fine late sixteenth-century North Lees Hall, with a cruck-framed outbuilding adjacent and a small area of garden earthworks, with a ruined sixteenth-century chapel at a distance which may be at the site of an earlier hall. A short distance away is one of the best-preserved Romano-British settlements in the region, often missed by walkers because of its dense bracken cover. The irregularly-shaped fields and lynchets around these settlements tell of centuries of gradual modification of the farming landscape. This stands in strong contrast with ruler-straight walls on the moors above, dating from the time of the Parliamentary Enclosure Award of 1830 when the land here was parcelled up but not improved. By the side of a stream there is a small ruined mill, last used for papermaking. In the early eighteenth century there was a water-powered lead smelter here and three white coal kilns for drying chopped coppice poles from surrounding woodlands. While coppice stools are now absent due to replanting with standards, these kilns show that the woodland here provided the smelting fuel. Running from the valley to and across the moors there are hollow-ways and paved paths that were part of the

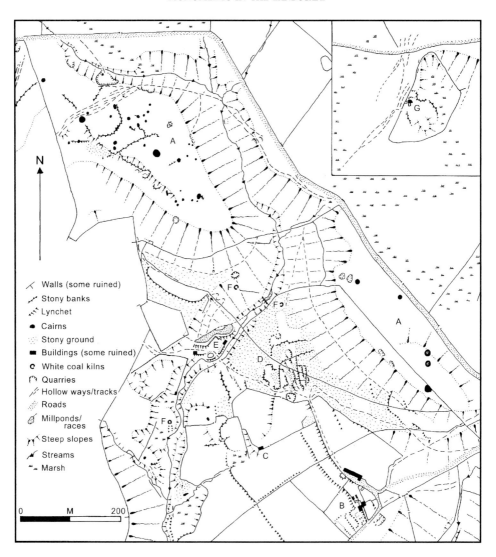

35 Part of the North Lees archaeological landscape (using the standard depiction for 1:2500 survey sheets). A: Prehistoric survivals, B: North Lees Hall, C: Chapel, D: Romano-British settlement, E: Mill/lead smelter, F: White coal kilns, G: The Buck Stone

communication network to and from the Peak District before the advent of turnpike roads. In contrast, a so-called 'Roman road' above Stanage Edge to the north is likely to be a 1771 road built to facilitate the movement of industrial products such as millstones. Nestled below Stanage Edge adjacent to one of the main older routeways there is a huge boulder known as the Buck Stone, surrounded by the ruined walls of an isolated moorland enclosure and a smaller predecessor. This stone has notches on three sides for timber roof supports, together with drip gullies and a curious carved stickman on its flat top where there are also notches for a 'railing'. While the lost buildings may have been associated with shepherding activity, they can alternatively be interpreted as an overnight stopping point for packhorsemen, perhaps in effect an isolated early 'inn'.

The North Lees landscape illustrates well the fact that altitude plays a major part in what survives from different periods. There is a strong contrast between the valleys, where settlement and agriculture have perhaps been near-continuous for two to four millennia, and the moorlands above, where prehistoric features can still be found because these areas have been upland grazing for the last 2000 years.

This area also illustrates that present appearances can be deceptive. All too often visitors to the National Park come to visit the unspoilt countryside and utter to themselves such banalities as 'isn't nature wonderful'. What they miss, as all landscape archaeologists know, is that the moorlands are the product of people's activities in the past. Even the heather wouldn't be here without continuous intervention from grazing; at this altitude the open landscape would revert to woodland if left to its own devices. Similarly, few realise the extent and impact of industry in the recent past. Few know that there was a lead smelter here that was regularly emitting plumes of poisonous fumes, or that there was surrounding managed woodland which provided fuel. On the moors nearby, above Stanage Edge, there were coal mine shafts dug in the eighteenth century, in an area that is now often perceived as a bleak wilderness.

The Bakewell open fields

A large part of the parish of Bakewell, one of the main traditional market centres of the Peak District, was surveyed in 2002. This community fieldwork project was carried out by pupils of Lady Manners School in the care of a small team of local people, National Park Rangers and the author (Barnatt 2002b).

One part of the survey area, to the west of the town, is illustrated here (36). Bakewell was unusual in that large parts of its six open fields survived in use until around 1810. Elsewhere on the limestone plateau the medieval open field pattern has been 'fossilised' by many hundreds of miles of sinuous drystone walls. These define small, narrow fields reflecting the earlier strip pattern and largely result from the gradual break down of the open field method of agriculture from late medieval times onwards. They create one of the key components of the Peak District's historic landscape (Barnatt 2003). A glance at an Ordnance Survey 1:25,000 map showing the land around places such as Monyash, Flagg and Chelmorton illustrates the distinctiveness of this pattern, with the land surrounding the villages standing in strong contrast with the rectangular fields on enclosed commons beyond.

This is not the case at Bakewell, where the Parliamentary Enclosure Award of 1810 led to the open field areas being divided into mostly straight-edged fields with the resulting loss of the earlier pattern. Despite the land above the town being agriculturally advantaged in regional terms, many earthworks of ridge and furrow and strip lynchets still survive, if intermittently. These illustrate the now-redundant

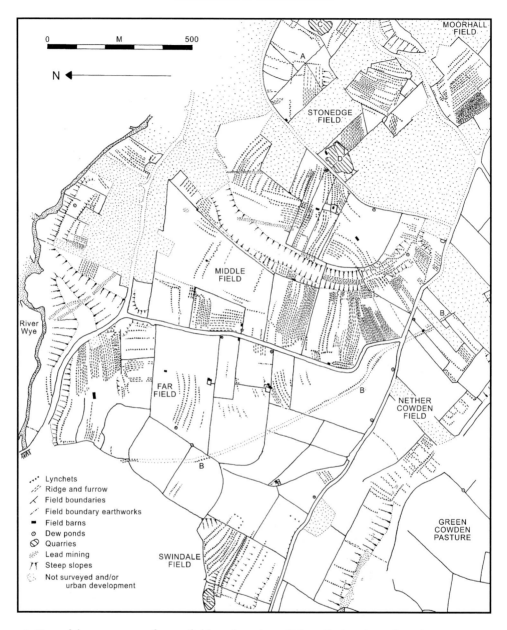

36 One of the core areas of open field earthworks at Bakewell, showing selected archaeological features, simplified from 1:2500 survey sheets. A: Bowling green, B: Derbygate, C: Parsonage Chert Quarry, D: Stonedge Pits – limestone, lime and possibly chert, E: 'Rottenstone' (silica-rich decalcified limestone) quarry

strip layout as present in about 1800. The names of the fields and their furlongs can largely be reconstructed from historical documentation. Higher on the limestone plateau such earthworks are rare as the soils are so thin. Thus, Bakewell also stands in contrast in that cultivation strip earthworks are well defined, and provides a key area, along with other low-lying areas around Chatsworth and Tissington, where they can be studied.

The land above Bakewell is also of interest in that it has more than its share of fieldbarns, in this case built after 1810. This reflects the dual economy, farming and other forms of income, of many of the occupants of Bakewell. One of the surprises of the survey was the identification of a square earthwork superimposed on the cultivation strips which is probably a seventeenth-century bowling green, sited to overlook the town, lying within 'Bowling Green Furlong' named in the eighteenth century. The Manners family, Earls and later Dukes of Rutland, have long been key players in Bakewell and this previously unrecognised feature complements other bowling greens at nearby Haddon Hall. Other features of note include the old pre-turnpike main road called Derbygate that once ran above the town, and quarries associated the local chert mining, which provided crushing stones for the pottery industry around Stoke-on-Trent.

As an exercise in local awareness raising and training this survey was a great success. While the survey work and quality control were time consuming, the benefits outweighed these. Many local people were introduced to the archaeological and historic landscape heritage of their town through the rich store of information on the past held in earthworks for those who have learned to read them. These insights have been gained either by taking part in the survey, or through the resulting exhibition and talks given, or by accessing the survey report in the local library or Old House Museum.

Beeley and the Chatsworth Estate

The area illustrated here is only part of an archaeological landscape survey of about 45sq km of the Duke of Devonshire's estate centred on Chatsworth House. This was undertaken between 1996 and 2000, and included parkland, enclosed farmland and moorland (Barnatt and Bannister 2002). An interpretation of the park and gardens has recently been published (Barnatt and Williamson 2005) and an overview of the archaeology across the Estate as a whole is in preparation (Barnatt and Bannister in prep).

The land around and above the village of Beeley in the Derwent Valley (37) provides a further example of a multi-period landscape with contrasts between moorlands and farmland below (Barnatt 1998; 2000b; Barnatt and Bannister 2002). However, unlike North Lees, the valley includes a focal village with medieval origins. The Derwent Valley and the limestone plateau to the west of here have many such villages, whereas in the northern and western parts of the Peak District there is predominantly non-nucleated settlement. Another contrast is that much land in Beeley was acquired by the Chatsworth Estate in post-medieval times and has an 'estate landscape' veneer.

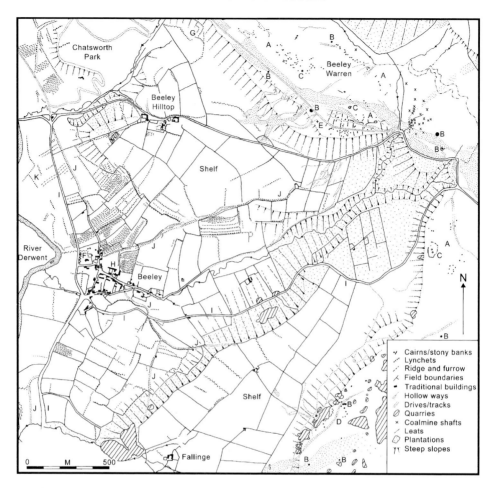

37 The archaeological landscape around the Beeley part of Chatsworth Estate, showing selected archaeological features, simplified from 1:2500 survey sheets. A: Prehistoric settlements, cairnfields and fields, B: Barrows, C: Stone circles and ringcairns, D: Funerary cairnfield, E: medieval cross base, F: Beeley church, G: Site of Doe Wood farm, H: The Dukes Barn, I: New nineteenth-century roads, J: Old lanes, K: Beeley Meadows

One of the highlights of the moorland is the extensive remains of settlements, with associated cultivation and monuments such as barrows and stone circles, dating to the Bronze and Iron Ages. There is a variety of clearance features and field boundaries, some of which, as on Beeley Warren, have co-axial layouts but at a radically smaller scale than those on Dartmoor (Fleming 1988). They are to be interpreted in a purely local context rather than indicating communal planning. These remains narrowly escaped destruction, as estate plans drawn in the 1850s show that it was intended to make Beeley Warren into a designed 'wilderness' with paths and plantings. Fortunately this never came to fruition. At a broader scale, in many cases it is not that the exceptional prehistoric survivals on the East

Moors were on land unsuitable for agricultural improvement in the nineteenth century, but that they were often set aside for grouse shooting by large estates. On Fallinge Edge there is a rare example of a small funerary cairnfield with a series of carefully designed circular and rectangular mounds. The detailed assessment of the prehistoric features on the Chatsworth Estate moorlands has led to a refining of the conclusions drawn during work on my PhD thesis, where a simple dichotomy between settlement areas (with stone circles and barrows) and large open pastures beyond (with barrows) was drawn (Barnatt 1986, 1987a, 1987b, 1989). Beyond the prehistoric fields the open pastures contain a scattering of small cairns and diminutive stone settings. While some of these cairns are probably funerary, others may be at places where small and short-lived cultivation episodes took place. The large barrows found away from the settlement zones are placed close to watersheds, at the upper limits of the pastures. These are offset from the watersheds so that visually they function in specific directions rather than signalling to all and sundry that the land was used. In other cases, as east of Beeley Warren, they are found in areas suitable for cultivation, but where there is no evidence that this took place; these may again be at boundaries between communities (Barnatt 2000a).

While the Chatsworth moorlands have been used for open grazing for the last two millennia they are still rich with archaeological sites from the historic period. These include extensive pre-turnpike hollow-ways, some at major routeways and one with an adjacent medieval cross base. There are also leats dug to provide water for the ornamental features in the gardens at Chatsworth. Extensive industrial features exist, including an eighteenth- to nineteenth-century colliery with a series of shallow shafts, and sandstone quarries where millstones, troughs, lintels and gateposts were made; many products broken during manufacture still litter this landscape.

The archaeology in the valley is very different. Today Beeley village has a medieval church with traditional farmsteads and cottages that were mostly built from the seventeenth century onwards. A detailed assessment made by the Estate in 1850 shows that, while some had roofs with traditional stone slates, a significant number of others had thatched roofs. This contrasts strongly with today; none are thatched and such roofs are now very rare in the Peak District. The enclosed fields that surround the village have evolved over centuries, but in parts cultivation strip earthworks survive from the time when there were open fields here.

In contrast to the valley landscape with its nucleated village, on the high shelf to the east there are isolated farmsteads. That at Beeley Hilltop has an early seventeenth-century hall and there are traces of medieval-type ridge and furrow nearby. This settlement, together with Fallinge to the south and another at Doe Wood, are documented from the thirteenth/fourteenth century; Doe Wood was abandoned in the decades around 1800. It is worth pondering whether such shelf settlements continued a tradition of non-nucleated living and farming first started here in prehistory.

While Beeley lies beyond the grand park around Chatsworth House, the Estate's influence on the landscape is obvious. The tenanted properties all have the traditional blue and white paintwork and the village has Estate buildings such as The Dukes Barn built in the late eighteenth century, and later used to house the estate work-horses and wagons. The farmland around the village is decorated with scattered trees and there are plantations on the steeper slopes above. Some roads were moved by the Estate in the decades around 1800, with the earlier traditional ones still visible as earthworks. Similarly, in the early nineteenth century the field boundaries between the main road and the river to the east were removed to give the approach to the landscape park from the south at Beeley Meadows a decorative 'parkland-like' appearance; this area was used to graze and show-off the estate work-horses.

Ecton Hill

Metal mining sites are amongst some of the most threatened archaeological remains in the Peak District. Whilst the surface features were once very common, over the last 100 years about 75 per cent of hillocks have been removed or badly damaged, either for the fluorspar, barites and calcite they contain or lost to agricultural 'improvement'. From the 1990s onwards, building on work by the Peak District Mines Historical Society and others, there has been intensive effort by the National Park Authority, in partnership with English Heritage and English Nature/Natural England, to assess the features that remain to establish conservation priorities across the orefield. This review has identified the most important surviving sites and landscapes for their historical, archaeological, ecological and historic landscape value (Barnatt and Penny 2004; Barnatt 2004; 2005).

One such site, at Ecton, amidst 'unspoilt' and picturesque scenery at a high ridge above the River Manifold is used here to illustrate the richness of the mining landscapes to be found (*38*). A preliminary assessment of the surface remains was carried out in 1996 as part of the author's personal research into Ecton, which has now been demonstrated to have been mined for copper since the Bronze Age (Barnatt and Thomas 1998) and has long been known to be a major copper, lead and zinc producer in the seventeenth to nineteenth centuries. In the seventeenth century one of the earliest uses of gunpowder in a British mine took place here (Barnatt, Rieuwerts and Thomas 1997). In the mid- to late eighteenth century, Deep Ecton Mine was one of the deepest and richest mines in Britain (Barnatt 2002a; Porter 2004; Porter and Robey 2000; Robey and Porter 1972). The surface survey allowed refinement of those core parts of Ecton Hill that were designated a Scheduled Monument.

Much of the archaeologically important evidence at Ecton lies underground and is beyond the scope of this short text, but at the surface there are a wide variety of important evocative ruins, deep openings and extensive waste hillocks, that together illustrate the development of the mining. High on the ridgetop there are many hillocks, some of which are at the site of prehistoric mining. Hammerstones have

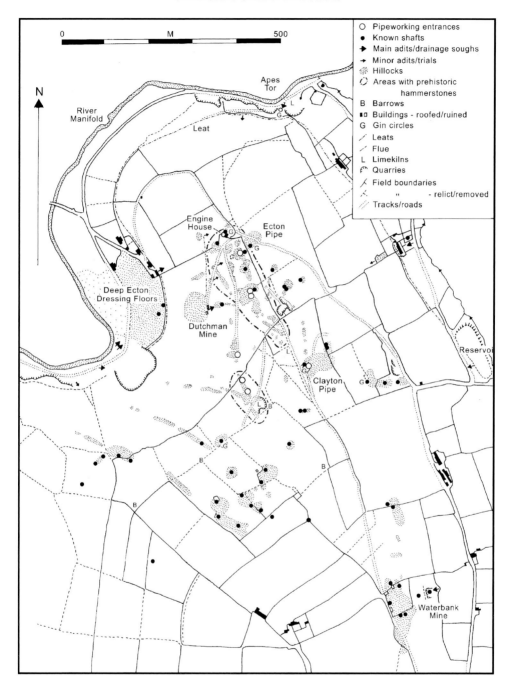

Pipeworking entrances
Known shafts
Main adits/drainage soughs
Minor adits/trials
Hillocks
Areas with prehistoric hammerstones
B Barrows
Buildings - roofed/ruined
G Gin circles
Leats
Flue
L Limekilns
Quarries
Field boundaries
" - relict/removed
Tracks/roads

38 A schematic plan of the Ecton Hill mining landscape

been found here, a few hillocks are perhaps original features while many others are later, the prehistoric finds having been moved with mine waste as early galleries were reworked. From deep underground an antler mining tool has been recovered, again displaced in post-medieval times, which has been radiocarbon dated to the first half of the Bronze Age. Immediately opposite the early mines there are roughly contemporary barrows.

Little is as yet known of medieval mining at Ecton but in the late medieval times the hill was at the heart of a documented deer park; the earliest field boundaries on the ridgetop probably relate to the fragmentation of this and renewed mining in the seventeenth century. Around this time firesetting, using coal as fuel, was employed to break rock underground (Barnatt and Worthington 2006), and from 1665 to 1668 gunpowder was used. In the eighteenth and nineteenth centuries the main pipeworkings under the hill at Ecton and Clayton Pipes were followed vertically down from the earlier ridge workings to over 300m below river level. This was only made possible with the driving of drainage soughs to the river and the use of underground engines to raise water to this horizon. The richest of these mines, at Ecton Pipe, was owned by the Dukes of Devonshire who, after the deposits had been proved by a company of miners working between 1723 and 1760, didn't renew their lease and had it worked 'in house'. It was developed as a 'state of the art' mine where investment led to substantial profits for the Dukes; the promise of great riches may well have been one factor that gave the fourth Duke the confidence to create the impressive landscape park at Chatsworth (Barnatt and Williamson 2005).

High on the ridgetop there is a 1788 Boulton and Watt engine house once used to raise ore; this is the only surviving eighteenth-century steam engine building with substantial remains in the Peak District. Original structures for final ore processing and smelting at the Dukes Mine, located close to the river next to Deep Ecton Level which went deep into the hill, have largely gone. However, nearby to the north the mine agent's house, the mine office and mine salesroom are now occupied as dwellings. The upper dressing floor, on a massive waste heap part way up the steep hillside, was for poorer grade ores that needed preliminary processing. This has eighteenth-century origins when ore was drawn up shafts from Deep Ecton Level, but was redeveloped later when a new level was driven to the main engine shaft, and has vestiges of circular buddles and other structures, which were used by both Deep Ecton and Clayton Mines. The course of a 1780s leat that supplied water for dressing, taken from a reservoir on the other side of the hill 1.4km away, fed by water from a drainage sough from the mines, can still be traced. This passes close to a shaft top at the northern end of the hill at Apes Tor, with an impressive gin engine platform cut into the cliff above. This shaft once led down to an underground canal that brought ore to be wound to the surface. Nearby there is limekiln where waste stone was burnt and then put to good use. Deep Ecton is a classic early example of an integrated mining operation created at the first flowering of the Industrial

Revolution. The Dukes not only controlled the mining, but also had their own smeltworks and at Whiston several miles away, with their own collieries providing much of the fuel, moved along a road network improved for the purpose.

By the early 1790s the richest ore deposits had largely been worked out, but the fame of Ecton was such that a series of nineteenth-century speculative mining ventures took place, with shareholders regularly loosing their investment. Many visible shafts and ruined mine buildings date to this period, as at Dutchman Mine and Watergrove Mine. These remains tell their own story, of misplaced optimism and exploitation of the rich and greedy.

PRESENT AND FUTURE SURVEY

While the National Park Authority has been undertaking rapid archaeological earthwork surveys continually since the 1980s, with 1-3 survey archaeologists working at any one time since 1989, there is still approximately half the National Park to assess. When the task is finally completed, it will be time to start again. The process of assessing and managing this valuable landscape is something like painting the Forth Road Bridge. A second round of survey will establish what still survives several decades down the line and identify the subtler features missed the first time round because the light was wrong, the grass too long or the heather too mature.

Many of the individual surveys undertaken have been carried out on farms and other properties where the land manager has expressed an interest in an agri-environment conservation agreement, with the survey informing what should be targeted. Thus, short-term conservation benefit is maximised. However, the surveys undertaken, and those in the future, will also inform conservation priorities, allowing a more mature assessment of all aspects of the archaeological resource by identifying the range and quality of surviving features and landscapes. Equally importantly, it will allow research to be carried out at what are demonstrably the most productive areas and best sites. Often over the years the discovery of new features has revealed previously unanticipated diversity in the archaeological resource and this in itself has led to new avenues of research into the wonderfully rich Peak District historic landscape.

ADDENDUM

Andrew Fleming has been one of the leading practitioners of landscape archaeology for many years, and has been instrumental in demonstrating what can be learned from approaching research at a landscape scale. My own work as Senior Survey Archaeologist for the Peak District National Park Authority has concentrated upon such surveys for the last two decades. My involvement started before then, from the 1970s onwards, carrying out detailed recording of the extensive prehistoric remains on the region's East Moors. Initially this was as an adjunct to my PhD thesis (Barnatt 1987b; 1989), which was supervised by Andrew. He played a significant part in teaching me the value of taking a landscape approach, learned whilst working alongside him on Dartmoor. For me the last 30 years of survey have been an intensely rewarding experience which has fostered a deeper understanding of the Peak District landscape and the people who have inhabited and helped shaped it.

ACKNOWLEDGEMENTS

Many thanks to the Peak District National Park Authority for supporting archaeological survey in the National Park over many years, to the many participants and the organisers of the Bakewell survey project, to Chatsworth Estate and English Heritage for commissioning the survey around Chatsworth, to Nicola Bannister and Heidi Taylor for their part in this work, to the late Geoff Cox for encouraging the work at Ecton and to Garth Thomas for help with the fieldwork.

BIBLIOGRAPHY

Barnatt, J., 1986 Bronze Age remains on the East Moors of the Peak District. *Derbyshire Archaeological Journal* 106, 18-100.

Barnatt, J., 1987a Bronze Age settlement on the gritstone East Moors of the Peak District of Derbyshire and South Yorkshire. *Proceedings of the Prehistoric Society* 53, 393-418.

Barnatt, J., 1987b *The Design and Distribution of Stone Circles in Britain: a reflection of social organisation in the Second and Third Millennia BC* (3 vols). Unpublished doctoral thesis, Sheffield University.

Barnatt, J., 1989 *Stone Circles of Britain: taxonomic and distributional analyses, and a catalogue of sites in England, Scotland and Wales* (2 vols). Oxford: BAR.

Barnatt, J., 1991 *The North Lees Estate, Outseats, Derbyshire: archaeological survey 1991.* Unpublished report, Peak District National Park Authority.

Barnatt, J., 1998 *Chatsworth Moorlands: archaeological survey 1997-8* (2 vols). Unpublished report, Peak District National Park Authority.

Barnatt, J., 2000a. To each their own: later prehistoric farming communities and their monuments in the Peak. *Derbyshire Archaeological Journal* 120, 1-86.

Barnatt, J., 2000b *Chatsworth Inbye Land: archaeological survey 1999-2000* (2 vols). Unpublished report, Peak District National Park Authority.

Barnatt, J., 2002a The development of the Deep Ecton Mine, Staffordshire, 1723-1760. *Mining History* 15, 10-23.

Barnatt, J., 2002b *The Bakewell Archaeological Survey.* Unpublished report, Peak District National Park Authority.

Barnatt, J., 2003 *A Landscape Through Time: the historic character of the Peak District National Park Landscape – aims, methods and user manual.* Unpublished report, Peak District National Park Authority.

Barnatt, J., 2004 *An Inventory of Regionally and Nationally Important Lead Mining Sites in the Peak District: archaeological importance* (2 vols). Unpublished report, Peak District National Park.

Barnatt, J., 2005 *Updated Inventory of Regionally and Nationally Important Lead Mining Sites in the Peak District – November 2005.* Unpublished report, Peak District National Park.

Barnatt, J. & Bannister, N., 2002 *Vestiges of a Rich and Varied Past: an archaeological assessment of the earthworks, field boundaries and buildings of the Chatsworth landscape* (2 vols). Unpublished report, Peak District National Park Authority.

Barnatt, J. & Bannister, N., in prep. *The Archaeology of a Great Estate: the Chatsworth landscape.* Bollington: Windgather.

Barnatt, J. & Penny, R., 2004 *The Lead Legacy: the prospects for the Peak District's lead mining heritage.* Bakewell: Peak District National Park Authority.

Barnatt, J., Rieuwerts, J. & Thomas, G.H., 1997 Early use of gunpowder in the Peak District: Stone Quarry Mine and Dutchman Level, Ecton. *Mining History* 13.4, 24-43.

Barnatt, J. & Smith, K., 2004 *The Peak District: landscapes through time.* Bollington: Windgather.

Barnatt, J. & Thomas, G.H., 1998 Prehistoric mining at Ecton, Staffordshire: a dated antler tool and its context. *Mining History* 13.5, 51-64.

Barnatt, J. & Williamson, T., 2005 *Chatsworth: a landscape history.* Bollington: Windgather.

Barnatt, J. & Worthington, T., 2006 Using coal to mine lead: firesetting at Peak District Mines. *Mining History* 16:3, 1-94.

Fleming, A., 1988 *The Dartmoor Reeves: investigating prehistoric land divisions.* London: Batsford.

Fleming, A., 1998 *Swaledale: valley of the wild river.* Edinburgh: Edinburgh University Press.

Porter, L., 2004 *Ecton Copper Mines under the Dukes of Devonshire 1760-1790.* Ashbourne: Landmark.

Porter, L. & Robey, J., 2000 *The Copper and Lead Mines around the Manifold Valley, North Staffordshire.* Ashbourne: Landmark.

Robey, J. & Porter, L., 1972 *The Copper and Lead Mines of Ecton Hill, Staffordshire.* Ashbourne: Moorland.

13

SOME ASPECTS OF EARLY LAND USE IN WEARDALE, COUNTY DURHAM

Tom Gledhill and Ros Nicholl

INTRODUCTION

This paper introduces some of the results of a landscape survey conducted in Weardale, County Durham. An archaeological survey of Stanhope Park revealed, among other features, several settlements and extensive field systems. These resemble settlements and field systems elsewhere in northern England, which have been securely identified as Roman in date. We hereby present our findings and discuss them with reference to dated sites.

Stanhope Park lies in Weardale in the North Pennines Area of Outstanding Natural Beauty, three miles west of Stanhope between the villages of Eastgate and Westgate. The park, which was created in about AD 1300 as a deer park for the Bishop of Durham, is about four miles long and three miles wide and straddles the River Wear. The land rises from 230m above sea level at the river to a height of 452m. Current land use is mostly agricultural, consisting of a mixture of pasture and hay meadow. Much of the land shows signs of having been ploughed in the fairly recent past.

One of the aims of the project was to answer questions raised by aerial photographs taken by Dennis Harding and discussed by Rob Young (1993 and see Young and Webster this volume). The aerial photographs show field systems and possible settlements considered to be late prehistoric. Both the extent and the date of these features were uncertain. A wider aim was to investigate the potential for previously unrecorded earthwork archaeology in Weardale. The deer park was selected as a starting point for this investigation because of the potential demonstrated by the aerial photographs and because it forms a discrete entity.

The survey took place between during January and March of 2004, 2005 and 2006. It was conducted in winter to minimise disturbance to ground-nesting birds and farm stock, and to take advantage of the short sward and low winter light.

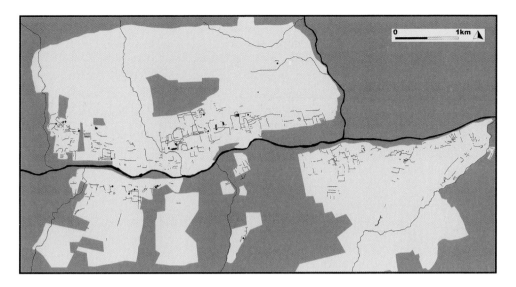

39 Walkover survey results. Lines represent rubble banks and lynchets, dots represent hut platforms

Each field was systematically walked and visible features were recorded manually on a map, given a written description and a GPS position. Following this walkover survey some features were selected for measured survey, including two settlement sites north of the Wear. The purpose of this measured survey was to investigate and record the form of the settlements and the relationship between the settlement and the field systems.

SURVEY RESULTS

The results of the walkover survey demonstrate that the late prehistoric features visible on aerial photographs form part of a landscape of rectangular fields and dispersed settlement, extending along the valley sides both north and south of the River Wear (*39*).

In the first phase of the survey in 2004 we recorded large numbers of relict field boundaries on the north side of the Wear. These take the form of long, fairly straight, earth and stone banks and lynchets, running down and across the hillsides, in some places forming narrow rectangular fields. Though fragmentary in some areas, these early field systems extend from Eastgate to Westgate and seem to form a continuous zone of early farming.

In phases 2 and 3 in 2005 and 6, south of the Wear, we again found both settlement sites and field boundaries, though here the lynchets are less well developed, and the field system does not appear to have been continuous, but is more fragmentary than north of the river.

During the 2004 walkover survey seven probable and two possible settlement sites were recorded within the field systems. These settlements mostly occupy scoops into the hillside ranging from about 20-60m in diameter. There are also at least 25 detached hut platforms dispersed throughout the field systems. The condition and visibility of the settlements varies, depending on past and present land management. In 2005 and 2006, on the south side of the Wear, a further seven settlement sites were located. These are more varied in form and location than those north of the Wear; one consists of a loose collection of hut circles and enclosures at the base of a scarp, three are enclosed settlements on small knolls, at another site, on sloping ground, possible hut platforms are dispersed among a complex of small lynchetted enclosures, and the remaining two are scoop settlements similar to those north of the river.

MEASURED SURVEY

Site A, a settlement associated with one of the better-preserved areas of the field system north of the river, is one of the settlements we selected for measured survey (40). The settlement was visible as a platform scooped into the hillside, surrounded by a rubble bank and appearing to contain at least three circular hut platforms. The enclosing rubble bank was observed to connect with the field system which extends southwards from the settlement. A fragment of rotary quern of Romano-British type was found with a quantity of pot-boilers in the modern ditch at the side of the farm-track immediately below the site.

The results of the measured survey demonstrate the character of this settlement. The scooped enclosure is subrectangular, about 50m from east to west, and 60m from north to south. The northern two thirds of the enclosure are very steep. Three clear hut platforms of approximately 7m internal diameter lie in a line at the base of this slope; a possible fourth platform near the south-east corner of the enclosure is cut by the modern track. A substantial lynchet forming part of the field system meets the enclosure bank at the western edge of the enclosure. A north–south aligned rubble bank forming one of the co-axial boundaries of the field system lines up with the east edge of the enclosure, though the junction has been removed by the modern farm track. A record of this relationship survives on Dennis Harding's aerial photograph which predates the construction of the track.

Site B, also north of the Wear was surveyed and was found to be smaller than site A, consisting of a trapezoidal scooped enclosure 30m in length, and 20m wide, with apparently only one hut platform at the south corner. Three small groups of stones along the south edge may be post settings, or perhaps part of the remains of a stone wall on this side of the structure. A westward extension of the hut platform may

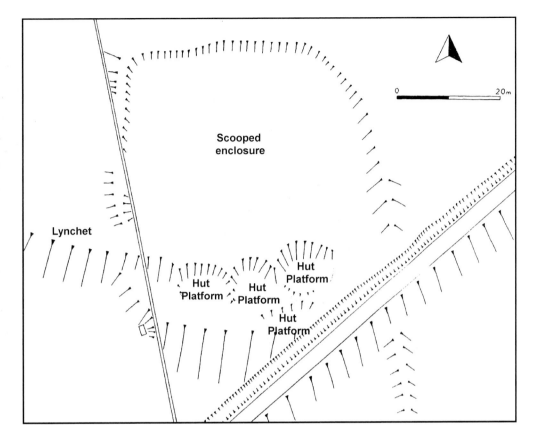

40 Measured survey of Site A. Hachures representing the slope at the back of the settlement have been omitted for clarity

represent an annexe or porch on the west end of the hut. This settlement is associated with the east end of a large area of well-preserved field system now cut by a quarry access road.

DATING EVIDENCE

Dating for the settlements rests partly on comparison with dated settlements elsewhere, discussed under 'Wider Parallels' below, but also on stray finds found close to settlement sites during the survey, such as the quern fragment at site A mentioned above. A second, much larger, piece of quern was found in a wall close to a settlement site south of the Wear. This fragment is half a rotary quern with a hole in the side for the handle, and shows evidence for the hopper. The style of this quern also suggests a Romano-British date. At a third settlement site, also south of the river, a small rim sherd of Romano-British pottery was found in rabbit disturbance close to the edge of a hut circle.

The dating of the field systems is based mainly on their relationship with more easily dated settlements. It is also based partly on relative dating; there is some direct evidence from the survey that the lynchets and rubble banks which form the field systems are the first in a sequence of boundaries visible in the park. This sequence includes the park wall and the boundary of an internal compartment of the deerpark called the Frith. Both of these boundaries appear to have been substantial walls parts which still survive to a height of about 2m, with a basal width of *c*.1.5m. These walls, which date to the creation of the park in about AD 1300 (Drury 1978), overlie a number of long, substantial, bank and ditch boundaries on the north side of the Wear. One of these incorporates a deer leap or salter, and is likely to relate to the exploitation of the medieval forest for grazing prior to the creation of the park. The banks and lynchets of the field systems are earlier still as they in turn underlie the bank and ditch boundaries.

WIDER PARALLELS

The settlements and field systems found in Stanhope Park have strong parallels elsewhere in the Pennine Dales. In Swaledale, Andrew Fleming and Tim Laurie have surveyed an extensive relict landscape of small rectangular fields with scooped and enclosed settlements, as well as a number of hut platforms dispersed amongst the fields. Excavation of one of the settlement platforms revealed a sequence of houses from Iron Age to Romano-British in date (Fleming 1998). Houses which were late in this sequence were securely dated by pottery which was predominantly from the second century AD.

The field systems associated with the Swaledale settlements seem to have an underlying regular pattern. East of the Village of Healaugh, for example, the Romano-British field system appears to be based on a series of parallel boundaries which run from south to north up the valley side. Field systems of this type, based on long parallel boundaries, are called co-axial, and were created in many parts of Britain during the later prehistoric, from the mid-Bronze Age onwards (see Bradley; Fulford; Williamson; all this volume). The field systems in Stanhope Park resemble those in Swaledale in that both are partly co-axial. In Stanhope Park this is easiest to observe in the central section north of the river.

In Swaledale and in Stanhope Park many of the Romano-British fields are strongly lynchetted; the height difference between the bottom of one field and the top of the next can be up to 1.5m. Lynchetting is thought to be caused by soil movement resulting from cultivation on sloping ground. The presence of lynchetting at field boundaries in Swaledale and Stanhope Park is therefore evidence for cultivation. The presence of quern fragments at settlement sites in Stanhope Park, and the recovery of a series of querns from the excavation at Healaugh suggest that grain was being grown.

Additional parallels for the settlements and field systems in Stanhope Park exist in Teesdale. At Forcegarth Pasture Denis Coggins and Ken Fairless (1980, 1986) excavated two settlements, one of which, Forcegarth South, is a scooped settlement very similar to site A in Stanhope Park. As in Swaledale and Stanhope Park, the settlements at Forcegarth are associated with a field system which includes heavily lynchetted boundaries, particularly east of Forcegarth Farm. Other parts of this field system, closer to the settlements, are more irregular, and un-lynchetted.

DISCUSSION

The Stanhope Park survey forms part of a growing body of evidence for late prehistoric settlement and land use in the uplands of northern England. Much of the dating evidence is Romano-British, but there is evidence to suggest that the field and settlement patterns developed over a period of time. In Swaledale Andrew Fleming (1998) has shown that a sequence of large-scale co-axial field systems belonging to the Iron Age are visible on the moorland above the modern farmland (inbye). The Romano-British fields associated with the settlement on the lower slopes on the modern inbye seem to be fitted into these earlier co-axial systems resulting in modification of the regular field pattern. The results of Andrew Fleming's excavations on the settlement site at Healaugh demonstrated similar time-depth for the settlement remains. As discussed above the pattern of Romano-British field boundaries in Stanhope Park closely resembles that observed by Andrew Fleming in Swaledale. Both appear to be modifications of a co-axial field system. In Stanhope Park, however, we lack the evidence for an unmodified Iron Age field system on the higher ground, nor has there yet been excavation to investigate the length of occupation of the settlement sites.

Andrew Fleming links the creation and use of large scale field systems in the Iron Age and Roman period to evidence of extensive woodland clearance seen in pollen profiles for the period across much of northern England. He refers to this clearance episode as the 'Great Brigantian *Landnam*' (Fleming 1988, 140). This evidence for widespread clearance is supported by the work of Chris Fenton-Thomas (1992) who brought together palaeobotanical evidence from 13 sites in the Tyne-Tees region for the period between c.800 BC and AD 900. He demonstrated that not only did levels of tree pollen reach a minimum in most areas in the Roman period, but also that pollen from plants associated with agriculture reached a peak. In the light of the palaeobotanical evidence for clearance and cultivation it seems probable that the patterns of settlement and land use observed in Stanhope Park and Swaledale are widespread. The apparent dearth of evidence for late prehistoric settlement in other North Pennine dales is therefore more likely to represent a lack of archaeological investigation than an absence of material.

Since the completion of the Stanhope Park survey additional features of a Romano-British type have been found elsewhere in Weardale. Volunteers involved in the survey have identified scoop settlements and lynchets several miles further up the Dale at Ireshopeburn. Without further work it is impossible to determine whether this represents a continuation of the pattern seen in Stanhope Park, or represents an isolated outlier. Further investigation including targeted excavation would also be necessary to determine the period of use of the Stanhope Park settlements and fields. Such research will help us understand a key stage in the development of the Pennine uplands.

ACKNOWLEDGEMENTS

We wish to thank the funding bodies, the AONB and Durham County Council, who made this project possible, and the Friends of Killhope, particularly Dick Graham and Margaret Manchester for managing the boring, administrative side of things. Great thanks to all the volunteers who suffered the wind, rain, hail and snow, and persevered in surveying under very difficult working conditions. We would also like to thank Russell Parkin for assisting with the production of the illustrations. We would most of all like to thank all the landowners who allowed us onto their land to undertake this project.

BIBLIOGRAPHY

Drury, J.L., 1978 Durham Palatinate forest law and administration, specially in Weardale up to 1140. *Archaeologia Aeliana*, Series 5, 6, 87-115.

Fairless, K.J. & Coggins, D., 1980 Excavations at the early settlement of Forcegarth Pasture North, 1972-74. *Transactions of the Architectural and Archaeological Society of Durham and Northumberland* new series 5, 31-38.

Fairless, K.J. & Coggins, D., 1986 Excavations at the Early Settlement Site of Forcegarth Pasture South, 1974-75. *Durham Archaeological Journal* 2, 25-40.

Fenton-Thomas, C., 1992 Pollen analysis as an aid to the reconstruction of patterns of land-use and settlement in the Tyne Tees region during the First Millennia BC and AD. *Durham Archaeological Journal* 8, 51-62.

Fleming, A., 1998 *Swaledale: valley of the wild river*. Edinburgh: Edinburgh University Press.

Young, R., 1993 Three earthwork sites in Weardale. *Transactions of the Architectural and Architectural Society of Durham and Northumberland* 9, 9-17.

14

BONES, BOWS AND BYRES: EARLY DAIRYING IN THE SCOTTISH HIGHLANDS AND ISLANDS

Robert A. Dodgshon

INTRODUCTION

Resolving the question of when dairying developed, and how it was organised, has generated considerable debate, primarily because of disagreement over the evidence by which we can attest to the presence and character of dairying in an archaeological context. Early discussions relied heavily on material such as bone assemblages and the quantitative study of animal age and sex composition. As Halstead pointed out, such an approach relies on making inferences about 'production goals' using 'the contentious analysis of slaughter patterns'(1996, 25; 1998), the assumption being that production for milk as opposed to meat would reveal itself through different slaughter patterns. A more recent approach has circumvented the ambiguity of such faunal evidence and, instead, has convincingly used traces of milk proteins and lipid residues found on surviving potsherds and vessels (e.g. Craig 2002; Craig *et al.* 2005; Copley 2005a; 2005b). Significantly, analysis of such evidence drawn from sites in eastern and south-eastern Europe suggests that dairying may have been practised by the very earliest farmers (Craig 2002, 97-107), and was part of the bundle of later, mid-Bronze Age developments labelled as the 'secondary products revolution' (Sherratt 1981).

Yet whilst such evidence has undoubtedly started to answer some of the most basic questions over the presence of dairying, it still leaves us with the question of how we resolve the long-running debate over what bone assemblages might tell us about how early dairying was organised. This paper re-examines how we might answer this question by setting some of the issues raised by the archaeological debate beside later documentary data for the Scottish Highlands and Islands, an area that has figured large in the recent debate over early dairying as well as in Andrew Fleming's more recent work.

BONE ASSEMBLAGES AS EVIDENCE FOR DAIRYING

The use of bone assemblages and inferred slaughter patterns as archaeological evidence for dairying has been critically reviewed by a number of authors (Halstead 1996, 1998; Legge 1981; McCormick 1992, 1998). Guided by the early work of Payne (1973), a key assumption underpinning such work was that the different forms of stock output – meat, milk and wool – can be associated with different slaughter patterns and that these different slaughter patterns are recoverable from the close analysis of bone assemblages. Thus, the management of stock for meat might be linked to a pattern of stock kill-off that emphasised juveniles and sub-adults, whilst a slaughter pattern associated with dairying might be expected to emphasise male infants (Halstead 1996). The killing of infant male animals served the purpose of freeing up milk for human consumption without compromising the ability of the herd or flock to reproduce itself. There are critical assumptions being made here, both about the ability of herds to sustain themselves if high slaughter rates were practised and the willingness of cows to suckle calves that were not their own, so it is not surprising that both have been a focus of attack by critics of the argument (e.g. Clutton-Brock 1981). Yet, as Halstead makes it clear, Payne's scheme of differentiation was consciously idealised. In reality, the characterisation of bone assemblages is likely to be blurred rather than clear cut as communities sought to mix different forms of output.

Over the past decade, the debate over how bone assemblages might be related to the presence of dairying has acquired a Scottish dimension. Bigelow (1987) reviewed evidence for a critical change in the nature of Norse domestic architecture during the medieval period, with early Norse hall houses, or *skali*, giving way during the eleventh and twelfth centuries AD to longhouses that incorporated byres. Bigelow saw this switch as driven by a growing exaction of butter and cheese as tax and ecclesiastical tithe and the pressure which this placed on the farm economy to find ways of intensifying dairy output. He proposed that the winter housing of stock, the accumulation of their manure in the byre during the winter months and the close contact between humans and animals, hearth and byre, that was enabled by the longhouse system served the purpose of raising milk yields through the warmer conditions which it produced for stock. As part of his case, Bigelow pointed to the way in which bone dumps present at sites like Sandwick and Jarlshof reveal a growing concentration on cattle, with the 'majority of these bones from very young calves, suggesting a slaughter pattern that would have maximised milk, rather than meat, production' (1987, 33).

Whilst Bigelow's case for an intensification of dairying over the eleventh and twelfth centuries AD was plausible, the bone assemblage data was not seen by everyone as giving unequivocal support to his case. Excavations carried out in the Outer Hebrides have produced a great deal of bone assemblage data for sites in the Uists, albeit dating from the Late Iron Age. On the one hand, they revealed a similar pattern to that highlighted by Bigelow for Sandwick and Jarlshof, with – amongst the cattle bones – a preponderance of bones relating to young or infantile stock. For example, at Baleshare, Hornish Point and Kildonan, all on the Uists, the percentage of bones derived from cattle under 10 months were 40 per cent, 27.3 per cent and 40 per cent (some of which were probably neonatal deaths), whilst at Dun Vulan, the figure was as high as 60 per cent (Parker Pearson, Mulville and Sharples 1996). In their 1996 paper, Parker Pearson and his colleagues were initially cautious about how this data should be interpreted, expressing caution about whether it indicated a high kill-off rate for young stock and, therefore, evidence for intensive dairying. Such a high kill-off rate, they argued, would have put herd replacement at risk. Further, they repeat doubts about whether traditional breeds would have gone on providing milk to other calves once their own calves were slaughtered. They concluded that we needed to keep open the possibility that the pattern of bone assemblages evident at these various sites might be explained by seeing them as only a proportion – a biased proportion – of the total animals being killed by the communities involved.

A more recent analysis of the problem by Craig, Taylor, Mulville, Collins and Parker Pearson (2005), one that applies new biomolecular methods to the problem of dairying in the Hebrides, has provided a fresh appraisal of what the bone assemblages might tell us and offers some telling insights. The analysis uses the debate over bone assemblages as a context for its study of lipid residues. Drawing on a wide range of Hebridean data, it restates the point that on sites across the Western Isles as a whole, the loading of assemblages towards the bones of infant animals forms 'a remarkably consistent feature of the cattle assemblages', with 'between 30 and 50 per cent of all ageable cattle bones dating from the 1st millennium BC to the 1st millennium AD [belonging to juveniles] (<1 year of age), the majority of which are neo-natal individuals less than one month old at death' (Craig et al. 2005, 91). However, this bias is now seen as 'the result of a considered economic strategy, rather than a sampling bias or natural mortality' (Craig et al. 2005, 92). They acknowledge that such a pattern of bone assemblage accords with one that would optimise milk output for human consumption, but restate the problems that such a high rate of juvenile slaughter would have posed for long-term herd viability, especially in a region that experienced endemically high levels of environmental risk. Amongst the alternative factors they introduce into the debate is the possibility that such a high level of juvenile slaughter was linked to the scarcity of winter fodder and the consequential need to ensure an adequate degree of stock survival from one winter to the next. Their review of the bone assemblage debate provides a context for their analysis of milk residues on potsherds from Bronze and Iron Age sites in the region. Using this biomolecular approach, they confirm – in a way that bone assemblages alone cannot – that dairying was a significant component of the farm economy, a component that was 'continuously exploited' from the Bronze Age down to later historic times. In a final summing up, they return to the evidence of bone assemblages, arguing that the clear and abundant biomolecular evidence for dairying makes it much more likely that the bias towards juvenile stock was linked to dairying since it was a pattern of slaughter that optimised dairying, though, whilst pointing us in this direction, they also restate the risks that this must have created for herd replacement especially in a region that suffered from low levels of winter stock feed.

The study by Craig and colleagues (2005) forms an important contribution to the debate because of the way it links biomolecular and bone assemblages together, using one to help remove some of the ambiguities of the other. Yet whilst it advances the debate in significant ways, it still leaves us with a bundle of questions about how such a system might have been managed, what demands drove it, how communities managed to maintain cows in milk once their calves were slaughtered and the role played by the problems of winter feed in any slaughter policy. I want to take up these questions using late medieval and early modern documentary evidence for the Scottish Highlands and Islands. The majority of the evidence is derived from unpublished documents housed in the National Archives of Scotland and a list of those used to inform following discussion is to be found after the Acknowledgements.

THE ORGANISATION OF DAIRYING AS REVEALED BY DOCUMENTARY SOURCES: OR HOW MANY COWS DID IT TAKE TO PRODUCE A PINT OF MILK IN THE SCOTTISH HIGHLANDS AND ISLANDS?

In principle, we can identify three levels or intensities of dairy output: that which is sufficient to supply domestic needs, that which is sufficient to supply domestic needs *plus* the needs of their tribute/taxation/rent bundle *or* marketing, and that which is sufficient to accommodate all these needs at the same time. The sort of intensification that Bigelow had in mind falls into the second category, with communities producing dairy produce not just for their own consumption, but also for the needs of tribute, taxation and/or rent. In the case of the latter, it could be paid directly in kind, or marketed in order to meet rent demands being made in cash. His case has wider significance, for all parts of the region, the Hebrides and mainland as well as the Northern Isles, were burdened with exactions of some sort by the medieval period. At first these appear as burdens or renders of tribute and hospitality. Even in the sixteenth century, there are still traces of an archaic system of hospitality in which every township in parts of the Hebrides was burdened with renders intended to support the local chief and his retinue, renders that could include cheese and butter (Skene 1880). Alongside these surviving traces of hospitality payments, we also find substantial payments of cheese and butter in early rentals, such as in sixteenth-century rentals for Ardnamurchan and Sunart (McNeil 1897). Arguably, the latter were simply the former in another guise, having been converted to a regular rent. In time, these rent payments of dairy produce were converted into cash payments but many estates continued to burden their touns with small payments, particularly of butter if not cheese, until well into the seventeenth century. As Bigelow rightly argued, when at their maximum, such payments would have been a powerful driver for the intensification of dairying.

Yet when trying to understand why particular forms of husbandry may have been adopted, the scale of what was being exacted forms only part of the equation. We have to see these exactions in the context of the very low yields of milk produced by traditional Highland and Hebridean breeds. In his mid-eighteenth century surveys of the Hebrides, Dr James Walker provides us with some figures for output on Skye: that from the best cows was one quart of milk per cow per day (that is, about 60 gallons during each lactation) but the average yielded only around one pint of milk per cow per day (or 30 gallons per cow for each lactation) (McKay 1980; cf. lowland figures in Hamilton 1945, and traditional alpine figures in Orland 2003). For comparison, a modern high-yielding cow would be expected to produce over 1200 gallons a year. When we set these levels of traditional milk output beside the average number of stock present in townships and the amounts of cheese and butter being exacted from them as renders or rent, we are forced to conclude that the latter consumed a substantial portion of what, to start with, were very modest levels of output. If we need a strong driver for the intensification of dairying, then it probably lies within this ecologically, economically and socially prescribed circle of output, consumption and exaction.

Bigelow saw the winter housing or byring of stock within an open longhouse system, with its warming effect on cattle having a beneficial, if marginal, effect on milk yields as part of this intensification. His point though, needs qualification. As Craig et al. (2005) note, cattle-based dairying was probably present and important in the Hebrides throughout the Bronze and Iron Ages. However, the archaeological evidence also makes it clear that that stock were not always routinely housed. There were phases, such as the medieval period, including the Late Norse period, when their housing on islands like the Uists appears exceptional rather than normal (Parker Pearson, Sharples and Symonds 2004). This helps me to make this point. The housing of stock was driven by a number of factors, of which its impact on milk yields was only one. An equally relevant factor was the need to accumulate stock manure for arable. When seen through the documentation of the early modern period, the Hebrides made some use of stock manure but the prime additive to arable was that of seaweed, a fact that reduced the need for the indoor housing of stock. Of course, the region also benefited from milder winters compared to the mainland, enabling stock to be kept outdoors. The archaeological evidence for the Uists suggests that communities there switched to the indoor wintering of stock in the eighteenth century (Parker Pearson, Sharples and Symonds 2004). The archaeological and documentary data are actually in full agreement here, for the latter makes it clear that on islands like the Uists, Lewis, Skye and Tiree, the practice of wintering stock outdoors had given way to their indoor wintering during the second quarter of the eighteenth century (Dodgshon 1993). In all probability, the shift was bound up with changes in the use of seaweed, with estates now capitalising seaweed as kelp and restricting its use as a field manure. On the mainland, the balance of controls was different. There, arable was heavily dependent on stock manure, though other manures like turf and ferns were used alongside it. The manure accumulated in byres over winter formed the prime source, at least for the arable nucleus of townships, that is, their infield. In the core of the Highlands, housing stock also protected them against the extremes of winter. Even without pressure to expand milk output, one would expect some stock to be housed, especially during the worst phases of the Little Ice Age. Indeed, for some contemporary commentators, this was the prime reason for housing (e.g. Millar 1909). Housing created its own demands, notably for hay, though even in the central Highlands, reports of cattle starving through lack of such feed as well as the modest acreages classed as meadow in eighteenth-century surveys suggest that hay making may not have been given priority ahead of other summer tasks like peat and turf cutting (Dodgshon 1993, 696).

Of the various themes that make up the debate over dairying during the first millennia BC and AD, the one that early documentary sources can shed most new light is the meaning that we can attach to certain forms of bone assemblages. They do so through what they can tell us about the precise organisation of dairy output. A starting point is provided by a series of detailed accounts drawn up by the Breadalbane Estate that covered its 'bow' farms in Perthshire. *Sensu stricto*, a bow farm was a specialised stock farm, the term bow referring to the byre that housed the stock over winter. In some sources, it was the farm used by chiefs or landlords to store the cattle which they gathered in as draught marts or rent. Its use on the Breadalbane Estate was different, being used to describe farms, or 'bowhouses' as they are referred to in some sources, which it set in bowgang: this was a form of tenure in which the estate provided the stock needed for the farm and took back a significant proportion of its output in terms of cheese, butter and calves. Yet though organised to produce stock, these bow farms still had a substantial arable sector, most also being given so many bolls of sowing, plough horses and plough gear by the estate alongside the stock also provided. In fact, some bow farms had arable sectors that were as sizeable as those in ordinary townships. What distinguished them was the emphasis given to cattle in their bowgang agreements and to dairy products and calves in their terms of rent, not their land use.

When specifying this rent, the various bow books that become available from the late sixteenth century onwards listed the amounts of cheese and butter to be paid. The way in which it did so is revealing. Each bow farm was required to pay so many stones of cheese or quarts of butter out 'of ilk cuple of newly calfit kye'. The payments of cheese were the greater, with payments usually being between seven and nine stones out of 'ilk cuple'. Thus, in 1639, the tenant of Claggan was required to pay nine stone of cheese out of 'ilk cuple', whilst the tenant of Clochran was required to pay seven stones of cheese out of each 'cuple' plus one stone of 'mail butter' and two quarts of fresh butter out of 'ilk cuple'. The reference to 'ilk cuple' is repeated across each entry, and in bow book after bow book. Precisely what it means is explained for us by comments that occur in various eighteenth-century surveys and reports for the region. In his Hebridean reports, for instance, Dr John Walker, reported that on North Uist, 'the common practice is to raise only one Calf on the Milk of two Cows', whilst in a report on the south-west highlands drawn up in 1768, Archibald Menzies referred to farmers in Kintyre as rearing 'one calf between every couple'. Likewise, in Coigach, a report of c.1755 noted that farms reared 'one Calf for every two Milk Cows, so that whatever number of Milk Cows the farm keeps they rear half that number of Calves'. Clearly, the couple system involved two cows calving, but only one calf being raised on their milk, a system that then freed the remaining milk produced by the two cows for the making of cheese and butter. Of course, the idea that one calf could be killed and then the surviving calf reared on the milk of two cows confronts the doubts raised by those who have argued that traditional breeds do not provide milk once their calf is dead. Craig *et al.* (2005) thought any such system would have required very careful management.

A hint of this management is provided at the end of the seventeenth century by Martin Martin. 'When a Calf is slain', he wrote, 'it's a usual Custom to cover another Calf with its Skin, to suck the Cow whose Calf has been slain, or else she gives no Milk' (1981, 155). What these comments make clear is that the couple system was a general feature of dairy production not just of bow farms. Its purpose was to ensure herd development whilst, at the same time, releasing milk for the making of cheese and butter within a system in which yields were low and margins tight. This and more is hinted at by the reporter in the third volume of the 1795 *Old Statistical Account* for Applecross: the cattle, he said, 'are for the most part coupled, i.e. have but one calf between every two cows; by these means the calf is better fed, a greater quantity of cheese and butter is manufactured, the bulling secured, and no superfluous stock kept on hand' (1795, 372). The reason why we are provided with extra detail in the Breadalbane Bow Books is because of the need to specify the bowgang arrangements, or terms of set, not because the couple system was exclusive to them.

Arguably, coupling closes the circle of evidence for early dairying. It confirms that communities in the Highlands did practice a slaughter policy of killing infant stock and that it was directly linked not so much to maximising gross milk output *per se* but to maximising that available for dairy products: cheese and butter. The documentary evidence enables us to add two further features to it as a system. First, some early rentals, including rentals for the Breadalbane Estate, record the payment of veals as part of a township's rent (e.g. Macphail 1920). In all probability, such payments were linked to the couple system and its early slaughter of calves. Indeed, we know from evidence for other parts of Europe that calves need only have been a few weeks old

when slaughtered for veal. Second, and linked in with the point some have made
about its effect on the sustainability of herds, the slaughter of infantile calves clearly
had an effect on herd structure. If the practice was to slaughter a half of all infantile
calves, presumably most of the males calves, then we would expect a herd structure
in which the number of one, two and three year old stock would always be one half
of the number of *milk* cows present, though this would assume that the milk cows
were what were called tidy cows, who calved every year. Additionally, we can expect
to find one or two bulls present depending on the size of the herd.

A number of sources enable us to set this presumed herd structure beside
real herds. Thus, in data drawn in 1770 for townships in Glen Strathfarrar and
Stratherrick, two straths north of the Great Glen, both display herd structures like
that just described, with the number of one year olds, two year olds and three year
olds being exactly half of the number of milk cows reported to be present. In fact,
so consistent is this pattern across all townships, we can detect it even at an aggregate
level. In Stratherrick, the 23 township had between them 542 milk cows, plus 271
one year olds, 271 two year olds and 271 three year olds. In Glen Strathfarrar, the
12 townships listed had between them 160 milk cows, plus 80 one year olds, 80 two
year olds and 80 three year olds. By comparison, earlier seventeenth-century herd
listings for the Breadalbane Estate reveal a different structure. A key feature is their
distinction between milk and farrow cattle. The latter referred to a milk cow that
had not calved that year. Their distinction with milk cows becomes fuzzy when
we come across farrow cows that were still yielding milk and whose stirks, or one
year olds, were treated as followers. Indeed, we can find sources that refer to the
payments of cheese and butter to be made from milk cows and to lesser payments
from farrow cows (e.g. Rogers 1880). In addition distinguishing between the number
of milk and farrow cows present, the Breadalbane herd listings also note the number
of one-year olds, two-year olds and three-year olds present. In each case, the latter
amounted to one half of the total number of *milk* cows but to only one quarter of
the total number of cows, milk and farrow. We can see this sort of herd structure
through tack or lease agreements. Good illustrations are provided by a 1680 tack
for Stronmilochan which, as part of the farm's bowgang agreement, listed the stock
provided as 32 cows 'new calfed cows coupled with there calves', 32 farrow cows
'with there stirks' (that is, their one-year olds), 16 two-year old queys, 16 three-year
old quays and two bulls, and a 1688 list for Craig on south Lochtayside which records
10 new calfit cows, 10 farrow cows, 5 three-year olds, 5 two-year olds and 5 one-year
olds. As the equal number of two- and three-year olds at Stronmilochan make clear,
we can assume that the unspecified number of calves coupled to the 32 'new calfed
cows' must have been half the number of such cows and, likewise, that the number
of stirks or one year olds must have been half the number of farrow cattle, so that the
total number of calves allowed to survive in each year amounted to half the number
of milk cows but a quarter of all cows, milk and farrow together, as at Craig. In fact,

in one source, a 1668 tack for Botuarie More, the precise number of 'new calfit kye' and their calves is made clear, with the estate providing '12 new calfed kye wt yr 6 calves 12 farrow kye & 6 3 year olds 6 2 year olds & 6 year olds'. A 1684 tack for Wester Stix defines an identical structure but adds the fact that the three-year olds had been put 'to ye bull'.

There are clear differences between the Stratherrick/Glen Strathfarrar lists and those cited for the Breadalbane Estate as regards the precise structuring of herds, notably the presence of farrow cows in the latter. In all probability, the latter documents the more traditional system of herd management, one that other sources enable us to take back to at least the fifteenth century (Rogers 1880). Under it, cows would have calved every alternate year so that, at any one point in time, the herd comprised milk and farrow cows though – as noted earlier – farrow cows could still produce milk in their farrow year even though they were not 'new calfit cows'. As the Breadalbane lists confirm, slaughtering half the calves born each year and coupling cows so as to rear the half that were left, produced a herd structure in which the number of calves equalled half the number of *milk* cows present but a quarter of all cows, milk and farrow. Such a herd structure probably provides us our best close-up view of how the traditional coupling system may have operated, with stock producing calves each alternate year until they were eight or nine years old, the herd being organised to maintain itself and to produce a surplus for cheese and butter.

By comparison, the Stratherrick/Glen Strathfarrar lists were compiled in the mid-late eighteenth century at a time when the growth of droving had affected the production decisions of farmers. Droving had its roots in the early seventeenth century but became much more significant after the Union in 1707. Though sheep had started to spread in the southern Highlands by the 1750s and 60s, they had not yet displaced cattle production in areas like Stratherrick and Glen Strathfarrar at the point when their lists were drawn up. In other words, the herd structure revealed by their lists may have had more to do with producing lean stock or stores than with maximising cheese and butter output. If we take the lists at face value and assume that the milk cows were all milk cows that had calved, but that only 50 per cent of the calves had been allowed to survive under presumed couple system, this would explain why the numbers of one-year, two-year and three-year olds were 50 per cent of the total number of milk cows present. Such an interpretation would require us to assume that all the cows present were 'tidy' cows, calving every year. It would produce a herd structure that would enable some stock to be sold each year, either by selling stock as they reached their fourth year or by selling off milk cattle after two or three calves. However, if the prime objective was now to sell lean stock, it would not make sense to have slaughtered so many calves at birth. That suited a low-output system geared to maximising cheese and butter output, but once the emphasis shifted to lean stock, it would have made more sense to use the milk available to rear as many calves to maturity as possible. An alternative would be to see the lists as bundling milk and farrow cows together, half and half. If this was the case, then the lists are unlikely to depict a couple system simply because the 271 milk cows would have produced 271 calves, but under a couple system, only 50 per cent or *c*.135 would have been allowed to survive not the 271 noted by the lists. A third possibility would be to see the 542 milk cows present as made up of both milk and farrow but with all calves being allowed to survive, giving a balance and age structure of 271 one-year, two-year and three-year olds, and perhaps 271 four-year old 'new calfit cows' and 271 five-year old farrow cows; though the milk and farrow cows might encompass a greater age spread if the strategy was to sell some stock once they became four years old. For reference, contemporary descriptions of stock leaving the Highlands describe most as four or five years old.

CONCLUDING REMARKS

I have tried to bring the archaeological and documentary evidence for early dairying in the Scottish Highlands and Islands together, albeit drawing such evidence from widely different chronological contexts. Yet, as Andrew Fleming has himself demonstrated in his work on Swaledale and St Kilda, when such data is used together, each can inform the other. In the case of dairying, the archaeological evidence confirms its deep-rootedness in the Highlands and Islands but raises questions about precisely how stock were managed for dairy produce and whether herds were sustainable if output relied on the slaughter of young juveniles. The documentary evidence can help answer such questions. Whilst we cannot say that the couple system, as we see it through seventeenth-century data, can be extended back in time unchanged, it does confirm that communities in the region had, at some point, evolved strategies of herd management that involved slaughtering young stock so as to release more for cheese and butter. As some have already argued, we can best explain such a system by rooting it in the cultural ecology of the region and the way subsistence margins were squeezed between poor levels of feed, the low milk yields of stock and the demands of chiefs and landlords. What the documentary evidence also tells us is that the coupling system creates a T-shaped herd structure, one in which the numbers of calves, one-, two- and three-year olds present would each have equalled half the number of milk cows present, or a quarter of all mature cows, if both milk and farrow cows were present. Yet if the couple system is to be a basis for interpreting early bone assemblages then we need to understand how these bone assemblages might map into a couple system. On the face of it, with young infantile stock accounting for between *c*.40-60 per cent of early bone assemblages (the Hornish Point data excepted), there is certainly a circumstantial case for supposing that a form of couple system was present.

ACKNOWLEDGEMENTS

Work on the Breadalbane Muniments was carried out as part of the Ben Lawers Historic Landscape Project.

The following records from the National Archives of Scotland have been used in this paper: GD112/9/3/3/3, Earle of Breadalbane's Rentall in Argyll Shire, 1680; GD112/9/5/7/2 Rental 1700; Breadalbane Muniments, GD112/9/16; GD112/9/9, Bow Book, 1616-1620; GD112/9/16, Bow Buik 1639-1642; GD112/9/20, Bow Book, 1660-1771; E729/9/1, Journal of Archibald Menzies, 1768; Forfeited Estates, E746/166; GD112/9/24 Rental 1669-1678; E769/72/5; 769/72/6; GD112/10/10; GD112/10/9; GD112/10/8; GD112/59/31/11; GD112/10/9.

BIBLIOGRPAHY

Bigelow, G.F., 1987 Domestic architecture in medieval Shetland. *Review of Scottish Culture* 3, 23-38.

Clutton-Brock, J., 1981 Discussion. In Mercer, R.J. (ed.), 218-20.

Copley, M.S., Berstan, R., Dudd, S.N., Aillaud, S., Mukherjee, S.J., Straker, V, Payne, S. & Evershed, R.P., 2005 Processing of milk products in pottery vessels through British prehistory. *Antiquity* 79, 895-908.

Copley, M.S., Berstan, R., Mukherjee, A.J., Dudd, S.N., Straker, V., Payne, S., & Evershed, R.P., 2005 Dairying in antiquity. III. Evidence from absorbed lipid residues dating to the British Neolithic. *Journal of Archaeological Science* 32, 523-46.

Craig., O.E., 2002 The development of dairying in Europe: potential evidence from food residues on ceramics. *Documenta Preahistorica* 29, 97-107.

Craig, O.E., Taylor, G., Mulville, J., Collins, M.J., & Parker Pearson, M., 2005 The identification of prehistoric dairying activities in the Western Isles of Scotland: an integrated biomolecular approach. *Journal of Archaeological Science* 32, 91-103.

Dodgshon, R.A., 1993 Strategies of farming in the western highlands and islands of Scotland prior to crofting and the clearances. *Economic History Review* 46, 679-701.

Halstead, P., 1996 Pastoralism or household herding: problems of scale and specialization in early Greek animal husbandry. *World Archaeology* 28, 20-42.

Halstead P., 1998 Mortality models and milking: problems of uniformitarianism, optimality and equifinality reconsidered. *Archaeozoology* 27, 3.

Hamilton, H. (ed.), 1945 *Selections from the Monymusk Papers (1713-1755)*. Edinburgh: Scottish History Society, third series, 39.

Hodder, I., Isaac, G. & Hammond, N. (eds), *Pattern of the Past: studies in honour of David Clarke*. Cambridge: Cambridge University Press.

Legge, A.J., 1981 Aspects of cattle husbandry. In Mercer, R.J. (ed.), 169-81.

Macphail, J.R.N. (ed.), 1920 *Highland Papers, vol. 3*. Edinburgh: Scottish History Society, second series, vol. 20.

Martin, M. 1699 *A Description of the Western Islands of Scotland*, reprinted 1981. Edinburgh: Mercat Press.

McCormick, F., 1992 Early faunal evidence for dairying. *Oxford Journal of Archaeology*, 11, 201-9.

McCormick, F., 1998 Calf slaughter as a response to marginality. In Mills, C.M. & Coles, G.M. (eds), 49-53.

McKay, M. (ed.), 1980 *The Rev. Dr. John Walker's Report on the Hebrides of 1764 and 1771*. Edinburgh: John Donald.

eÉ

McNeill, G.P., 1897 *Exchequer Rolls of Scotland, xvii, 1537-1542*. Edinburgh: H, M, Register House.

Mercer, R.J., (ed.) 1981 *Farming in British Prehistory*. Edinburgh: Edinburgh University Press.

Mills, C.M. & Coles, G.M. (eds), *Life on the Edge: human settlement and marginality.* Association for Environmental Archaeology, 13. Oxford: Oxbow.

Old Statistical Account of Scotland, 20 vols, 1791-99. Edinburgh.

Orland, B., 2003 Turbo-Cows: producing a competitive animal in the nineteenth and early twentieth centuries. In Schrepfer, S.R. & Scranton, P. (eds.), 167-89.

Parker Pearson, M., Sharples, N. & Mulville, J., 1999 Brochs and Iron age society: a reappraisal. *Antiquity* 73, 57-67.

Parker Pearson, M., Sharples, N. & Symonds, J. 2004 *South Uist: archaeology and history of a Hebridean island*. Stroud: Tempus.

Payne, S. 1973 Kill-off patterns in sheep and goats: the mandibles from Asvan Kale. *Journal of Anatolian Studies* 23, 281–303.

Rogers, C., 1880 *Rental Book of the Cistercian Abbey of Cupar Angus*. London: British Topographical Society, 2 vols.

Schrepfer, S.R. & Scranton, P. (eds.), 2003 *Industrializing Organisms. Introducing evolutionary history*. New York: Taylor and Francis.

Sherratt, A.G., 1981 Plough and pastoralism: aspects of the secondary products revolution. In Hodder, I., Isaac, G. & Hammond, G.L. (eds), 261-305.

Skene, W.F., 1880, *Celtic Scotland: a history of ancient Alban. vol. iii, land and people*, appendix, 428-47.

15

WHO ARE YOU CALLING MARGINAL? A NINETEENTH-CENTURY SQUATTER SETTLEMENT IN UPLAND WALES

Sarah Tarlow

Many of the landscapes for which Andrew Fleming is best known – Dartmoor, the uplands of North Yorkshire and the island of St Kilda, for example, are regarded as 'marginal'. Fleming's inter-disciplinary landscape studies have been significant in critically examining the relationship between economically marginal areas and the social and cultural lives of those who used and inhabited them in the distant past. This chapter considers another 'marginal' landscape: the nineteenth-century squatter settlement of Rhos Gelli-gron.

Although both its original construction, taking advantage of Welsh 'tai-unnos' tradition, and its current state, on a boggy, unpopulated upland sheepwalk, seem 'marginal', the history of the site shows that, at its height in the mid-to late nineteenth century, it was a thriving and well-integrated part of the local economic and social scene.

'SQUATTER' SETTLEMENTS IN WALES

Although squatter settlements are known from many parts of Britain, there are an unusually high number in upland Ceredigion and they constitute a distinctive part of its landscape and settlement history. The Historic Landscape Characterisation of upland Ceredigion notes eighteenth- and nineteenth-century squatter settlement at Cnwch Coch, Ffair Rhos, Blaen Sychnant, Ystumtuen, Rhos y Gargoed/Rhos Marchnant, Berthgoed, Bryngwyn Bach, Ponterwyd, Tyngraig, Gwar Castell, Bwlchddwyallt/Blaengorffen, Pen-Rhiw-Newydd, Mynydd March, Bont Goch and Rhos-y-Gell as well as the settlement that is the focus of this study. Nearly all of these settlements date from the late eighteenth or early nineteenth century. Although often absent from formal estate maps and inventories, they are visible historically through

41 Rhos Gelli-gron settlement from the north. Trees are unusual in this upland landscape and mark the position of former hedges and gardens

landowners' attempts to remove them, and archaeologically in the modern landscape (*41*). The original squatters were people from various backgrounds among the lower ranks of society: predominantly younger sons of tenant farmers, artisans, and workers in the mines and quarries (Howell 1977). The land onto which they moved was generally common land in the ownership either of the Crown or of one of the large estates (in upland Ceredigion the great estates of Nanteos, Hafod and Trawscoed dominated private land ownership).

The origins of this particular site are obscure, but local oral historical evidence and analogy with similar sites in the area makes it almost certain that the site was first occupied by squatters under the traditional Welsh practice of the 'tai-unnos' ('one-night' or 'overnight' house). According to one late eighteenth-century source:

The Party Incroaching assembles his relations & Friends to his Assistance & they run up a Structure & inclose a small Quantity of Ground between sunset & sunrising the next morning. In this Structure without any Alteration they must reside a year & if

in that time he has met with no interruption he claims such ground & Structure as
his freehold property, pulls down the first rude Edifice & constructs another of more
permanence & encroaches gradually on his Enclosures.
(Cited from the Trawsgoed papers by Wiliam 1995, 24-5)

Other sources further specify that smoke must be rising from the building by sunrise,
and that the area enclosed is demarcated by the throw of an axe (or hammer or
stone) from the door of the cottage (Carter and Jones 1996). Rees (1936) claims that
having a kettle boiling in the new shanty before midnight was essential. The original
turf and thatch buildings were replaced over the following couple of years by a stone
structure; the original turf buildings have all vanished now, and there is nothing that
distinguishes a stone squatter cottage architecturally from other poor rural houses in
the area. They are generally built in vernacular style, but may have some Georgian
elements such as symmetrical windows or gable end chimneys.

The established local landowners were generally hostile towards the squatters. For
them, the problem with the squatters was not that they were necessarily trespassing on
their land (although they sometimes were) but that they were occupying Crown land
upon which the landowners themselves had designs. In fact Thomas Johnes of Hafod,
despite being a Crown agent responsible for safeguarding Crown land from illegal
encroachments, appropriated more land than anyone else in the county, enclosing
nearly 7000 acres for himself (Williams 1955). In the case of the squatters at Cnwch
Coch, aesthetic reasons also pertained. Colonel Vaughan, the landowner, wanted their
homes removed because they were 'miserable looking Huts' and spoiled the view
from his house at Trawscoed (Morgan 1997). In the end those particular squatters
were allowed to remain and agreed to pay rent to the Vaughans, which was not an
uncommon solution to disputes between squatters and landowners.

It was not only the great landowners who were unhappy about the presence
of squatters on the common, however. Legitimate commoners might resent the
appropriation of land they had previously used for grazing and peat-cutting, and fear
for their livestock. Squatters were occasionally a target for the transvestite 'Rebecca'
rioters. On 28 September 1843 a group of men dressed as Rebecca and her daughters
entered a tai-unnos on Llandybie common, about 10 miles from Rhos Gelli-gron.
They made the old woman living there kiss a gun and swear that she did not recognise
any of them before turning her out and destroying the house (Williams 1955). The
potential expense that a squatter settlement might present to the parish meant that
many of the more settled parishioners worried that such settlements might attract
paupers. The Board of Guardians of Tregaron resolved in 1816, in a minute that could
well allude to the houses on Rhos Gelli-gron:

We shall not suffer any fence to be erected on the Common or Mountain opposite
the Parish of Caron … in order to enclose into field or fields any part thereof – and

we do hereby unite in determination that we shall march in a body and demolish any such inclosure which may be made (Davies 1998, 328)

However, on other occasions the squatter cottage represented a way of reducing people's dependency on the parish and encouraging economic self-sufficiency. In 1807 the parish guardians of Llanwnda and Llandwrog, Caernarfonshire, encouraged paupers to build on the common where they would not be a burden on the rates (Howell 1977). Moreover, the original building of a tai-unnos would require the co-operation of many people in the area and could therefore not easily be accomplished in the face of united local opposition. Trefor Owen cites a Welsh poem written around 1780 by Thomas Edwards (Twm o'r Nant) about an old and infirm mole-catcher, hoping to build a house on a mountain near Llanuwchllyn (Merioneth). The mole-catcher, Ffowc Sion, asks everyone to give whatever they can, especially wood or money. He hopes that his friends the carpenter, slater and blacksmith will not forget him but will give their labour for a day or two (cited in Owen 1970).

Undoubtedly the early squatter settlements in the late eighteenth century were considered by many to be squalid, poor, dirty and, given the nineteenth-century association between physical and moral uncleanness, sinful places. However, David Williams's (1955, 81) characterisation of the squatter as 'an outcast, an Ishmael in society, living on the verge of destitution, and predisposed … towards criminal acts' is probably too harsh a verdict. It certainly would not suit the chapel-going families of late nineteenth-century Rhos Gelli-gron.

RHOS GELLI–GRON

Rhos Gelli-gron is in the parish of Caron-uwch-clawdd, and lies east of the great bog of Cors Caron and about three kilometres south of Pontrhydfendigaid on the lower slopes of Bryngwyn Bach. The common land is poorly-draining rough grassland. The settlement (42) is bounded on the north by the River Fflur which flows into the Teifi at Cors Caron, and on the east by the small farm (41 acres) of Gwndwn Gwynne, which was owned by the Powells of Nanteos at the time of the establishment of the settlement.

Most of the houses of the settlement are simple one- or two-cell buildings of stone and clay mortar. Most houses have lean-to extensions and some have evidence of an upper storey or a full or half loft. Some of the houses are associated with small, simple outbuildings, probably stores or animal buildings. Each house has a small area of land enclosed with a stone wall, or a bank and ditch (43). Typically, the land is divided into a small garden area immediately adjacent to the house, and one or two small fields beyond. In the mostly treeless upland landscape,

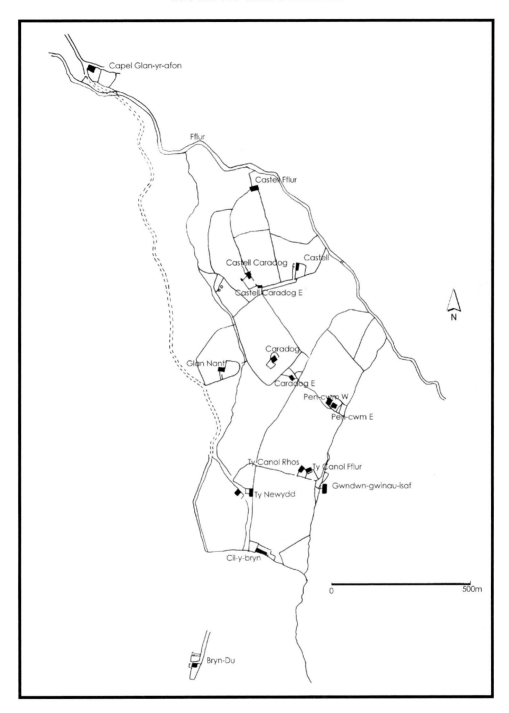

42 Rhos Gelli-gron site plan

43 Pen-cwm E

the site is conspicuous today for its many trees. These include apples and rowans originally planted as garden trees and hawthorns and beeches that were planted as hedges.

ORIGINS OF THE SITE

The *Cambrian Register* reported in the 1796 volume, actually published in 1799, that there was a village above Pontrhydfendigaid that had 'not many honest labourers but robust, athletic miners of no religion.' The oldest dwellings – Castell and Castell Caradog – appear on the 1839 tithe map as already well-established homes. Their inhabitants show up on parish records from 1821. A sketch map from the 1820s in the Sites and Monuments Record shows a settlement on the common. By 1839 Castell Caradog had two fields called 'Hengae' and 'Cae Newydd' – old field and new field – which suggests that the farmstead had already undergone expansion. Some dwellings, such as Castell Fflur, seem to have expanded to two adjacent houses; in the case of Castell Fflur from at least 1841 both households contained families called Jones who were probably related.

THE SETTLEMENT IN ITS HEYDAY

By the third quarter of the nineteenth century there were about 20 households on the common. It was a confident period in the life of the settlement – the houses constructed at this time are comparitively large and well-built with internal staircases and glass in the windows, and from the 1880s the community had its own chapel and school house. How did its inhabitants make a living? Each household had a small garden attached and test pits in the garden belonging to Castell revealed a rich, loamy garden soil with ample evidence of manuring. Two low mounds west of Castell Caradog may be the remains of corn-drying kilns, by analogy with Irish corn kilns of this period (Gailey 1970). In addition, stone animal pens, probably pig sties, were adjacent to most of the older houses. An English visitor to South and West Wales in 1801 records the Welsh practice of positioning pig sties by the gable end of the house – and the absence of other outbuildings:

> The people in the Country, not even opulent Farmers, never build any Temples to Cloacina, but sacrifice to that Goddess in the open air, the place generally appropriated for the Altar is the gable end of the House, and therefore it often happens that you are rudely taken by the Nose on your approach to it, and to compleat the business the Pig stye is frequently attached to the other end. (Martyn 1801, 125)

The plots were too small to sustain a family without additional income, however. The censuses from 1841 onwards give the main male occupations at Rhos Gelli-gron as farmer, labourer and miner. Chances are that most able-bodied adult men of the settlement combined farming their own plots and running a few sheep or cattle on the common with seasonal work in the mines or quarries or on farms. The women took care of the gardens and knitted stockings. One account of the area describes poor families gleaning tufts of wool from the common to spin, knit and sell (Knowles 1998).

Table 1: *Male and female heads of household at Rhos Gelli-gron, from census data*

	1841	1851	1861	1871	1881	1891	1910	1918	1930	1943
Men	11	11	13	9	8	1	6	3	5	3
Women	1	1	3	9	10	11	5	2	0	0

44 The line of a banked trackway between the fields of Castell and Castell Caradog

The census material shows an interesting pattern (*Table 1*). In contrast to most other areas, in the late nineteenth century Rhos Gelli-grom returned many more women heads of household than men. This might suggest that adult males were living away from home at the time the censuses were carried out in early April, perhaps at the mines which were furnished with barrack accommodation for their male workers. So we might imagine a community in which women constituted the stable core population, with men working away for part of the year, and older unmarried girls perhaps working in domestic service. Younger children probably participated in economic activities, but by the 1870s the census was describing some of the settlement's children as 'scholars' and they appear on the Pontrhydfendigaid school register from around the same time.

Although each house and its plot was the property of a single family, there is considerable evidence of co-operative activity too. Roads run up to and around the site and ditches mark the fields (*44*). Keeping the land adequately drained was probably the greatest problem for the settlers and it is likely that the cutting, recutting and maintenance of ditches was a constant chore. Like the road building and repair it is likely to have been undertaken collectively. Similarly, the construction and operation of the Calvinistic Methodist Chapel was a communal endeavour. Inhabitants of the tai-unnos constituted not only the congregation and the classes but also provided the teachers – Lydia Jones of Gwndwn Gwynau and Rees Jones of Pencwm were both Sunday school teachers at the chapel (Rees Jones 1974).

However, although it is tempting to see this settlement as an instance of collective and co-operative action by the poor in the face of economic and social struggle, the site is actually more remarkable for the independence of the new households. The houses do not cluster, but are widely dispersed. They are not orientated towards each other but all face either north or west, even in the case of Ty Newydd, for example, which thus faces out onto the common rather than towards Cil-y-bryn, or Castell Caradog which in turn faces away from Castell. Moreover, the houses seem to be located at points where the natural topography largely screens them from their neighbours. This is a very differently organised settlement to its Irish equivalent. The nineteenth-century village on Slievemore Mountain, Achill Island, County Mayo, although inhabited at the same time and by people of the same socio-economic group as Rhos gelli-Gron, is organised so that the houses are adjacent to each other, and the gardens beside the houses do not necessarily belong to that house but may belong to another house in the village (Horning, pers. comm.). The Irish village plan speaks of an altogether more communitarian style of living.

Some light may be cast on the Welsh settlement by the work of A.K. Knowles (1998). Whereas many historians of nineteenth-century rural Wales have attributed the development of squatter settlements to a rapid growth in population and a consequent 'land hunger' (e.g. Howell 1977; 1993; Moore-Colyer 1998), Knowles points out that the people of north Ceredigion did not choose under the pressure of expanding population to emigrate to the valleys, London or North America. Knowles instead asks the question why, given the extremely low fertility of the land, the absence of large or even medium-sized towns and high competition for tenancies, did the population of north Ceredigion continue to rise in the nineteenth century? Her answer centres around the possibility for poor young couples to enclose for themselves small amounts of land from the common. Although the areas of land enclosed – not usually more than about six acres and sometimes much less – were too small to support a couple without additional income, Moore-Colyer (1998) estimates that even in the more fertile south of the county at least 30-35 acres would be necessary to achieve self-sufficiency, the squatters had multiple and flexible strategies for family survival. These included casual, seasonal or temporary wage labour on farms or in industry, and entrepreneurial or casual industrial or craft production, such as the stocking knitting that the women of the area were known for, or the labour in mines or quarries in which the men partook. According to Knowles, the northern Cardi's preference for an inadequate holding in Ceredigion rather than the possibility of a wealthier existance elsewhere relates to the particular importance of land and land-holding in the local *mentalité*.

> The postponement of emigration from Mynydd Bach [the area adjacent to the site] reinforces the importance of continued access to land to the social fabric of this region. So long as land was available for colonisation, the region could continue to retain population, even though encroachment resulted in small, poor farms which were incapable of supporting families on them. (Knowles 1998, 91)

The attachment of the people of north Cardigan to their land was strong, even in Wales, and was also sentimental, practical and cultural. People of the area had long been identified by the name of their place: local surnames are fairly few and therefore Cardis used to, and still do, distinguish themselves by the name of their farm, house or village.

THE END OF THE SITE

Ultimately, of course, even a profound attachment to land was not enough to prevent large-scale emigration in the twentieth century. Like the rest of mid- and West Wales the Pontrhydfendigaid area experienced a sharp decline in population during the first half of the twentieth century and the settlement on the common was eventually abandoned. Members of two households appear on the 1945 electoral register but the site must have been entirely abandoned soon after that. The availablity of paid work in the nearby mineral mines and works was important for the economy of the site and with the closure of the mines came hardship not only to the inhabitants of Rhos Gelli-gron common but right across the region. The nearby lead and silver mines and works closed in the 1910s and 1920s, with the lead ore works at Esgair Mwyn the last to close in the area in 1926 (Knowles 1998).

While some of the houses seem just to have been abandoned, there is evidence that a process of deliberate 'decommissioning' was sometimes undertaken. Usable architectural elements such as window panes, doors, roof slates and perhaps flooring materials were removed from some of the buildings, notably at Pen Cwm and Caradog where the rubble contains only a few roof slates, and those are broken. The symbolically meaningful 'pentan' or fireback stone seems to have been deliberately removed from some of the houses. At Caradog, for example, a hole has been made from the outside of the chimney and the pentan removed. According to Iorwerth Peate (1944) the pentan was a characteristic feature of a medieval house but, like other features he identifies as medieval such as wicker fire hoods and doors next to the fireplace in the gable end, they are known from several houses at this eighteenth to nineteenth-century site. The pentan was the sign of an occupied house in the Middle Ages and there were legal sanctions against taking them away. Thus, the deliberate removal of the pentan could well have been a necessary part of the process of abandonment.

MARGINALITY?

So how 'marginal' was the squatter settlement on Rhos Gelli-gron? As is so often the case when dealing with the comparitively recent past, our superficial familiarity with terms and concepts can lead us astray.

When we think of squatters in rural areas we think of hippies in trees, people operating outside and perhaps in opposition to the established order of things. Is this an approriate idea to bring to the late eighteenth century? Not entirely.

At the time of the first encroachments on the common, the settlers might have been perceived as, or perceived themselves as, fighting against the staus quo. Lord Lisburne of the Nanteos estate, who had plans for the common, sent men to evict squatters – possibly from this common. Even 'the highly moral and discriminating Rebecca' was unsympathetic to them, says Howell (1993, 70). On the other hand, the regular payment of fines for squatting was sometimes just seen as a way of paying rent, and where encroachments were small and the land not particularly valuable, this could be the most profitable way of using the land as far as the owner was concerned. The dwellers on the common might not have perceived themselves as much different in lifestyle or aspiration from their town-dwelling neighbours. They were baptising their babies, some of whom were, admittedly 'natural' children, and burying their dead at the local church from the first decade of the nineteenth century, according to parish records, and their transfer from the established church to the Methodist chapel in the 1850s was absolutely typical of the area.

The status of the dwellers on the common also changed over the course of the settlement's history, and some of the better-off squatters actually bought their land. At the same time, other members of the Rhos Gelli-gron communities were recipients of parish relief, or described as 'paupers' in the census. Interestingly, despite the 'workhouse test' promoted by the government and reformers of the day which specified that poor relief should only be given to those so desperate for it that they would be willing to enter the workhouse, the Tregaron Union was evidently still giving 'outdoor relief' – a dole to paupers staying in their own homes.

The character of the site must have been very different in 1800, full of those robust and irreligious miners, to how it was in 1840, a confident settlement, building new houses and enclosing new fields, to 1880, dominated by women and opening a new chapel, to 1920, when most of the houses had been abandoned and the last few, very poor inhabitants were moving out.

Although we are perhaps more inclined to seek evidence of extreme poverty and hardship – and we can find it – was the site on the common any worse than in nearby towns? An account of neighbouring Tregaron from the 1847 *Blue book* makes Rhos-Gelli-gron sound unexceptional:

> The extreme filthiness of the habits of the poor, though observable everywhere, is as striking in this place, if not more so, than elsewhere, inasmuch as in a town it might be expected that a little more of the outward observance of cleanliness and decency would be met with, Dung heaps abound in the lanes and streets. There seemed seldom to be more than one room for living and sleeping in; generally in a state of indescribable disorder and dirty to an excess. The pigs and poultry form a usual part of the family. In walking down a lane which forms one of the principal entrances to the town, I saw a huge sow go up to a door (the lower half of which was shut) and put her fore-paws on the top of it and begin shaking it: a woman with a child in her arms rushed across the road from the other side of the way, and immediately opened the door and the animal walked into the house grunting as if she was offended at the delay, the woman following and closing the door behind her. Even the churchyard gives evidence of the absence of necessary outbuildings in the town, and several of the tombstones were covered with half-washed linen hanging to dry.

So perhaps the question is something like: how can we find a way of telling people's stories that is subtle enough to acknowledge the heterogeneity, the complexity and the changing character of communities of the recent past. Compared with prehistorians, historical archaeologists have abundant data – historical and archival sources, oral histories, standing structures and surviving landscapes – literally surviving in the case of the planted rows of beech (not native to the area) along the banks. So it is not true that the poor are hard to find. Nor is it the case that the poor are entirely left out of Welsh histories (although they sometimes are). Rather, their role is often collective, passive and undifferentiated, as 'population' helplessly blown about by the winds of politics, economics or other people's philosophies, or as 'waves' of migrants, or the hapless laboratory for some Improver's innovative ideas. Yet motivation, dissent, experience, complexity, innovation, aspiration and emotion were not the exclusive properties of the journal-keeping, letter-writing classes.

Writing the histories and archaeologies of 'marginal' people involves balancing the need to represent the conditions within which they lived – in this case poverty and insecurity, against the desire to show the complexity of their experiencess, their values and other accomplishments (cf. Potter 1991). Responsible representation must include both the adversities with which the site's inhabitants had to contend and an acknowledgement of their achievements and the richness of their lives, in terms of the things which are likely to have been meaningful to them, like building the chapel, improving their gardens or, probably most of all, maintaining an independent family land holding. In the attempt to reconstruct something of the texture and depth of past people's experiences, perhaps we can find a way to bring the margin to the centre.

BIBLIOGRAPHY

Carter, R. & Jones, W., 1996 *Houses and Homes in Wales*. Llandysul: Gomer.

Davies, A., 1998 Poor law administration in Cardiganshire, 1750-1948. In Jenkins, G. & Jones, I. (eds), 323-41.

Gailey, A., 1970 Irish corn-drying kilns. *Ulster Folklife* 15/16, 52-71

Howell, D., 1977 *Land and People in Nineteenth-century Wales*. London: Routledge and Kegan Paul.

Howell, D., 1993 The agricultural community of Cardiganshire in the eighteenth century. *Ceredigion* 12, 64-86.

Jenkins, G. & Jones, I. (eds), 1998 *Cardiganshire County History, vol 3, Cardiganshire in Modern Times*. Cardiff: RCAHMW.

Knowles, A.K., 1998 The structure of rural society in north Cardiganshire 1800-1850. In Jenkins, G. & Jones, I. (eds), 76-93.

Martyn, T., 1801 *A Tour to south Wales*. National Library of Wales manuscript 1340c.

Moore, D. (ed.), 1970 *The Irish Sea Province in Archaeology and History*. Cardiff: Cymdeithas Hynafiaethau Cymru.

Moore-Colyer, R.J., 1998 Agriculture and land occupation in eighteenth- and nineteenth-century Cardiganshire. In Jenkins, G. & Jones, I. (eds), 19-50.

Morgan, G., 1997 *A Welsh House and its Family: the Vaughans of Trawsgoed*. Llandysul: Gomer.

Owen, T., 1970 Social perspectives in Welsh vernacular architecture. In Moore, D. (ed.), 108-15.

Peate, I., 1944 *The Welsh House*. Liverpool: Brython Press.

Potter, P., 1991 What is the use of plantation archaeology? *Historical Archaeology* 25, 94-107.

Rees, D.C., 1936 *Tregaron*. Llandysul: Gomer.

Rees Jones, J., 1974 *Son Am Y Bont*. Llandysul: Gwasg Gomer.

Wiliam, E., 1973 Adeiladau Fferm Traddodiadol yng Nghymru. *Amgueddfa* 15.

Wiliam, E., 1995 'Home-made homes': dwellings of the rural poor in Cardiganshire. *Ceredigion* 12, 23-40.

Williams, D., 1955 *The Rebecca Riots: a study in agrarian discontent*. Cardiff: University of Wales Press.

16

MONUMENTALISING PLACE: ARCHAEOLOGISTS, PHOTOGRAPHERS AND THE ATHENIAN ACROPOLIS FROM THE EIGHTEENTH CENTURY TO THE PRESENT

Yannis Hamilakis

A couple of years ago, I was sitting with a friend at the café in the popular area of Theseion, opposite the Acropolis, in Athens. It was early evening, the site was beautifully and atmospherically lit, and we were both gazing at it admiringly. I, then, in a provocative mood, made the comment that what we are seeing in front of us is a construct of the nineteenth century, not a Classical site at all. I still remember her shock, and of course an argument, friendly but passionate, began. She was not an archaeologist, but a secondary school teacher. Yet, her surprise was the typical reaction I would have got from the vast majority of visitors and admirers of the Acropolis, Greek and non-Greek alike.

I was, of course, only partly right in my statement, for the sight/site in front of us was, and still is, also Classical. Yet, in its present shape, it is primarily a monumentalised ruin, a nineteenth-, twentieth- and twenty-first-century landscape. It is this process of monumentalisation that I want to trace in this short note, paying particular attention to two devices that have had a major impact in it: the device of archaeology and the device of photography. I will conclude the article by returning to the present, in an attempt to explore some pathways towards its possible de-monumentalisation.

The well-known image (45), an engraving by William Pars from the 1760s, from the *Antiquities of Athens*, by Stuart and Revett (1787), despite its somehow romanticised nature, gives a nice impression of the site in question, prior to its transformation. A palimpsest of buildings, activities and more importantly, times and temporalities: in addition to the Classical temple of the Parthenon, we can still see the Ottoman mosque inside it, and many other buildings of various origin and use. A commercial photograph (46) by the French photographer, Felix Bonfils, taken in the late 1860s or the early 1870s, roughly 100 later (cf. Hamilakis 2001; Szegedy-Maszak 2001), conveys a different sight: the solitary presence of the Parthenon, nothing else. The process of

45 An eighteenth-century representation of the Parthenon and the surrounding buildings on the Athenian Acropolis; in the cella of the Parthenon, the Muslim mosque is visible. *Illustration by W. Pars, from Stuart, J. and Revett, N. 1787, The Antiquities of Athens, vol. 2, pl. 1*

monumentalisation of this site, the process of creating a modern landscape, was well under way.

Some background information is needed here. Greece, part of the Ottoman Empire when Stuart and Revett visited, had been a nation-state since the 1830s, and the Acropolis was the most sacred specimen of the national imagination; an imagination which was largely constructed on the basis of continuity and cultural allegiance with the Classical past. In this locale, orientalist colonialism, western modernity and national imagination converged, leading to its transformation. Along with all the trapping of western modernity, scientific archaeology as a distinctive modernist device, was by the mid-nineteenth century firmly established in the area. Most of the people who were instrumental in the creation of the archaeological apparatus in Greece at the time, were part of the entourage of the first Bavarian king, Otto. The archaeological device started work even before the foundation of the new state, and in its first years produced the Acropolis that will be become known and endlessly reproduced, for the centuries to come. This project involved a series of strategies: strategies of demolition, which I prefer to call strategies of ritual purification, as happened with the new nation-state, the sacred specimens of the western imagination were liberated, or better, cleansed from the matters out of place, the remnants of 'barbarity'; there were also strategies of rebuilding

46 A photograph by Felix Bonfils (late 1860s or early 1870s) showing the Parthenon. *Felix Bonfils Photographs Collection. Manuscripts Division. Department of Rare Books and Special Collections. Princeton University Library. Reproduced with permission*

and recreation, with the restoration, reconstruction or the complete rebuilding of Classical buildings; strategies of demarcation, with the physical and symbolic erection of fences that separated these ruins from the web of daily life, thus creating peculiar heterotopias; and finally, strategies of exhibition.

The development of modernist archaeology in the West is of course the outcome of broader social, political and intellectual processes: capitalism with its emphasis on things as commodities, humanism, with its belief in progress, rationality and the ability to learn about the past from material things, colonialism with its desire for things from elsewhere, and nationalism, as a new, seemingly but deceptively secular way of imagining space, time and territory. Greece was not formally colonised, but it underwent many of the processes of the colonial project; for example, modernist archaeology was set up primarily by westerners but also some Greeks who were educated in western countries. For the new nation-state, archaeology was of course one of the most powerful devices upon which the national myth of origin could be built. Other devices, such as national historiography or folklore (*laographia*), were, of course important, but archaeology offered the material truths, the physical proofs of the assumed continuity, the tangible links with the earth and territory.

The new apparatus of modernist archaeology needed to produce its object of study, the national archaeological record. One of the paradoxes of national archaeology is that it presents itself as the objective process of recovering, collecting, studying, exhibiting and protecting the material past, yet in practice, national archaeology, as with all modernist archaeologies, *produces* its object, it does not simply recover and collect it. I referred to some of the practices employed in this process of production above. This highly selective production process involves as much destruction and demolition as it does protection and care. I referred to this destruction and demolition process as a purification device; when, in 1875, the medieval tower of the Propylaia of the Acropolis was demolished by the Athens Archaeological Society with the financial backing of Schliemann, L. Kaphtantzoglou, one of the protagonists of the demolition, wrote:

> ...the badly-built Turkish minaret, once sited on the pediment of the Parthenon, and the barbarian tower, which used to inappropriately occupy the Propylaia, were un-necessary, shameful additions, like the droppings of the bird of prey flying over it... In such a sacred place, we consider it to be impious and improper to preserve the dark relics of the passing waves of barbarity (1878: 302)

Through their demarcation and delineation, that is the separation of antiquities from the web of daily life, antiquities in essence become a new category; they become monuments, now existing in peculiar, other places, places of different order, where the normal rules of sociality and temporality do not apply. Their fencing off, demarcation and separation from daily lives and routines, marked both physically and symbolically this change of status. But it also meant that their mode of appreciation and their engagement with humans had now changed significantly; while before that engagement was a fully embodied and kinaesthetic one, from now on, it will be primarily one based on visual appreciation, involving organised archaeological sites, complete with entrance fees and guards, or specially selected repositories, i.e. museums.

Modernist archaeology is also a device that engages in extensive recreation and rebuilding, almost the forging of the archaeological record, as the compete rebuilding, initially in the 1830s, of the small Temple of Athena Nike on the Acropolis, showed (Mallouhou-Tufano 1998; Hamilakis 2007). Above all, national modernist archaeology recollects the fragments, constructs a whole, either a pre-existing whole of a desired moment, as in the case of the Athenian Acropolis of the fifth century BC, or an imaginary whole. A good example of this process is an enigmatic image (47), but a likely interpretation of it is that we are seeing a (now-disappeared) creation by the first native Greek archaeologist, Kyriakos Pittakis (cf. Kokkou 1977). He used to collect fragments of marble and other stones from the Acropolis and the area around it, fragments of a different date and origin, and construct what he called *pinakes*, frames: walls of artificial buildings, a mélange of different periods, objects

47 A photograph by Felix Bonfils (late 1860s or early 1870s) showing an artificial wall, possibly by the first Greek archaeologist, K. Pittakis. *Felix Bonfils Photographs Collection. Manuscripts Division. Department of Rare Books and Special Collections. Princeton University Library. Reproduced with permission*

and iconographic themes. This was his way of protecting these loose artefacts from destruction and pillaging.

These last two photographs, however, are specimens that testify to a much broader phenomenon. They are nineteenth-century commercial photographs, part of the much wider trend that involved many, primarily western but also some local photographers, who were producing hundreds of images of Classical monuments and then circulating them widely, either individually by catalogue, or as photographic albums (cf. Hamilakis 2001; Szegedy-Maszak 2001). But, as it should have become clear from the above, these photographers were depicting themes that were *staged by archaeology*. Modernist archaeology can be seen as an *exhibitionary discipline*, a device that reworks the material traces of the past and produces themes that are offered for primarily visual consumption and dissemination. The photographic and the archaeological are devices that were developed collaterally within the imagination of western modernity. In fact, there is a lot to be gained by studying the two devices side by side, and exploring their converging effects of monumentalisation of place and locality. Photography embraced archaeology from the first moment of its inception; in fact, as the 1839 speech by F. Arago to the French Chamber of Deputies (considered as the public announcement of the invention of the daguerreotype process) indicates, it was promoted as a device which could help enormously in the copying of hieroglyphics and other antiquities (Lyons *et al.* 2005). The first daguerreotypes of the Acropolis were produced that very same year. Photography and archaeology also share an epistemology of evidential truth ('seeing is believing'), as well as the fundamental principle of historicism, that is to narrate things as they really were. They also both attempt to freeze time: photography with capturing time and space in an image, and archaeology through fighting decay and loss and restoring the material traces of the past, but above all, by arresting the social life of a building or object. Finally, they are both techniques for the management of attention, and they both developed within a regime of autonomous gaze. The study of nineteenth-century photographs of archaeological monuments therefore, would allow us to trace the collateral development of the photographic and archaeological, as distinct but related representational devices of western modernity.

These images were taken by commercial photographers, who were responding to the demand for certain stereotypical images of Classical antiquity. From the many ruins of Greece, only a small number became the themes of photography, and in most cases, a photographic canon was established, determining the choice and the framing of the subject, the angle, the depiction of scale and so on. Photographs of Classical ruins became a currency in a new visual economy (cf. Sekula 1981; Poole 1997) where more people than before, the emerging middle classes, were participating. Luckily for many, photography was invented more or less at the same time as the nation-state had imposed severe restrictions on the export of antiquities. It was no longer possible to carry Classical antiquities out of the country, as now they were property of the Greek State. Yet, you could capture antiquities through photography: you could now carry a photographic image of the Classical ruin, or better, a ruin recreated and staged by archaeology as an object to be captured by the camera and gazed at. But photographers did not simply respond to the demand for certain images. Due to the dominant photographic canon which most of them adhere to, they were also producing and were helping to disseminate and consolidate certain, repetitive stereotypical 'seeings' and images of Classical antiquity. Photographs became the signs in a new universal language of perceiving Classical antiquity. To return to our context, a dominant theme in this representational canon is the portrayal of nineteenth-century Athens as a monumental land: as a place of ruins and monuments, but devoid of people, modern activities, city life or industrial development. Yet the Athens of the mid-nineteenth century was a buzzing European capital with plenty of the signs of fast urbanisation and industrialisation. This is the colonial gaze in action. Greece was still portrayed, mostly by western photographers, as belonging to another time, the time of Classical Greece, not the time of mid- and late nineteenth-century Europe.

48 A postcard bought at the entrance of the Acropolis in 2007

My main argument, therefore, is that both modernist archaeologists and commercial photographers contributed to the monumentalisation of the place, they both created the landscape we today call the Athenian Acropolis. They produced a spectacle, a staged theme, an object to be gazed at, rather than a complex, multi-cultural and multi-temporal locale, to be experienced in a multi-sensory mode. Roland Barthes (1981) reminds us that photographs partake in a form of primitive theatre, and the connections between theatre and archaeology have been pointed out by Tilley (1989) and Pearson and Shanks (2001), among others. The photographic and the archaeological produced and continue to reproduce a mnemonic canon, a memory of the site that is more about forgetting; forgetting the complex and immensely interesting biography of the place; they still condition the experiential encounter of today's visitors: how to approach the site, where to stop, where to stand, what to gaze at and from which angle, what is worth photographing etc. More importantly, they attempted to erase the multi-temporal nature of the site: a multi-temporal nature enacted by buildings, objects and artefacts created at different times since prehistory, but lasting, enduring and living in the present. The practices of demolition and ritual purification, selective representation, cropping and framing out, all attempted to glorify the singular temporality of the Classical.

49 An architectural fragment from the classical temple of Erechtheion with an inscription in Ottoman Turkish. *Photograph by Yannis Hamilakis*

Have they succeeded? Well, to a large extent, yes, judging from my friend's reaction, from the visitor's encounter with the site, from the dominant public perceptions, from the official histories and representations of the site, from the guides, postcards (*48*) and tourists snapshots. Except that materiality has the annoying habit of being hard to resist. In the spring of 2000 I produced a photographic object myself (*49*). It depicts a piece of worked marble, an architectural part coming from a Classical monument, but with an inscription in Ottoman Turkish on it. It was lying almost unnoticed near the Erechtheion, not sign-posted, not part of any tourist itinerary. I learned later that the original piece was part of the west façade of the Erechtheion. In 1805, the piece was inscribed with the inscription which praises the strong fortress of the Acropolis and the zeal displayed in its fortification and construction by the then Ottoman governor of Athens; the piece was incorporated into a contemporary vaulted entrance near the Propylaia (cf. Paton 1927). What time is this photograph and what time is the piece it depicts? This piece embodies in a rich but concise way many of the themes that I have been developing in this article. It disrupts the created singular temporality of the present, as well as the temporality of Classical antiquity, by bringing into the fore the temporality of the Ottoman life of the Acropolis. But it does more than that. It constitutes the resistance of materiality, a materiality that endures and lasts, despite various processes of purification, recreation and photographic monumentalisation. It embodies material agency: the agency of things rather than persons to intervene in the present and unravel the temporal and in this case, the material, representational, monumental and archaeological consensus.

It also shows us perhaps a possible way towards de-monumentalisation: we cannot reverse almost 200 years of archaeological and photographic monumentalisation, but we can produce new images, point to other material presences, the cracks in the edifice, the traces of a complex and rich biography, be it this re-used and multi-temporal fragment, a canon from the time when the Acropolis was a fortress, or the metal plaque installed recently to commemorate the removal of the swastika from the Acropolis in 1941 (see Hamilakis and Yalouri 1999).

ACKNOWLEDGEMENT

It is a pleasure to acknowledge that this piece and a book-length, wider study (Hamilakis 2007), results, in part, from the encouragement of Andrew Fleming.

BIBLIOGRAPHY

Barthes, R., 1981 *Camera Lucida: reflections on photography* (trans. R. Howard). New York: Hill and Wang.

Hamilakis, Y., 2001 Monumental visions: Bonfils, classical antiquity, and nineteenth-century Athenian society. *History of Photography* 25, 5-12, 23-43.

Hamilakis, Y., 2007 *The Nation and its Ruins: antiquity, archaeology, and national imagination in Greece.* Oxford: Oxford University Press.

Hamilakis, Y. & Yalouri, E., 1999 Sacralising the Past: the cults of archaeology in modern Greece. *Archaeological Dialogues* 6, 115-35.

Kaphtantzoglou, L., 1878 On the demolished Turkish tower at the Athenian Acropolis. *Athinaion* 6, 287-308.

Kokkou, A., 1997 *The Care for the Protection of Antiquities in Greece, and the First Museums.* Athens: Ermis (in Greek).

Lyons, C., Papadopoulos, J.K., Stewart, L.S. & Szegedy-Maszak, A., 2005 *Archaeology and Photography: early views of ancient Mediterranean sites.* Los Angeles: The Getty Museum.

Malouhou-Tufano, F., 1998 *The Restoration of Ancient Monuments in Modern Greece.* Athens: The Athens Archaeological Society (in Greek).

Paton, J.M. (ed.), 1927 *The Erechtheum.* Cambridge, MA and Princeton: Harvard University Press and the American School of Classical Studies at Athens.

Pearson, M. & Shanks, M., 2001 *Theatre/Archaeology.* London: Routledge.

Poole, D., 1997 *Vision, Race, and Modernity: a visual economy of the Andean image world.* Princeton: Princeton University Press.

Sekula, A., 1981 The traffic in photographs. *Art Journal* 41, 15-25.

Stuart, J. & Revett, N., 1787 *The Antiquities of Athens*, vol. 2. London.

Szegedy-Maszak, A., 2001 Felix Bonfils and the traveller's trail through Athens. *History of Photography* 25, 13-22 and 23-43.

Tilley, C., 1989 Excavation as theatre. *Antiquity* 63, 275-80.

17

THE IMAGINARY, THE IDEAL AND THE REAL: RECENT LANDSCAPES IN CENTRAL SICILY

Mark Pluciennik

Some time ago Chris Gosden and Lesley Head (1994, 113) noted that the term 'landscape' was a 'usefully ambiguous concept', encompassing 'both the conceptual and the physical'. As with Andrew Fleming's recent critique of post-processual landscape archaeology, they were primarily concerned with prehistory. Fleming argued that the lack of past cultural and conceptual context means that prehistoric landscape archaeology is particularly vulnerable to becoming 'an arena full of opportunity for the fantasist and the ideologue' (2006, 277-8). Understanding the potential relationships between the conceptual and the physical might reasonably be expected to be, if not easier, perhaps better delineated for more recent periods. On the other hand, evaluating the various factors which go to make any recent social and historic landscape specific and characteristic is perhaps more difficult, given the wealth of data, scales and contexts on which any interpretation can draw. Here we suggest that the empirical, the textual, the social, the pictorial, the geological, the political, the disciplinary and many other strands need to be interwoven to form understandings of contemporary and historical central Sicilian landscapes. Fantasists and ideologues might be said to inhabit these landscapes too, although not necessarily in the form of contemporary archaeologists.

Since medieval times the landscapes of central and western Sicily have been characterised as densely populated 'agrotowns' set amidst the surrounding deserted agricultural estates or *latifondi*. These historical, geographical and other perceptions of desolate rural landscapes have themselves become part of the 'Southern Question' in Italian politics – the way in which societies and people in southern Italy and Sicily have been deemed, among other things, backward and conservative, as well as corrupt. However, over the last two centuries these areas have also been the scenes of attempted revolution and direct state intervention, as well as less spectacular forms of resistance and expressions of desire for change. The systemic and institutional

50 Borgo Antonino Cascino, Enna, Sicily

contexts may range from local and national understandings of global capitalism, and the rôles of the church and the state, to issues of ownership of specific plots, access to patronage, availability of 'marginal' agricultural land, and from feelings of economic and political confidence in the future to crises of agriculture or rural employment. All these, we would argue, are indirectly 'visible' in contemporary central Sicily, given that we know some of the relevant contexts also from other, non-archaeological sources. Here we examine some of the ways in which these complex and inter-related factors are manifested in the rural landscapes around Enna. What we experience today is thus an amalgam of the imaginary, the ideal and the real: derived from images of what a proper agricultural countryside should look like and how people in it ought to behave; from ideas and attitudes associated particularly with a unified Italian state, and from the ways in which people have practically engaged with, owned, exploited, managed, moulded and intervened in the landscape.

The image of the hamlet Borgo Antonino Cascino (*50*), is surely recognisable as part of a quintessentially Italian, and more specifically Tuscan, landscape. Its elements (tower, cypresses) and even its situation atop a small rise are familiar especially from nineteenth-century paintings, as well as contemporary tourist images. Those of the Roman *campagna*, another great attraction for artists of the period, would typically include remnants of a massive Classical ruin too. Both supposedly captured traditional or even timeless aspects of rural existence, often emphasised by the presence of a small figure of a shepherd or other rural worker, seemingly oblivious to the rise and fall of empires. Yet Borgo Cascino is placed in the centre of Sicily; it is largely surrounded by the extensive and borderless sweeps of wheatlands typical of *latifondo* ownership, and at 70 years old is a relative newcomer. Borgo Antonino Cascino is in fact a materialised imaginary. Rather than representing or having stimulated local feelings of a deeply rooted *Italianità* or national and historical identity, however, it is physical evidence of another aspect of modern Italian political life: *meridionalismo*, or the 'Southern Question': a question repeatedly posed largely from the north since the late nineteenth century, and typically meaning 'what shall we do with the problematic South?'

In 1876 Leopoldo Franchetti and Sidney Sonnino, two former law students in their late twenties, travelled extensively through Sicily. Both were to become successful politicians; both had an interest in the functioning and administration of the economy within the newly unified Italian State. No doubt they also wanted to see for themselves the potential as well as the problems of integrating Sicily. Neither was prepared to ascribe the alleged problems of southern Italy to innate backwardness or inability. As liberals they were closer to the analysis of Pasquale Villari, who in his 'Letters from the South' had explored the legacy of Bourbon corruption, the sources of banditry, and the effects of illiteracy and the structure of land ownership. He had suggested that moral and political reform (and the formation of a modern and liberal middle class) could expunge the 'parasitic' elements from southern society. Italian political unification had largely been driven by interests from the north and was associated with increasing industrialisation, despite the fact that Garibaldi's march of liberation physically began and gained support in western Sicily. This issue of *meridionalismo* still structures much of Italian politics today, with resentment in a rich north (typified by Umberto Bossi's *Lega Nord*) against a needy and corrupt South, fuelling political and economic claims for regional autonomy or federalism.

Franchetti and Sonnino were from Tuscany (born in Florence and Pisa respectively). Apart from the urban glories of their native cities, they would also have been familiar with their rural hinterlands in which there were nucleated villages and small towns, and a substantial number of landed farmers. The contrast with central and western Sicily, where large *latifondi* devoted to extensive cereal cropping and grazing were most common, could not have been greater. Those who physically worked the land were generally extremely poor, and dependent on vicious and unbalanced systems of share-cropping to gain a bare living. Given the annual leases, the share-croppers had no incentive or opportunity to live near 'their' land, but rather agglomerated in provincial towns. Franchetti and Sonnino were shocked to see the state of the Sicilian peasantry and the structures which sustained the system. Written, one feels, at the end of a long hot day in the saddle (*51*), they commented:

> One can travel by horse for five or six hours from one town to another and never see a tree or a shrub. One rises and falls, now passing through fields, now climbing

51 Contrada Fico d'India, Enna, Sicily: a classic 'latifondo' landscape

by steep paths scoured by water; one passes by the crests of hills; valley follows valley; but the view is always the same; everywhere solitude, and a desolation which crushes the heart. Not a single peasant house. (Franchetti and Sonnino 1877, 14)

Were they right? This may seem a curious question to ask. The passage in question is generalised and may represent a crystallisation of their experiences and memories, though they could have had a specific journey in mind. Rural settlement in Sicily and the south of Italy generally, whether in nucleated villages or dispersed houses, *was* typically much rarer than in the centre and north, as shown by the census of the same time, with only five per cent of the population of the province of Caltanisetta described as living in the countryside (Jacini 1883). In contrast with Tuscany and the Po Valley, where around half the populace could be categorised as rural dwellers, the Sicilian interior was rather characterised by 'agrotowns' such as Enna in the very centre of Sicily, and from where peasants might have to walk for several hours to reach their year's allotment of land.

However, recent archaeological and archival work, as part of the Archaeology of the Torcicoda Valley Project (Mientjes *et al.* 2002; Pluciennik *et al.* 2004) would suggest that at least by the time Franchetti and Sonnino were on the move, there was considerably more activity in the countryside than their description implies. It is true that there is little evidence of dispersed peasant or farm houses set among the fields. Those few that exist are in ruined state and are difficult to date precisely. No detailed official survey or Land Registry is available between 1840 and the early 1930s. In addition, historians have tended to work in family or estate archives (e.g. Cancila 1983; Davies 1985; Riall 1999) which then naturally give an excellent but primarily top-down picture of activity on, but not necessarily between or beyond the *latifondi*. In typical archaeological fashion, then, we might ask: what about the workers?

In fact, archaeologically we can identify at least three areas of labour and activity in this countryside, beyond the frequent but seasonal and archaeologically largely ephemeral work of cultivation (sowing, weeding, harvesting) carried out by the share-croppers and by salaried wage-earners directly employed on the estates. These comprise investment in the *latifondi*, mills and their associated infrastructure and neighbouring dwellings, and the extensive and long-term work of clearance, terracing and construction, typified in our area by Contrada Torre.

LATIFONDO INVESTMENT

Historians, economists and others often point to the Sicilian *latifondi* as examples of the perils of rent capitalism and also as a source of that particularly Sicilian problem, the Mafia. In brief, from early modern times onwards, for reasons of status, nearness to patronage, court activity and royal, judicial and political power and institutions, the owners of the large estates had tended to establish themselves and build their primary *palazzi* in Palermo and/or Naples, the centres of the Kingdom of the Two Sicilies. Increasingly during the eighteenth and particularly nineteenth centuries, the estates were leased out to those termed *gabelloti* for three, six or nine years. These *gabelloti* sub-let on an annual basis to the share-croppers. The dependence of the nobility on cash flow from the *gabelloti*, and the interests of the *gabelloti* in extracting as much as possible in terms of crops and labour over the term of their lease, meant that investment in, and the productivity of these rural estates was often minimal in comparison with 'improved' agriculture elsewhere in Italy and Europe. The Mafia as a widespread phenomenon, it is generally agreed, arose and was first named in the mid-nineteenth century. It represents a particular form of exploitation of and extortion directly from poor rural populations, and indirectly from the large landholders – threats of violence sometimes serving to ensure that only a single low offer for a particular lease was made by *gabelloti* or their associates. The *masserie* or estate centres were thus primarily dedicated to working requirements, with extensive buildings for stabling, machinery repair, and storage, often arranged in part around a courtyard. They were not country residences for leisure, pleasure or display, and were without the buffering gardens or parks familiar from villas or elite rural residences elsewhere. In the Torcicoda area there are also examples of *masserie* with churches or chapels, for the use of share-croppers and families employed directly by the estate, rather than any general rural populace. However, within this working environment we have many examples of later nineteenth-century and perhaps earlier twentieth-century new buildings and/or expansions of older ones, in areas away from the estate centres: as secondary centres of stalling for draft animals, but also including proper ovens, suggesting a degree of permanent residence, presumably by estate workers. Such buildings are easily recognised not only by their locations within *latifondo* landscapes, but also by their dressed stone doorways, windows and cladding. Precisely what this evidence means is so far unclear: it could refer to changes in agricultural practices including the range of activities, the mode of organisation of estate workers, or more general expressions of status or economic confidence and a demonstration of agricultural 'investment', for instance.

MILLS, ROADS, HOUSES

The Torcicoda River often serves as a boundary: nowhere is this clearer than in the centre of its course where it has cut into the rock to form a 70m-deep gorge called the Vallone Cateratta. This zone is characterised by a very different landscape to those of the surrounding *latifondi*, not only topographically, but also in terms of human activity. At the western end there is a rare example of an isolated house with small cleared fields and substantial enclosures for sheep. In little more than a kilometre there are the remains of six watermills and their associated leats; there are more mills further downstream beyond the gorge mouth. At least one of these goes back to late medieval times, but the extant structures are primarily of later nineteenth-century or early twentieth-century date. Typical of these is the Mulino Nuovo ('New Mill') on the eastern side (52), which a stone incorporated into a rebuilt wall suggests was perhaps 'new' in 1666, and with a date for the rebuilt water tower ('botte') of 1871.

The leat which feeds the water tower also shows three phases of reconstruction. This mill is associated with a series of structures, mainly houses, but also stalling for animals, in the adjacent rockshelter; others exist in the two rockshelters on the opposite side of the gorge, built of roughly squared stone blocks with a clay daub covering. These houses show every sign of having been permanently occupied. Here, and elsewhere in the gorge, are also the remains of cultivation terraces. At some point, perhaps again the second half of the nineteenth century, a well-built cobbled road with stone-walled parapets was built leading from the fields above, past the two rockshelters on the southern side of the gorge, crossing the river by a now-destroyed stone bridge to a well-built platform above a leat for two mills further downstream, and finally ascending to the rockshelter above the mill (53). Archival work by Antoon Mientjes has shown that although these mills could be owned by families, groups or institutions such as the Church, they were typically leased out to the operators.

52 Mulino Nuovo, the associated rockshelter and houses

Judging by the nature, extent and quality of the stonework still visible in the buildings and infrastructure, milling must have been a profitable business, despite the expense of necessary maintenance. But poor agricultural workers also lived here (in the houses within the western rockshelters, for example). At least in the later nineteenth and earlier twentieth centuries, and quite possibly before, the Vallone Cateratta must have been the focus of much busy movement and intense activity in this narrow zone literally carved out in the centre of the 'deserted' *latifondo* landscape.

BOUNDARIES AND BUILDINGS

A few kilometres to the north-east is another less dramatic though still steep-sided valley running approximately east to west. Along most of the southern slopes are the remnants of terraces and buildings: we have intensively mapped part of this area in the Contrada Torre. Here one can also trace field roads and field walls, features now comprising 2-3m wide linear spreads of stone clearance piles running up- and down-slope, and which also function as boundaries dividing the hillside into segments. The buildings vary from houses and at least two wells, to wine presses and smaller

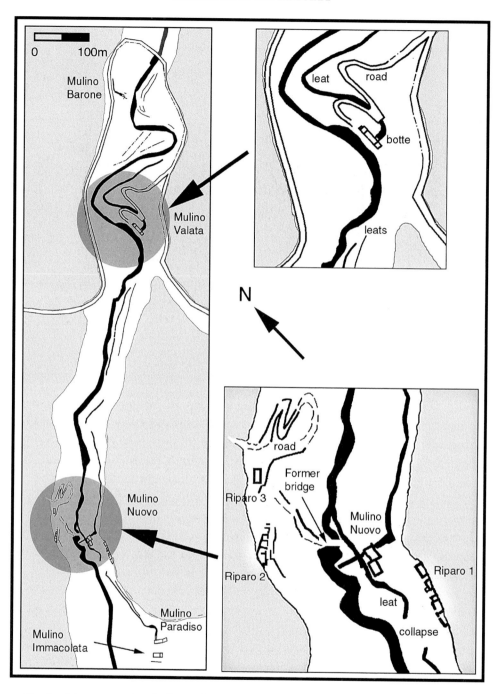

53 Details of the constructions in the southern part of the Vallone Cateratta

54 Contrada Torre. Antoon Mientjes by one of the terrace walls

buildings. The terraces (*54*), built to trap, contain and retain soil, vary in size, shape and function: some semi-circular constructions are typical of those built for olive or other fruit trees. Archival work here has shown that the pattern of ownership in this area reflects this much more fragmented and diverse use, with much vine growing as well as cereals, almonds, olives, cherries and prickly pear. (Pluciennik *et al.* 2004).

Although survey has shown evidence of longer use in this area (valley bottom fields contain Roman as well as later ceramics), and at one place there is a rock-cut tomb of Classical type towards the top of the slope, both archival and archaeological work suggests that the existing remains are primarily from the eighteenth, especially the nineteenth, and the earlier twentieth centuries. It is worth emphasising that while this landscape is very visible archaeologically, and of course well known to local people, including shepherds and recreational hunters, it is much more difficult to 'see' historically. Although this zone, and others like it, show a sustained and intense input of time and labour over several generations, trying to trace the people who owned and worked this area in previous centuries is similarly laborious and time-consuming, owing to the ways in which previous censuses and current archives are organised. That is, the structure of the Land Registers and cadastral maps do not allow simple correlation of plots of land with named people; the censuses from Enna (formerly Castrogiovanni) which include inventories of possessions including land, are organised by street and area. Nevertheless, such information as we have to date shows that land in this area was often owned directly (not leased), by people from the middle or lower (but not lowest) portions of Sicilian society – a priest, a cobbler, a wealthier peasant. Sometimes such land was used as collateral for other ventures: the lease of a mill or mills in the Vallone Cateratta, or a beneficial marriage, for example. We have therefore argued that the material remains of the efforts invested here, in this initially unpromising terrain, also represent an archaeology of aspiration and upward mobility (Pluciennik *et al.* 2004): another example of how natural variation in the landscape can provide niches and interstices which, given the right circumstances, can be taken advantage of and confer status in a political, social and economic, as well as more utilitarian sense.

COLONIAL ENDEAVOURS

Despite this evidence of local and rural initiative, and indeed many repeated uprisings aimed more directly at land reform and redistribution throughout the nineteenth century and immediately after the First World War, nationally the 'problem' of the South continued to be framed in terms of *meridionalismo* – explaining 'the peculiarities of the South in relation to the rest of the country' (Morris 1997, 2; cf. Dickie 1997, Epstein 1992). In the recently-unified Italian state, Sicily and the peninsular South, including their agriculture, were seen as under-developed in comparison with the industrialising North. Within Italy, the perception of southern rural landscapes and their inhabitants was largely *not* one of a romanticised classicism. The issue of *meridionalismo* continued to be discussed and acted upon during the inter-war period. Although in Sicily, under the Fascists regional agencies established to carry out public works and land improvement, little was achieved (Duggan 1989). Instead, migration from the countryside (or rather provincial towns) to cities in Sicily, elsewhere in Italy and abroad continued, and in response the Fascists introduced the policy of ruralisation. 'To 'ruralise' means to hold the peasants to the soil, or, if they have left it, to bring them back to it' explained a Fascist official in 1930 (cited in Schmidt 1938, 43). There was much rhetoric extolling rural virtues, leading to slogans such as 'Return to the land'. 'People who abandon the land are condemned to decadence ... I have willed that agriculture take first place in the Italian economy', wrote Mussolini. At the same time, noting the appalling condition of much rural housing, he proposed that 'within a few decades all peasants and farmworkers must possess large, healthful houses, in which the rural generations can live through the centuries, in which the race will find a secure foundation' (Mussolini 1931, cited in Schmidt 1938, 168). But partly through the recalcitrance of the large landowners, little if any improvement could be seen in rural areas. Thus in the summer of 1939 Mussolini announced that the Sicilian *latifondo* 'will be destroyed by the rural village ... [which will] have water and roads' (cited in Stampacchia 1978, 586). In October the sites of the first eight new Sicilian rural villages were inaugurated, including that of Borgo

Antonino Cascino; the following January the legal framework for agricultural reform was approved. Twenty thousand family farmhouses, each with 25ha of improved land, were planned for the next decade. The reforming law included the foundation of the *Ente di Colonizzazione del Latifondo Siciliano* (ECLS: Corporation for the Colonisation of the Sicilian Latifondo) – the title showing clearly the vision of these foundations and reforms as pioneering settlements analogous to those in Africa, for example, and the import of northern ideas to educate and guide the southern locals. Not only ideas: some of the inhabitants of these villages and farmhouses were to be part of a reverse migration from north to south, living exemplars of a healthy Fascist peasantry.

Thus Borgo Antonino Cascino was built on a low hill, with administrative offices, a church dedicated to the Virgin Mary, houses and a rural school constructed around a central square. At least five farmhouses were constructed nearby to standardised plans, and 20 in the wider area. Our *Casa* 3 still retains a plaque recording its establishment by the ECLS in Year XVIII of the Fascist era (1940). The structure and layout materialises the state-set goal of self-sufficiency ('*autarchia*' – also a national aspiration) within a family farm (*unità poderale*), and neatly expressed also by the three trees – olive, apple and almond – planted to the side of the house. Four of these fascist-period houses are now abandoned, and the land re-incorporated into large cereal fields. In these (and slightly older buildings elsewhere), there is evidence of re-use for pastoral purposes during the middle of the twentieth century, with the insertion of mangers. Borgo Cascino in the 1950s also saw further state-inspired and funded attempts at land reform including renewed building of houses with small (2-3ha) plots; most of these are now refurbished, improved and occupied as permanent or weekend houses. The church is still used; there is an annual *festa*, and Borgo Cascino is known locally for its *ristorante-pizzeria*. The land reforms of the 1940s and 1950s largely failed in their own terms, but the resultant structures and niches have often been exploited in different ways.

DISCUSSION

By analogy with archaeological sites, landscapes are sometimes described as palimpsests, though that perhaps lacks the sense of dynamism. To evoke the sense of movement as well as stasis, they can be thought of as the intersection, inter-penetration and overlaying of traditions, time-depths, intentions, paths, practices, ideas, interventions, geological and topographic conditions and social, political, economic and environmental processes – all changing and accreting at different rates and rhythms. They also demonstrate horizontal variation in all these aspects. Landscapes also comprise real and implied relationships. As such their characterisation demands specific parameters referencing real places, people and histories. Within the small area of central Sicily described above – supposedly a classic 'deserted' *latifondo* zone – there are at least four areas which can be considered separate though inter-connected and partly synchronous landscapes. Some, such as Contrada Torre, are organic in development, building on pre-existing elements, and with a time-depth extending over perhaps several centuries: the slow sedimentation of aspirations and social mobility within a capitalist system. The *latifondo* landscape itself, although not without changes, is persistent and long-lived in form, although maintained as such through different political and socio-economic agencies (old noble families, the *nouveaux riches* aspiring to nobility, *gabelloti*, etc.). Other elements are more obviously imposed, the direct results of top-down political interventions such as the Fascist and post-war rural houses and land divisions. In the context of Italian nationalism the form and fact of Borgo Cascino references not only the centre, directly, which was Rome, but also another heartland of the imaginary, Tuscany, the supposed home of the first and purest form of the Italian language, for example. This use of rural landscape as a repository and symbol of national identity was widespread at the time: Black Forest peasants in Germany, the villages of rural England, the Aegean in Greece (e.g. Schama 1995; Leontis 2005). However, these national interventions and impositions can also be seen partly as responses to specific local conditions and grievances. These latter were sometimes manifested in political action such as occupations, and are evidenced materially in the refusal to abandon claims to the land represented by the late 'pastoral horizon': waiting for land reform. Such actions are also expressions of longer-term processes and attitudes seen through the move into, cultivation and use of interstitial areas such as the gorge, for example. Other aspects of landscape also have a national political dimension and represent horizons of change or at least intensification of activity such as the apparent late nineteenth-century burst of (re)building on the *latifondi* and at the mills, plausibly linked to the reunification of Italy during the 1860s and a growing sense of political and economic confidence. All these changes are, archaeologically-speaking, within the shortest of time-frames, and some are perhaps better described as events, rather than processes.

The idea of 'landscape' is clearly not only 'usefully ambiguous', but also comprises many different variables, values, scales and perspectives (in both senses of the word). Is it possible or desirable to attempt to offer histories, or interpretations which unify these sometimes disparate elements? Social landscapes (which are primarily what archaeologists are interested in), always relate to and reference entities beyond their physical boundaries. Similarly events relate to processes, practices to traditions and structures, material forms to sometimes nebulous or unarticulated concepts or feelings (aspirations, confidence, values, etc.). Chronological gaps and spatial absences can be as stimulating to thought as positive encounters. None of this comes into focus, though, without the encounter in the first place: 'landscape archaeology' with all its ambiguities.

ACKNOWLEDGEMENTS

The physical and conceptual work on which this paper is based has been a collaborative venture involving many people: thanks are especially due to Antoon Mientjes, and to Enrico Giannitrapani and Mike Morley.

BIBLIOGRAPHY

Cancila, O., 1983 *Baroni e popolo nella Sicilia del grano*. Palermo: Palumbo.

Cherry, J., Margomenou, D. & Talalay, L. (eds), 2005 *Prehistorians Round the Pond: reflections on Aegean prehistory as a discipline* (Kelsey Museum Publications 2). Ann Arbor: Kelsey Museum.

Davies, T., 1985 *Famiglie feudali siciliane. Patrimoni, redditi, investimenti tra '500 e '600*. Caltanisetta – Roma: Salvatore Sciascia Editore.

Dickie, J., 1997 Stereotypes of the Italian south 1860-1900. In Lumley, R. & Morris, J. (eds), 114-47.

Duggan, C., 1989 *Fascism and the Mafia*. New Haven: Yale University Press.

Epstein, S., 1992 *An Island for Itself: economic development and social change in late medieval Sicily*. Cambridge: Cambridge University Press.

Fleming, A., 2006 Post-processual landscape archaeology: a critique. *Cambridge Archaeological Journal* 16, 267-80.

Franchetti, L. & Sonnino, S., 1877 *La Sicilia nel 1876. Volume 2: I contadini*. Firenze: G. Barbèra.

Gosden, C. & Head, L., 1994 Landscape – a usefully ambiguous concept. *Archaeology Oceania* 29, 113-6.

Jacini, S., 1883 *Frammenti dell'inchiesta agraria* (seconda edizione). Roma: Forzani (Tipografi del Senato).

Leontis, A. 2005. Greek Modernists' discovery of the Aegean. In Cherry, J., Margomenou, D. & Talalay, L. (eds), 133-49.

Lumley, R. & Morris, J. (eds), 1997 *The new history of the Italian south*. Exeter: University of Exeter Press.

Mientjes, A., Pluciennik, M. & Giannitrapani, E., 2002 Archaeologies of recent rural Sicily and Sardinia: a comparative approach. *Journal of Mediterranean Archaeology* 15, 139-66.

Morris, J., 1997 *Challenging meridionalismo. Constructing a new history for southern Italy*. In Lumley, R. & Morris, J. (eds), 1-19.

Pluciennik, M., Mientjes, A. & Giannitrapani, E., 2004 Archaeologies of aspiration: historical archaeology in rural central Sicily. *International Journal of Historical Archaeology* 8, 27-65.

Riall, L., 1999 Nelson versus Bronte: land, litigation and local politics in Sicily, 1799-1860. *European History Quarterly* 29, 39-73.

Schama, S., 1995 *Landscape and Memory*. London: HarperCollins.

Schmidt, C., 1938 *The Plough and the Sword: labour, land, and property in Fascist Italy*. New York: Columbia University Press.

Stampacchia, M., 1978 Sull' 'assalto' al latifondo siciliano nel 1939-43. *Rivista di Storia Contemporanea* 7, 586-610.

18

THE LLANBADARN FAWR 'GRAVESTONE URN': AN OBJECT HISTORY

Zoë Crossland, Michael Freeman, Paula Jones and Brian Boyd

Walking through the picturesque graveyard of Llanbadarn Fawr, Aberystwyth, the urn carved on an 1843 gravestone would make any archaeologist stop and look twice (55). Rather than referencing a Classical tradition of urns and weeping willows more usually found on nineteenth-century funerary monuments, it shows an accurately illustrated cinerary urn, such as would be found in the local landscape lying under a Bronze Age barrow or, perhaps more usually today, in the display cases of a museum. The text beneath remembers William Hughes of Lluestgwilym, who died at the young age of 19. The inscription translated from the Welsh reads: 'Here is buried William, second son of Lewis and Mary Hughes, of Lluestgwilym, who was born on the 5th of April 1824 and died on the 26th of September 1843'. Beneath the personal information the *englyn* or short verse in Welsh is full of sentiment and attempts to make sense of the brevity of William's life. It may be translated as: Life is but one moment – and worthless/ Are the days of our lives/ From our coming into the world/ it is an unwholesome journey to the tomb's entrance.

On first glance the inscription seems to end with these lines, but fold back the grass at the base of the stone and another inscription is revealed (56), this time in English: The Urn delineated at the top of this Stone/ was turned up in ploughing over the remains/ of a Tumulus, in a Field called Caerodyn on/ the Farm of Pyllau issa, in the adjoining Parish/ of Llanfihangel Glyndroed alias Creuddyn,/ in the Month of November 1840. it contained a/ great quantity of human bones & had the mouth/ downward/ R.K.

The gravestone's idiosyncratic linking of Christian commemoration and burial, ancient and 'pagan' practices of cremation, and a scientific interest in the urn's origins, seems curious within the context of the nineteenth-century churchyard. Although cemetery monuments that referenced the ancient past were increasingly common in early to mid-nineteenth century Britain (their popularity growing in tandem with

Above: 55 Cinerary urn depicted on William Hughes' gravestone. *Photograph by Michael Freeman*

Right: 56 The full inscription. *Photograph by Michael Freeman*

the development of garden cemeteries), the designs were usually neoclassical, Egyptian or Gothic in origin (Mytum 1989; 2000). To draw on ancient indigenous funerary traditions like this was highly unusual (although Celtic crosses and designs would become popular later in the century). The erection of classically themed memorials placed the dead within a constructed tradition that emphasised continuity between the achievements and accomplishments of past civilisations and those of the nineteenth-century present (Tarlow 2000), excluding the poorly understood barbarian past of Britain from the narrative of historical progression. However, the gravestone explicitly links the British urn with this Classical tradition, evoking the more conventional funerary urns carved on other gravestones through its style and decorative motifs. The similarities suggest that the same stonemason carved the different gravestone urns – Classical and British – all in bass-relief, flanked by two rosettes, and framed by the projecting top edge of the stone. The Pyllau-Isaf urn was probably viewed as part of a history that related directly to the British or Celts described by Classical authors, and may be understood as part of a burgeoning interest in British archaeology and the history of Wales. Six years after the urn's discovery, the first issue of *Archaeologia Cambrensis* described the earliest period of British monuments as 'Celtic, Cymmric, Gaelic, Erse &c.' (Jones 1846, 14), illustrating the perceived link between the Celts and Britain's ancient past. The gravestone therefore makes a strong statement about the value of British archaeology, in comparison with the material remains of the Classical past.

The only other example of a British Bronze Age urn used as a funerary monument known to us is that of the Peak District antiquarian and enthusiastic barrow-digger, Thomas Bateman (1820-1861) at Middleton-by-Youlgreave in Derbyshire. While Bateman's monument clearly references his antiquarian interests, in the case of William Hughes his connection with the urn is not apparent. The 1847 tithe map for Llanfihangel y Creuddyn indicates that the tenant at Pyllau-Isaf was William Evans, and the land was held by Ernest Augustus Vaughan Lisburne, one of the major landowners for the county, whose seat was in the adjoining parish of Llanafan at Trawscoed (Crosswood). The gravestone therefore records a find not from the Hughes' land, but from the farmland of Evans. No mention is made of the relationship between the two families or farms. The connection, if any, between the urn and the life and death of William is left unstated. Maybe William was involved with its discovery on the farm of Pyllau-Isaf? We can also ask more broadly about how the urn was situated within an emerging archaeological discourse, while also embedded in an understanding of Welsh history that was tied to landscape and language. The intertwined biographies of the Llanbadarn Fawr gravestone and the urn that it recorded reveal how both were caught up with changing understandings of the past and of its commemoration through archaeological practice. In tracing the circuits within which the urn travelled after its discovery, the ways in which it was drawn upon in the creation of collective understandings of British history and identity are disclosed. The urn was carved at a moment of increased interest in 'ancient memorials of a national and medieval character, in place of the exclusive admiration of objects … of foreign origin' (Way 1844, 1-2). The gravestone simultaneously reveals the ways in which discoveries like the urn began to be made as objects of archaeological knowledge, and how this knowledge was drawn upon in the production of the Welsh past as one which encompassed a history relevant to Britain as a whole.

INCENDIARY HISTORIES

That past mortuary traditions were used to reflect on modern burial practices is made clear in a variety of nineteenth-century literature. The nineteenth century saw more variety than there had been for centuries in the ways in which the dead were buried. Increasingly they were placed in a diversity of locations: chapel burial grounds, churchyards and municipal cemeteries, and as debates over the hygienic disposal of the dead intensified in the 1840s, the differences in past mortuary practices seem to have been increasingly upon peoples' minds (Walker 1839; Collison 1840). In England certainly cremation was still seen at this period as barbaric, even by those who had an interest in promoting a diversity of approaches to disposal of the dead. George Milner, director of the Hull General Cemetery Company, noted the variety of forms of burial practice over the course of Britain's history, pointing out that the Ancient Britons burnt their dead but also making sure to emphasise that:

> Cremation has long since ceased to be practiced by civilised nations; and the sepulchral urn, is known to us of the present day, but as a classical emblem, decorating the mural tablets in our religious edifices, or ornamenting other sepulchral mementoes, erected to the illustrious dead (1846, 32)

The association of cremation with pagan beliefs like those of the Ancient British was a great hindrance to the development of the modernist project of rational and hygienic cremation, a fact not lost on Gorini, the Italian scientist who developed the technology for modern cremation in the 1870s. He noted that the task that lay before its proponents was 'not confined to the mere burning of the dead, but extends to burning and destroying superstition as well, purifying the religion of the urns from the prejudices in which it has been wrapped' (quoted in Leaney 1989, 123). Indeed, many Church notables were not only opposed to cremation, but even to its symbols on funerary monuments (Tarlow 1992). Because cremation was frowned upon from the perspective of Christian burial, it tended to be associated with liberal or progressive ideas, and a degree of anti-clericalism, especially on the continent (Leaney 1989). Cremationists in Britain were also often viewed as radicals, a view reinforced by individuals like Dr William Price of Llantrisant who, in 1884 publicly burnt the body of his son, Iesu Grist, who had died at just a few months old (ap Nicholas 1973). A radical free thinker, modern-day druid, and Chartist, Price's interest in cremation was fed by his druidical interests. The cinerary urns recovered from burial mounds seemed to show that the Ancient Britons and their antecedents had cremated their dead, and for those like Price who viewed themselves as heirs to the druidic tradition, cremation was not be viewed as barbaric but as part of their British heritage.

In the 1840s, however, it is unlikely that the practice of cremation was of primary interest to the Hughes family. Although ancient cremation in Britain had been noted and commented upon since Thomas Browne published *Hydriotaphia: Urn Burial* in 1658, it was not until the last decades of the nineteenth century that the great debates over cremation as a modern mode of disposal of the dead would take place (Jupp 1997; 2006). Instead the urn is more likely to have referenced a British history and past that had been claimed by many in Wales: a Welsh construction of a proud and unbroken tradition that provided an alternative to the Classical heritage more commonly proclaimed on gravestones.

Wales had been closely linked with the deep history of Britain for centuries. From the sixteenth century Britain's archaeological relics had been constituted in relation to the perceived antiquity of Wales and Welsh traditions and language. John Leland and John Bale linked the ancient druids of Classical antiquity to the medieval Welsh order of bards (Morgan 2005), and this druidical connection was followed up with well-known enthusiasm by antiquarians such as John Aubrey and William Stukeley, who interpreted Stonehenge as a druidic temple (Piggott 1968; 1989), although Stukeley (1740) suggested that it predated the arrival of the Celtic Welsh. The Honourable Society of Cymmrodorion founded by Lewis and Richard Morris in 1751, claimed in contrast to Stukeley, that the Welsh were the aboriginal inhabitants of Britain, and chose a druid and St David to stand on either side of their coat of arms to assert this claim (Morgan 2005). This illustrated the somewhat counter-intuitive pairing of druids with early Christianity in Britain, influenced in part by William Stukeley's suggestion that druidic beliefs and Christianity were grounded in similar attitudes (1740). In the later eighteenth century, Iolo Morganwg integrated this view of druidism as a form of proto-Christianity into his remaking of druidic tradition, asserting that the knowledge and wisdom of this tradition had been retained by the Welsh bards with their conversion to the new religion, situating the Welsh (particularly, and conveniently, the Glamorgan Welsh) as inheritors of a proud tradition, preserved and remembered through bardic lore and poetry (Suggett 2005). Suggett notes that although Iolo never published his History of the Bards, his ideas were in common circulation, making their way into print through Colt Hoare in the early nineteenth century. The incorporation of the Ancient British past into the stream of Christian tradition was accepted by Anglican antiquarians, as illustrated by the first meeting of the Cambrian Archaeological Association (to which we will return), when a visit was made to the landscape around the ruined Cistercian monastery at Strata Florida. The same evening, the Dean of Hereford made an after-dinner report about the excursion:

> A spot, such as they had that day visited, also raised in his mind thoughts of the most exalted nature ….When they looked around them at the wonders of the creation, and the immense progress man had made … they could not fail to be struck with admiration and awe, lest their ruins might in after ages be the only remains of the greatness we once possessed. When they therefore surveyed the ruins of ancient structures, they ought to fill us with feelings of a similar nature, and teach us … that those who inhabited this land, while they were destitute of that blessed Religion which we now enjoyed, had inculcated those habits without which we could not be good Christians, viz. self-denial and charity, and had considered it their first duty to render homage to their God (Anon. 1847, 359)

This speech was well received. The journal records 'loud cheering' upon the Very Rev. Dean's conclusion, indicating that there was broad agreement that the people of the past were not entirely ungodly. The Ancient Britons and their incendiary practices were thereby accommodated by Anglican antiquarians, who focussed on evidence of continuity rather than of threatening rupture.

The origins and history of the Ancient British were mapped out as much through studies of language like those of Edward Lhwyd (Morgan 1981) as through historical documentation, oral traditions and fieldwork (Jarvis 2005). Morgan makes the point that the Welsh language itself was closely tied to the sense of history and the past, noting that when Goronwy Owen wrote to Richard Morris about the proposed Cymmrodorion Society he spoke of Welsh almost as a national monument (Morgan 1981, 67) stating that the Society should '[lay] open its worth and beauty to Strangers': both the language and the past should be carefully curated and cared for. In the plans of the Morris brothers for the Society of Cymmrodorion language would be closely tied to the ancient landscape. In 1761 Lewis Morris wrote 'But by all means the bringing the people to love and caress their language and antiquities and to be masters of it, is the first step of establishing national honour in their hearts as Cymmrodorion' (cited in Morgan 1981, 85).

Within the context of the great interest in the landscape, history and language of Wales in the eighteenth and nineteenth centuries, the 'graveyard urn' of Llanbadarn Fawr can be made sense of not as an anomalous gravestone tucked away in the corner of a parish church, but as part of the re-making of Welsh identity and history in relation to the local landscape and with an eye to its wider significance in the history of Britain.

LANGUAGE AND LANDSCAPE OF RECORD

The resurgence of interest in Welsh history and culture in the eighteenth century, was expressed and promoted through popular books like Theophilus Evans' *Drych y Prif Oesoedd*, as well as more scholarly publications such as Lhuyd's *Archaeologia Britannica*, but also by an increasing interest in the local landscape and monuments among gentry and farmers alike (Morgan 1983). Iolo Morganwg's belief in the druidic origins of prehistoric monuments led him to see their cataloguing and description as an essential task in the documentation of Welsh history, and he planned sites and recorded stratigraphy with some accuracy (Suggett 2005). The famous druidic ceremony that he directed at Primrose Hill on 21 June 1792 was physically and metaphorically situated within a recreated archaeological landscape of standing stones, locating the newly constructed tradition within historical time and space, mediated by the similarly situated Welsh language, which seemingly had preserved tradition while recreating it anew. The rocking stone (Y Maen Chwf) near Pontypridd was another focus for meetings by Iolo and his supporters (Walters 2005), and would be the focus of druidic rituals carried out by the cremationist Dr William Price of Llantrisant in the later nineteenth century.

By the early nineteenth century county histories like Meyrick's *History and Antiquities of the County of Cardigan* were increasingly popular, both drawing upon and encouraging local interest in archaeological finds. Certainly burial mounds and other archaeological features were interpreted as part of an impressive and proud history, whether through antiquarian attempts to connect them with the druids, or in contemporary local traditions which made sense of landscape features in terms of remembered oral histories. The two may well have been connected. On Anglesey, the Anglican vicar Henry Rowlands of Llanidan claimed to find evidence of druids in place names and in the standing stones they had left behind (Rowlands 1723). When in the 1870s the future General Pitt Rivers investigated burial mounds on the island he noted local traditions which remembered the barrows as the final resting place of various Ancient British princes, commemorating them in names like *Carnedd Howel* or Howel's Cairn (Fox 1870). It seems probable that the Llanbadarn Fawr grave's depiction of a cinerary urn from the local landscape expressed in part this interest in local heritage and the affirmation of links between Wales and the Welsh language of the mid-nineteenth century and its 'British' heritage. The parents of William (who had presumably paid for the gravestone) had not only illustrated the urn but felt it necessary to give its provenance and details of its discovery, locating it firmly within the local landscape. While the gentry were at the forefront of promoting the interest in the Welsh past in the eighteenth century, the gravestone in Llanbadarn Fawr churchyard suggests a broader interest among the more affluent tenant farmers and middling sorts by the mid-nineteenth century, particularly among the

Anglican population. This was an interest that was echoed and reinforced by the growing popularity of eisteddfodau.

That the memorial for William expressed a feeling of connection with the local landscape and history is reinforced by the choice of language made for the stone's inscription. A large minority of gravestones at Llanbaradrn Fawr were written entirely in Welsh, with the rest mostly in English. Comparison with Mytum's work in Welsh-speaking Pembrokeshire is illuminating (Mytum 1994; 2002). In the churchyards and burial grounds of North Pembrokeshire Welsh was a minority choice until at least the middle of the nineteenth century. Where a bilingual inscription was chosen, then it followed a regular pattern. The introductory statement (*in memory of*; *here lies* etc.) and personal details would be in English, and the Welsh part of the inscription was in these cases restricted to the epitaph, or a verse from the Bible. This used Welsh for text that was simultaneously more personal, private and often emotive, but less important in terms of conveying identifying information. Mytum (2002) argues that this particular pattern of language use was chosen because it allowed individuals to make a statement about Welsh identity and language, while making the biographical details broadly accessible through the use of English. He suggests that this illustrates a concern with intelligibility in the arena of public record.

In contrast to the North Pembrokeshire graveyards, Welsh seems to be more common in the Llanbadarn Fawr churchyard: a substantial proportion of gravestones are inscribed in Welsh and in contrast to North Pembrokeshire, inscriptions tend to be entirely in Welsh or entirely in English, with fewer bilingual inscriptions (see Gilbey & Penglais School History Society website). Significantly, at both Llanbadarn Fawr and the graveyards studied by Mytum in North Pembrokeshire, when the introductory statement and personal details on gravestones were written in Welsh, then the epitaph or biblical verses were never in English. Bilingualism worked only one way: English was used for personal details and Welsh for epitaphs, but never vice versa. The urn tombstone is unusual in that it simultaneously breaks with and reinforces these conventions. The entire stone is inscribed in Welsh: introductory statement, personal details, and epitaph. The description of the urn however, moves into English. While the gravestone is unconventional in terms of language use within the churchyard, its deployment of English builds upon the language's position as the medium of public record and historical documentation, and illustrates a concern with intelligibility in matters of antiquarian interest. However, while it reinforces English's status as the language of public life, it does not mark it out as the only language of posterity. The rest of the gravestone is inscribed entirely in Welsh, speaking of a confidence in the continuation of the Welsh language and of future Welsh speakers to read it. While the English text, in its intended audience of future antiquarians (Welsh, English or otherwise) reveals a conviction that Wales' past is of significance for the history of Britain as a whole, the Welsh personal information and *englyn* express assurance in the future of the language and culture of Wales. In the carving of the gravestone past and future were brought together, articulated through an assertion of Wales' place in history.

A POTTED HISTORY

The interest in Welsh language, landscape and history was part of the coming into being of archaeology as a discipline, and the urn's peregrinations through Wales at the meetings of the Cambrian Archaeological Association trace out the network of associations between gentleman scholars, tenant farmers and visiting English antiquarians through which the modern discipline emerged. In his chapter, in the *Cardiganshire County History* Stephen Briggs described the complicated post-excavation history of the urn, tracking down its various sightings through back-issues of *Archaeologia Cambrensis* (Briggs 1994). Grimes' *Prehistory of Wales* notes that the urn may have been found with a pygmy cup and bronze pin (neither of which were mentioned on the gravestone). It is described thus:

> Decoration (corded): on internal bevel of rim: three horizontal lines; on collar: alternating triangles with filling of oblique lines, with two enclosing lines above and below; on shoulder: a row of roughly triangular impressions. Lower part missing. Diameter 18.5cm, original height about 20cm (Grimes 1951, 210)

At some point in the decades after its discovery, the urn seems to have become confused with other finds from Penyberth (Gloucester Hall), leading to some perplexity both over its original provenance and where it ended up (Peate 1932). On top of this is the puzzling appearance of the bronze pin and a small earthenware pygmy cup, both of which are undocumented on the gravestone. Arguably, their association with the urn seems to derive from the urn's post-excavation history of touring and display, rather than from the original context of excavation, as will be explored below.

Sometime after 1851 Thomas Owen Morgan seems to have acquired the material from Pyllau-Isaf, subsequently giving it to the University College Museum, Aberystwyth, from where they were donated to the National Museum of Wales. Morgan was a London barrister with an estate near Aberystwyth who had a great interest in the local history and archaeology of Ceredigion. His *New Guide to Aberystwyth* was a popular local guidebook, running to five editions between 1848 and 1869. The first edition was dedicated to the Cambrian Archaeological Association in acknowledgement for selecting Aberystwyth as the location for their first Annual Meeting in 1846. Tracing the urn's history through the records of the Association's meetings illustrates the intellectual context within which the urn was situated, and the way it, and other artefacts were employed in the reworking of the

British past. At the first Annual Meeting of the Cambrian Archaeological Association, held between 7 and 9 September 1847, a 'very curious Ancient British *cist ludw*' was amongst the items on display at the public rooms during the Association's outing to Strata Florida (Anon. 1847, 359). *Archaeologia Cambrensis* recorded that this was a vessel for holding ashes, found in the parish of Llanfihangel y Creuddyn in 1844 and exhibited by its owner, a Mr James. Despite the discrepancy in the date of the find (which is recorded on the gravestone as 1840) this seems likely to have been the cinerary urn depicted on William Hughes' gravestone. How the urn came into James' hands is unknown.

Three and a half years later, in the April 1851 issue of *Archaeologia Cambrensis*, T.O. Morgan reported on the recent discovery of an urn containing calcined bone and a bronze pin at Penyberth (Gloucester Hall). In this report he also noted the earlier find of what was probably the 'graveyard urn' in November 1840 at a site about 10 miles distant. He described the 1840 find as an earthen vase, with burnt remains found at the centre of a tumulus on the farm of Pyllau-Isaf in the parish of Llanilar. This misattribution to Llanilar rather than Llanfihangel y Creuddyn is presumably because the farm lies near the boundary between the two parishes (57). Morgan noted that the Pyllau-Isaf urn was broken on raising but that the fragments had been put together and were now in the possession of an archaeological friend (1851, 164-5). In October 1851 the journal noted that the vessels and bone found at Gloucester Hall (Penyberth), had been on display in a temporary museum arranged for the Tenby meeting of the Cambrian Archaeological Association (1851, 334). This exhibit demonstrated the latest archaeological theories, based on Thomsen and Worsaae's work outlining the three-age system. Their work had not yet been translated into English when the Pyllau-Isaf urn was found, but in July 1851 a positive review of Worsaae's volume was published in *Archaeologia Cambrensis*, and by the Tenby meeting in October of the same year, the prehistoric antiquities on display were ordered chronologically, listed as 'Primeval Antiquities' – 'Stone Period' and 'Bronze Period'. This marked a shift from the 'Celtic, Cymmric, Gaelic, Erse &c.' which previously had been thought to encapsulate the oldest elements of the British past. The reports from 1851 show an interest in comparison between sites and vessels, and the creation of new narratives about the past through the physical ordering of material objects. However, in the process of classification and comparison, the potential for future confusion arose. The record of the Tenby meeting noted that the Gloucester Hall urn contained a small cup not mentioned in Morgan's report made earlier in the year, and by this date the bronze pin has slipped out of view.

At this point then, there were at least two urns and a small cup doing the rounds of local Cambrian Archaeological Association meetings. They were clearly popular items for display. Sixteen years after its discovery the Pyllau-Isaf urn was apparently exhibited at the 1856 Welshpool meeting. Two cinerary urns were on show, one large

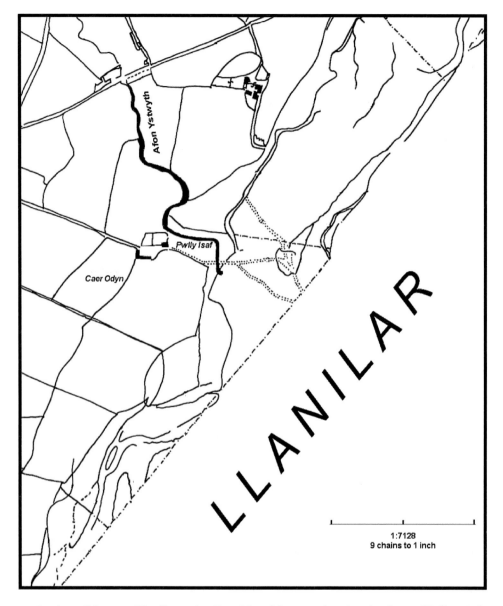

57 Section of the 1847 Llanfihangel y Creuddyn tithe map showing the farm of Pyllau-Isaf and the field (Cae'r Odyn) where the urn was discovered. Note that Llanilar parish lies just across the Ystwyth river

and one small, but both apparently found in the same tumulus, on the farm of Pwll-isa in Llanilar. These had been lent by T.O. Morgan (Anon. 1856), who had perhaps acquired the urn from his 'archaeological friend' by this point. By this date more discrepancies had appeared. The vessel was again recorded as found in Llanilar parish rather than Llanfihangel y Creuddyn, and it now seems to have gained a companion urn which was not mentioned in earlier reports, nor indeed on the gravestone. By 1868 an urn, apparently the one from Pyllau-Isaf, had become firmly associated with a small pygmy cup, which although recorded as found inside the urn, may have come from Penyberth or elsewhere (Stanley and Way 1868). Both ultimately ended up catalogued together in the National Museum of Wales in Cardiff (also see item 427 in Savory 1980, 149).

Reviewing the evidence in 1925 Peate suggested that the cinerary urn now held at the National Museum was the one found at Penyberth or Gloucester Hall, noting the disappearance of the bronze pin (Peate 1925), but then in 1932 published a short piece entitled 'New light on a Cardiganshire cinerary urn' in *Archaeologia Cambrensis* (1932, 201-2), which made the following correction:

> My attention has now been drawn by Mr Arthur R. Sansbury, B.SC., University College of Wales, Aberystwyth, to a tomb stone in the church yard at Llanbadarn-fawr, Cardiganshire, on which is depicted (see figure) the urn referred to in my 1925 note… The urn, now in the National Museum of Wales, described in 1925, is obviously that of the Llanbadarn inscription, and I am grateful to Mr Sansbury for bringing the inscription to my notice.

Finally then, we come back to the gravestone, a seemingly stable point within this object history that has allowed some decoding of the later history of the urn, once it left the security of its home under the barrow in Cae'r-odyn field on Pyllau-Isaf farm. The Hughes family were oddly prescient in their decision to document the artefact on William's gravestone, allowing twentieth-century clarification of misattributions and inaccurate records that appeared remarkably soon after the urn was discovered. If only every archaeological artefact found in the nineteenth century had such good contextual information! The gravestone carving makes the broken urn whole again, and mounts it upon a pedestal, but it also shows an understanding of the ambiguities of archaeological evidence and a concern with recording the context of discovery. The particular history of the urn necessarily receded once it was brought into practices of antiquarian classification and display, and this tension is expressed on the gravestone in the difference between the description, almost hidden at its base, recording how the urn was found turned downward, and the illustration which produces the urn as whole, upright and unbroken. The gravestone's concern with documentation may be situated within changing practices of historical marking and commemoration that were taking place both within the cemetery and in the antiquarian community more broadly at this time. The documentation of the urn brings it into a new tradition of object histories, also seen emerging in the pages of *Archaeologia Cambrensis*, one which no longer had faith in objects alone to tell their complicated stories, but realised the value and importance of context: the emergence of an archaeological mode of remembering.

CONCLUSION

In the churchyard of Llanbadarn Fawr we glimpse the appearance of an archaeological mode of thought outside the confines of universities and antiquarian societies. Histories of archaeology's coming into being focus on the role of the clergy, gentry and wealthy professionals, who made up the membership of these associations of interested amateurs. John Hughes Esq., who owned the land that William's parents farmed was in attendance at the first meeting of the Cambrian Archaeological Association, as was the vicar of Llanbadarn Fawr, but the tenant farmers and labourers who made up his parish are missing from the reports of meetings and events in *Archaeologia Cambrensis*. Their voices are heard sporadically in reported speech in the journal (e.g. Morgan 1851), when gentleman antiquarians were notified of discoveries within their fields. They may also have taken an interest in the archaeological objects on display in the public rooms of the Association's meetings, such as the one at Strata Florida where the Pyllau-Isaf urn was exhibited. The depiction of the urn on the Llanbadarn Fawr gravestone suggests that an archaeological mode of thought emerged within a widespread interest in the past among the equally emergent middle classes and is also intimately tied to their histories.

Certainly antiquarian societies would open up to the middle classes increasingly over the course of the later nineteenth century, but the urn and gravestone point to a broader-based interest. Archaeology emerged as a discipline together with a widespread concern with memory and commemoration, as Jensen (1998; 2000) has noted, and may itself be viewed as a form of commemorative practice, one which tied the present, and all the dramatic and ongoing changes that were taking place, to a stable and seemingly durable past. Antiquarian labour not only curated the memory of the past but also looked towards the future remembrance of the present. Anxious that the achievements of the nineteenth century would be recognised and remembered by posterity, British archaeological remains were increasingly valued by antiquarians (regardless of their apparently pagan and barbarian origins), drawn into a stream of tradition that by the end of the century would have a more evolutionary cast (Mack 1997).

The intertwined biographies of urn and gravestone reveal the collective understandings that were drawn upon in the urn's production as an object of antiquarian interest, pointing to the societal interest in memory, and the sense of the relevance of Welsh heritage to an increasingly valued British archaeology (Chapman 1989). The concern with the physical traces of human existence was also expressed through changes in memorialising practices associated with the dead, which struggled against the erasure of individual histories. Laqueur has noted the resonance of burial grounds as places for imaginative play, as they simultaneously demonstrate the limits of the thinkable while giving moral force to new ideas and practices. From the second half of the eighteenth century onwards funerary monuments show an increasing awareness of the ways in which the past could be known and recorded through objects, both referencing the past and ensuring that memory was durably inscribed with an eye to an imagined future audience (Jensen 2000). It is perhaps no coincidence that Iolo Morganwg, that great excavator, and indeed fabricator of Welsh tradition, was also a capable stonemason who carved gravestones and memorials – notably a draped urn at St Illtud's church, Llantwit Major (Morgan 2005; Suggett 2005).

In this context the Llanbadarn Fawr gravestone was an ideal venue to record archaeological information, enduringly tying together the image of the urn with the details of its discovery in a local setting designed for memorialisation. Indeed, time has proved it better than the journals, notebooks and scraps of card and paper on which such contextual information was typically recorded. In the context of the local landscape and the remembered experience of excavation, the details provided on the gravestone commemorate a short life, and evoke the memory of discovery; of an urn turned downwards in a field on the farm of Pyllau-Isaf. The stone also however, expresses a new interest in a common and Ancient British past, linking it pictorially with claims to Classical heritage. The gravestone illustrates the new approach to objects, producing them as part of a scientific discourse of documentation, but it also reveals an anxiety about the preservation of memory in its realisation that objects divorced from context lose something irrevocably unless efforts are made to preserve them; something that archaeologists still struggle with today.

ACKNOWLEDGEMENTS

Thanks to Mair Humphreys of Ceredigion Archives, and to Samuel A. Jones for help with translation from Welsh to English. Thanks also to the staff of the archives at the National Library of Wales, Aberystwyth for their assistance with the tithe maps.

BIBLIOGRAPHY

Andeersson, A-C., Gillberg, Å., Jensen, O.W., Karlsson, H. & Rolöf, M.V. (eds), 1998 *The Kaleidoscopic Past. Proceedings of the 5th Nordic TAG Conference, Göteborg, 2-5 April 1997*. Göteborg: Gotarc Serie C, Arkeologiska Skrifter, 16.
Anonymous, 1847 First Annual Meeting of the Cambrian Archaeological Association. *Archaeologia Cambrensis* (Series 1) 2, 352-72
Anonymous, 1851 Tenby Meeting of the Cambrian Archaeological Association. *Archaeologia Cambrensis* (Series 2) 2, 334.
Anonymous, 1856 Welshpool Meeting of the Cambrian Archaeological Association. *Archaeologia Cambrensis* (Series 3) 2, 366.
ap Nicholas, T.I., 1973 *A Welsh Heretic; Dr. William Price, Llantrisant*. London: Foyle's Welsh Co. Ltd.
Briggs, C.S., 1994 The Bronze Age. In Davies, J.L. & Kirby, D.P. (eds), 124-218.
Browne, T., 1658 *Hydriotaphia: urn burial or, a discourse of the sepulchral urns lately found in Norfolk*. London: Hen Brome.

Caygill, M. & Cherry, J.F. (eds), 1997 *A.W. Franks: nineteenth-century collecting and the British Museum*. London: British Museum Press.

Chapman W., 1989 Toward an institutional history of archaeology: British archaeologists and allied interests in the 1860s. In Christenson, A.L. (ed.), 151-62.

Charmaz, K., Howarth, G. & Kellehar, A. (eds), 1997 *The Unknown Country: death in Australia, Britain and the USA*. London: Macmillan.

Collison, G., 1840 *Cemetery Interment: containing a concise history of the modes of interment practices by the ancients*. London: Longman, Orme, Brown, Green, and Longmans.

Christenson, A.L. (ed.), 1989 *Tracing Archaeology's Past*. Carbondale: Southern Illinois University Press.

Davies, J.L. & Kirby, D.P. (eds), 1994 *Cardigan County History, Volume 1, From the Earliest of Times to the Coming of the Normans*. Cardiff: University of Wales Press.

Evans, T., 1716 *Drych y Prif Oesoedd*. Cardiff: Gwasg Prifysgol Cymru (re-issue of the first edition, 1961).

Fox, A.L., 1870 On the opening of two cairns near Bangor, North Wales. *The Journal of the Ethnological Society of London* 2, 306-24.

Gilbey, A.W. & Penglais School History Society, Aberystwyth. (www.llanbadarnchurchyard.org.uk/index.html)

Grimes, W.F., 1951 *The Prehistory of Wales*. Cardiff: National Museum of Wales.

Hobsbawm, E. & Ranger, T. (eds), 1983 *The Invention of Tradition*. Cambridge: Cambridge University Press.

Houlbrooke, R. (ed.), 1989 *Death, Ritual and Bereavement*. London: Routledge.

Jarvis, B., 2005 Iolo Morganwg and the Welsh Cultural Background. In Jenkins, G.H. (ed.), 29-49.

Jenkins, G.H. (ed.), 2005 *A Rattleskull Genius. The Many Faces of Iolo Morganwg*. Cardiff: University of Wales Press.

Jensen, O.W., 1998 The cultural heritage: modes of preservation and the longing for eternal life. In Andeersson, A-C., Gillberg, Å., Jensen, O.W., Karlsson, H. & Rolöf, M.V. (eds), 99-118.

Jensen, O.W., 2000 Archaeology and death in modern society. In Jensen, O.W. & Karlsson, H. (eds), 67-78.

Jensen, O.W. & Karlsson, H. (eds), 2000 *Archaeological Conditions. Examples of Epistemology and Ontology*. Göteborg: Gotarc Serie C, Arkeologiska Skrifter, 40.

Jupp, P.C., 1997 Why was England the first country to popularize cremation? In Charmaz, K., Howarth, G. & Kellehar, A. (eds), 141-54.

Jupp, P.C., 2006 *From Dust to Ashes: The replacement of burial by cremation in England 1820-1997*. Hampshire & New York: Palgrave McMillan.

Leaney, J., 1989 Ashes to ashes: cremation and the celebration of death in nineteenth-century Britain. In Houlbrooke, R. (ed.), 118-35.

Lhuyd, E., 1707 *Archaeologia Britannica*, London.

Mack, J., 1997 Antiquities and the public: the expanding museum, 1851-96. In Caygill, M. & Cherry, J.F. (eds), 34-50.

Meyrick, S.R., 1808 *The History and Antiquities of the County of Cardigan*. London: Longman.

Milner, G., 1846 *On Cemetery Burial, or Sepulture, Ancient and Modern*. Hull, London & York: W.R. Goddard, Longman and Co, Hargroves.

Morgan P., 1981 *The Eighteenth Century Renaissance*. Llandybïe, Dyfed: C. Davis.

Morgan, P., 1983 From a death to a view: the hunt for the Welsh past in the romantic period. In Hobsbawm, E. & Ranger, T. (eds), 43-100.

Morgan, P., 2005 Iolo Morganwg and Welsh historical traditions. In Jenkins, G.H. (ed.), 251-68.

Morgan, T.O., 1848 *New Guide to Aberystwyth and its Environs Comprising Notices, Historical and Descriptive of the Principal Objects of Interest in the Town and Neighbourhood*. Aberystwyth: J. Cox, Pier Street.

Morgan, T.O., 1851 Discovery of a sepulchral urn, or vase on the farm of Penyberth. *Archaeologia Cambrensis* (Series 2) 2, 164-5.

Mytum, H., 1989 Public health and private sentiment: the development of cemetery architecture and funerary monuments from the eighteenth century onwards. *World Archaeology* 21, 283-97.

Mytum, H., 1994 Language as symbol in churchyard monuments: the use of Welsh in nineteenth and twentieth-century Pembrokeshire. *World Archaeology* 26, 252-67.

Mytum, H., 2000 *Recording and Analysing Graveyards.* York: Council for British Archaeology and English Heritage.

Mytum, H., 2002 A comparison of nineteenth and twentieth-century Anglican and Nonconformist memorials in north Pembrokeshire. *Archaeological Journal* 159, 194-241.

Peate, I.C., 1925 Incense cup and cinerary urn. *Archaeologia Cambrensis* (Series 7) 5, 203-5.

Peate, I.C., 1932 New light on a Cardiganshire cinerary urn. *Archaeologia Cambrensis* 87, 201-2.

Piggott, S., 1968 *The Druids.* New York: Praeger.

Piggott, S., 1989 *Ancient Britons and the Antiquarian Imagination: ideas from the Renaissance to the Regency.* London: Thames and Hudson.

Rowlands, H., 1723 *Mona Antiquae Restaurata. An Archaeological Discourse on the Antiquities, Natural and Historical of the Isle of Anglesey, the Ancient Seat of the British Druids.* Dublin: Printed by Aaron Rhames for Robert Owen.

Savory, H.N., 1980 *Guide Catalogue to the Bronze Age Collections.* Cardiff: National Museum of Wales.

Stanley, W.O. & Way, A., 1868 Ancient interments and sepulchral urns found in Anglesey and North Wales, with some account of examples from other localities. *Archaeologia Cambrensis* 23, 217-93.

Stukeley, W., 1740 *Stonehenge, A Temple Restor'd to the British Druids.* London: Innes & Manby.

Suggett, R., 2005 Iolo Morganwg: stonecutter, builder and antiquary. In Jenkins, G.H. (ed.), 197-226.

Tarlow, S., 1992 Each slow dusk a drawing-down of blinds. *Archaeological Review from Cambridge* 11, 125-40.

Tarlow, S., 2000 Landscapes of memory: the nineteenth century garden cemetery. *European Journal of Archaeology* 3, 217-39.

Walker, G., 1839 *Gatherings from Graveyards, Particularly those of London.* London: Longman and Co.

Way, A., 1844 Introduction. *Archaeological Journal* 1, 1-6.

Worsaae, J.J.A., 1849 *The Primeval Antiquities of Denmark.* (Trans. W.J. Thoms). London: J.H. Parker.

19

LOVE LETTERS, LOVE STORIES AND LANDSCAPE ARCHAEOLOGY: REFLECTIONS ON WORKING IN THE NORTH PENNINES

Rob Young and Jane Webster

In 1999 one of us (R.Y.) reviewed Andrew Fleming's masterful study of the Swaledale landscape – *Swaledale: the Valley of the Wild River*, for the journal *Antiquity*. In its closing pages Andrew notes with disapproval that 'writing about a well-loved place becomes like writing a love letter, in which it is important to insist that the beloved is unique and special' (1998, 154). Coming from a man whose own relationship with landscapes in Dartmoor, St Kilda and Swaledale has been marked by a passion that has bordered, by his own admission, on the obsessional, this may seem an oddly unsympathetic remark. The point Fleming is making, however, is not that we should not 'love' our landscapes, but that researchers have tended to idealise *their* landscapes (as lovers idealise each other), ignoring the realities, problems and potentials of what should properly be an ongoing relationship with the land. Thus, he goes on to say: 'Should we not try to get away from the local study as love letter and try to write about the conflicts, the uncertainties, the paradoxes, the unfinished and the unfolding – in short to convey some sense of an ongoing relationship between researcher and landscape, between the present and the past?' (1998, 155).

Love is not written out entirely here however. Indeed, we take Fleming to mean that archaeologists should be writing not landscape love letters, but landscape love *stories*: evolving tales that embrace the present as well as the past, and others as well as ourselves. Fleming's own elegiac accounts of his work in some of the remotest landscapes of the British Isles may surely be best seen in precisely this light, and this contribution similarly takes Fleming's critique of love and landscape as its own starting point.

Focusing on our ongoing upland research project in the North Pennines, we chart our changing relationship with a landscape that we have known for many years. What started out more than 20 years ago as precisely the kind of 'love letter' described by

Fleming has evolved into the sort of love story that today, we hope, would meet with his approval.

WEARDALE 1973–98: ROB'S RESEARCH

Writing in 1833, the great lead mine manager and engineer Thomas Sopwith said 'There are not perhaps in all England three contiguous dales of greater interest and beauty than the mining dales of Tyne, Wear and Tees yet they are comparatively unknown to the public' (1833, 16). His comment has a ring of truth even today. The Wear Valley has been of great industrial importance to the north-east of England, but Weardale (the upper section of the Wear Valley, west of Bishop Auckland) remains sparsely inhabited, under funded and poorly understood.

The area has no tradition of landscape archaeology, but it has seen concerted local archaeological interest since the nineteenth century. Towards the end of that century, however, the area was written off by no less a figure than the great Canon Greenwell himself. Having dismissed the archaeological potential of County Durham as whole, Greenwell went on to say of the dales that 'the west of the county, consisting of a tract of high land which has never been cultivated, would in other similarly circumstanced parts of England have been occupied with the cairns and barrows of the people who once lived there but such monuments are almost entirely lacking on the Durham moorlands' (1877, 440).

This was also a view that most of the regions 'academic' archaeologists held in the 1970s and this situation set me off on a youthful (and no doubt youthfully arrogant!) campaign to prove the Canon and several members of the archaeology department at Durham University wrong in their assumptions about Weardale's archaeology. I commenced my doctoral research on 'Aspects of the Prehistoric Archaeology of the Wear Valley' in 1975, and realise now that my feelings about the Wear Valley (and Weardale in particular) were akin to Fleming's notion that the loved one was unique and special. I was born and bred in County Durham and it has always been my spiritual home, no matter where I have lived and worked.

In 1977 I began excavation and survey work at Crawley Edge, above Stanhope, where the late Lesley Lister had identified the first recorded cairnfield site in the county (Young and Welfare 1977, 1978; Young, 1992). A year later I published a general discussion on the Bronze Age archaeology of Weardale (Young 1978) and in 1980 I also identified the first barrow sites in the dale (Young 980, 1988). In the same year, I discussed Weardale's prehistory in the Durham Archaeology Committee's report on 'The Archaeology of the Durham Dales'. In 1986 I turned my attention to archaeological formation processes in the dale (Young 1986, 1995a, 1995b), and 1987 saw the publication of *Lithics and Subsistence in the North-East of England* (Young 1987). Throughout the 1990s I continued to publish on Weardale's archaeology, producing among others, papers on earthwork survey and stone axe distributions (Young 1993, 1994).

Looking at these publications against the backdrop of Fleming's comments, I have come to consider that my early writing on Weardale attempted to point out, to anyone who would read them, the potential importance and uniqueness of this one valley in the North Pennines. Mine was certainly an unqualified love and it provoked some animated discussions with colleagues at Leicester University about the importance and worth of 'local' and 'regional' archaeological research. But even as I defended my corner here, I was reifying 'my' landscape and its archaeology and turning it simply into a 'subject' to be studied. I remain convinced of the importance and worth of good, well thought out, local archaeology projects (after all, one person's archaeological doorstep is often the focus of another's internationally recognised research, and to propose that proximity necessarily breeds research of parochial importance is simply insulting). Yet, I am forced to concur with Fleming's observations that 'in a sense we can now almost write local studies in our sleep' (1998, 154). As he goes on to say: 'Sooner or later most parishes and regions in Britain will have their chroniclers. These studies will often be very detailed; after all it is deep local knowledge which gives their authors their authority. But there is a danger that these studies will become neat little packages' (1998, 154).

One such hermetically sealed package of my own devising was the Bollihope Common Archaeology Project, begun in earnest in the mid-1980s, and designed primarily as a student training exercise.

ORIGINS OF THE BOLLIHOPE COMMON ARCHAEOLOGY PROJECT

The Bollihope Burn is a tributary of the Wear and Bollihope Common lies on the edge of what is today the North Pennines Area of Outstanding Natural Beauty. The authors have co-directed the Bollihope Common Archaeology Project since 1998, but its inception dates back to 1976 when R.Y. was drawn to the Common by Dennis Harding's air photograph of the enclosure at Peg's House with its associated longhouse. Brian Roberts (1978) had carried out pollen analysis in the immediate area in the early 1970s and he had surveyed a small enclosure and a round house (site No. 15) (58) located further up the valley from Peg's House. This prompted a site visit and further discoveries were made.

From 1986 R.Y. worked at Leicester University and generations of Leicester students have contributed to the production of a general plan of the Common's upstanding archaeology. This work along with related palaeoenvironmental research, has contributed a great deal to our understanding of the development of this part of the North Pennines. It has also thrown up intriguing issues for future resolution.

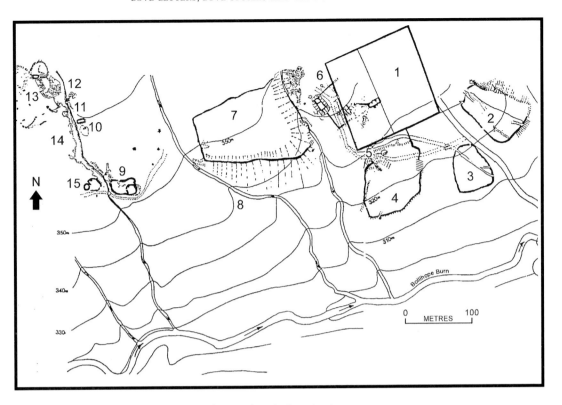

58 Bollihope common. Figures relate to descriptions in the text

For example, the nineteenth-century enclosure of Peg's House cuts the top of a large enclosure. A small flush bog overlies the eastern wall of the latter, and coring for pollen samples has revealed that bog formation commenced some time in the twelfth to thirteenth centuries AD. On the basis of available radiocarbon dates, observation of the stratigraphy of the underlying sediments and calculations of the rate of peat accumulation, it is argued that the enclosure may be of tenth-century date. If this is so then the hut platform on its northern side is of particular interest and is deserving of future excavation. This date also ties in well with that obtained from charcoal samples extracted from lead slag (see below) and may indicate an important pre-Norman element present in the Bollihope landscape.

Peg's House Enclosure itself (1) is a rectangular, dry-stone walled structure, used as a sheepfold. It encloses nearly four acres and is owned by four local farmers. The walls are 1.75m high and probably of eighteenth- or early nineteenth-century date. Inside the enclosure there are several earthwork features, the main one being a clear longhouse with slightly bowed sides and associated enclosure walling. This is earlier than Peg's House and on a different alignment to it.

Peg's House appears on the 1858 Ordnance Survey map, and it is referred to as 'an allotment', in the Halmote Court records for 1807 (Manchester, pers. comm.) but it was not included in the late eighteenth-century Enclosure Act for Weardale. Drury believes that it was, therefore, constructed around 1807 (Linda Drury pers. comm.). It is unusual to find a single, large enclosure like Peg's House, on an unenclosed common, and there is nothing comparable anywhere else in the dale.

Sites 2, 3 and 4 represent collapsed dry-stone enclosures. No. 4 is of particular interest. It measures c.80-100m across and on the north, uphill, side towards Peg's House there is a small sub-rectangular hut/building platform scarped into the hillside. The eastern wall of the enclosure runs beneath a small bog, the importance of which has been discussed above. The northern edge of the enclosure has clearly been robbed of stone in the construction of Peg's House.

A modern sheep shelter has been constructed at 5, while the building and related enclosure walling of site 6 is another intriguing feature on the Common. This appears to be an eighteenth- or nineteenth-century building, of dry-stone construction, that seems to have been sited on earlier foundations. It has its own enclosure that is, in turn, cut by Peg's House and it was probably robbed during the latter's construction. This building appears on the Ordnance Survey map of 1858 as a sheepfold. Pottery from rabbit burrows along the edge of the structure suggests eighteenth- to nineteenth-century activity and fire brick from the interior rubble suggests the presence of an oven, possibly on the southern gable wall.

To the east of site 6 is another massive dry-stone built contour enclosure (7). Its walling has slumped down the valley side on the southern and eastern edges, but the structure and related bank and ditch are well preserved to the north and west. There are no obvious features within it, and downslope from this enclosure, to the south, is another small, sub-rectangular dry-stone structure, associated with several small coal pits. There is one large heap of shale overburden to the east of the structure and the pits (8).

Site 9 consists of a sub-rectangular dry-stone enclosure built over the levelled foundations of an earlier circular structure. On the NW corner, collapsed stone indicates the presence of buildings, subsequently confirmed by excavation in 2005-6. Work in 1990 revealed a scatter of bloomery slag (iron) in the SW corner of the site, and this too has been shown by excavation to be the site of a Romano-British furnace. Eroding from the streamside, to the west of this enclosure, along its course up to site 13, are large concentrations of both iron and lead slag.

Moving up the eastern side of this stream, site 10 is a sub-rectangular dry-stone building, associated with the remains of a furnace, possibly for lead smelting, and another small sub-rectangular building is located at 11. This was partly destroyed when the stream was widened for drainage improvement in the late 1970s. Site 12 is a small sub-circular stone-built platform of uncertain date and function.

Site 13 at the head of the stream is a classic, well-preserved, medieval/post-medieval shieling site. This is an area of enclosures and clearance cairns, associated with a series of dry-stone structures that are probably huts. To the north of this cluster, and not shown on the map is the site of Brian's Folds, which again appears on the first edition of the Ordnance Survey map.

Moving south, down the western side of the stream there is an area of industrial activity (14) represented by several furnaces cut into the stream terrace. Large fragments of highly vitrified furnace lining have been recovered here and charcoal from a slag sample taken from the east of the stream in this area has produced a tenth-century AD radiocarbon date. Analysis of slag from a feature at the stream edge showed the presence of 70-90 per cent lead oxide. This is unlikely to be a waste product from lead smelting as the remaining lead content is very high. As a result, two alternative interpretations are possible: the slag may represent an intermediate residue from a two-stage lead smelting process, or it is a waste product from silver refining. Either way, these deposits will repay further research.

Site 15 was a small sub-rectangular enclosure with a circular stone-built hut. It also had a horseshoe-shaped feature attached to the hut and the enclosure had an east-facing entrance. The site was well preserved and was the target of our first excavations on the Common. The whole of the fell side to the west of the stream is littered with small cairns.

As this summary suggests, the survey work carried out at Bollihope indicates that lead exploitation in the area dates back to at least the Norman period. Documentary records (particularly those of the Bishops of Durham for the medieval period) show that mining and smelting were undertaken throughout the medieval and post-medieval periods, and three adits on the south side of the Bollihope Burn probably date to the eighteenth or nineteenth century, as they resemble other horseshoe-shaped adits from this period. It is important to note in this context that from the 1840s to the 1860s, the North Pennine dales (comprising Weardale, Teesdale, Alston Moor and Allendale) formed the most important lead-mining area in the world, with 30 per cent of Britain's lead coming from the region. Bollihope Common is therefore potentially a most important locale for the exploration of continuity and change among lead-working communities over the (very) long term. We come back to this point below.

EXCAVATIONS FROM 1998-2000

In 1998 my relationship with the Bollihope landscape entered a new phase, as Jane Webster became co-director of the project and we began the first stage of a long-tern excavation programme on the Common.

Our initial excavation target was a roundhouse complex (No. 15), and our aim was to answer questions about changing social and economic relations during the Iron Age/Romano-British transition, as well as dating some of the features identified in the field survey. We were (and still are) particularly interested in examining traditional models of 'upland desertion' in the Late Bronze Age/Iron Age and we also wanted to test whether some of the ritual deposition activities now being recognised on Iron Age domestic sites in southern England also occurred in the north. At the same time, we were interested in levels of 'Romanisation' among Romano-British households in a location that, whilst remote, is only 58km from Hadrian's Wall, and 40km from the Roman fort at Piercebridge.

At this stage, however, our involvement with the landscape and the sites was still largely like that of the literate lover. We had a relationship that was 'special' and only 'shared' with others smitten by the same bug. In other words the project retained, at this time, an air of exclusivity: we turned up for one month each year, bringing a community of diggers with us, and engaged in only limited ways with the community around us.

BOLLIHOPE COMMON 2000–PRESENT: A COMMUNITY STORY

Between 1998 and 2004 we excavated site 15 in its entirety. It remains the only Iron Age/Romano-British farmstead in the north-east to have been completely investigated (Young and Webster 2006). In 2005 and 2006 work commenced on a further enclosure, site 9. This revealed evidence for a two-phase circular building, abutted by a later enclosure wall and also the remains of a Romano-British iron-smelting site and related charcoal making pit (59). The recovery of several fragments of multi-coloured Roman glass from vessels and bangles in 2006 also raises some interesting questions about the nature of the links between the Bollihope sites and the wider contemporary community. These discoveries were made against the backdrop of a changing relationship with the landscape, and an evolving interest in community archaeology.

The year 2000 brought developments that together altered our sensibilities in relation to the North Pennines landscape. The first of these was the impact of the foot and mouth outbreak of 2000. The north-east was particularly badly affected, and for two years we were unable to gain access to the Common at all. This enforced lay-off made us re-think our attitudes to Bollihope. Through conversations with our good friend, the late, and much missed, Denis Coggins (archaeologist and farmer) and others, we learned some important lessons about the tensions and potential problems of upland farming that have impacted upon our views about what it is like to inhabit a landscape, and to invest in it (in all senses of that word), rather than simply 'study' it.

The year 2000 also saw the birth of our son Adam and in 2001 R.Y. became the Archaeologist for the Northumberland National Park. This necessitated a shift northwards and we moved to Stanhope, a Weardale village just to the north of Bollihope Common. No longer simply visiting academics, we now lived in the area

59 Excavation at site 9

that we were researching – and we soon found out that local interest in our work was enormous.

When Adam started nursery school he happily told staff and pupils that his mother and father 'were archaeologies', and local people began approaching us about our work, and the possibilities for joining in. From such simple beginnings, we began to grasp that we had wholly failed to tap into a well of local interest in a landscape that was not just *ours*, but *theirs*. In 2004 we opened up the excavation project to local volunteers (of all ages), who were invited to come along and dig alongside the undergraduates who still make up the majority of the annual excavation team. In exchange for their time, we provided volunteers with exactly the same range of training experiences we offered our undergraduate diggers.

The results were so encouraging that when the season ended, we sought for new ways to broaden the scope and local appeal of our research. In 2005 we approached the North Pennines AONB for a small grant to develop our community outreach, and the supportive AONB staff in turn pointed us towards other local organisations with an interest in community and heritage issues. Money and help in kind have subsequently been forthcoming from the AONB Partnership, The Durham Association, the Weardale Community Partnership and the Dales Centre in Stanhope. We have put some of that money towards volunteer transport costs, and the rest has been invested in basic excavation kit that can be used by volunteers who want to work on the site, but may not want to invest in their own trowels and buckets. Each season, we also offer a series of guided site walks (with free transport provided) and evening talks, and continue to be astounded by the large numbers of people prepared to turn out on a damp Thursday evening for a walk across Bollihope Common. There is a lot of good, grass-roots archaeology going on in Weardale, and many of the volunteers who come to us have also contributed to local fieldwork and conservation projects led by Ros Nicol, Tom Gledhill, and Ian Forbes (Director of the Killhope Lead Mining Museum). Together we have begun to train local people to excavate and to survey. With Ian Forbes, we are currently exploring initiatives that will enable us to provide training in the recognition, classification and survey of lead-extraction sites in the Bollihope and Killhope regions.

We have also developed very close links with local primary schools in Weardale and Teesdale. Every year since 2004 we have hosted regular visits by school parties, and have developed a schools' information pack, focusing on the Bollihope roundhouses, which is sent out in advance of school visits. The Museum of Antiquities at Newcastle allow us to borrow a range of real and reproduction artefacts (including a much-loved model roundhouse) that are of enormous value in bringing the site alive to children, and staff from the Museum have generously contributed their time to the project, by offering talks and finds-identification sessions. The presence of children on the site has had some unlooked-for, but most pleasing, consequences. Many of the undergraduates who train with us have an interest in working with children, and at the suggestion of some of the 2005 excavation team we developed a 'children's tour', which undergraduate volunteers now offer to every child who comes to the site. In 2006, a group of undergraduates who had worked with children at Bollihope played a leading role in the establishment of a new branch of the Young Archaeologists Club, based at the Museum of Antiquities in Newcastle (60).

Undergraduates coming to Bollihope today work in a different kind of environment to that experienced by students before 2004. They rapidly come to see that they are taking part in something that extends beyond their fieldwork training requirements and our academic research. They work alongside people of all ages, and are keen to impart what they have learned to these visitors. As a result, when they visit the village in the evenings they are among friends rather than strangers. It has been much the same for us too. Since 2004, we have signally altered our relationship with the landscape we are studying, and the kind of archaeology that we are doing.

60 Excavation in progress, Bollihope Common

The Bollihope experience has shown us that there is a fundamental difference between the landscape as a place in which to live, and the landscape as an object of study. The Bollihope Common Archaeology Project is today characterised by a two-way exchange of views and experiences, as 'incoming' students and resident 'local archaeologists' encounter each other each year. There is a shared strength of feeling about 'place': something that archaeologists who are not part of the communities that they study can only glimpse. Perhaps most importantly, local people are producing their own archaeology as opposed to simply consuming 'expert' opinion. Certainly, the input of local knowledge into the project has given us a far more nuanced understanding of how the landscape works, and that has also led to a shift in our own interests.

We have become much more interested in the more recent history of Bollihope Common, and the social and industrial archaeology of the extraction industries in particular, but have only been able to move in this direction by drawing on the expertise of other, locally based fieldworkers (such as Tom Gledhill and Ian Forbes) whose expertise are far greater than our own. We are able to do that because we, and they, share both a community, and a communal interest.

We believe that since 2004 we have made a break with the notion of the local study as love letter. The letters haven't necessarily been burned, but our awareness and understanding of how to fully engage with landscape and archaeology in a pro-active and more socially inclusive way has meant that their 'secrecy' is outdated and their sentiments have been more widely shared. As Doris Day would have said: 'Our secret love's no secret any more'!

BIBLIOGRAPHY

Dodgshon, R.A. & Butlin, R.A. (eds), 1978 *An Historical Geography of England and Wales*. London: Academic Press.

Fleming, A., 1998 *Swaledale: The Valley of the Wild River*. Edinburgh: Edinburgh University Press.

Greenwell, W., 1877 *British Barrows*. Oxford: Clarendon Press.

Manby, T.G. & Turnbull, P. (eds), 1986 *Archaeology in the Pennines: Studies in Honour of Arthur Raistrick*. Oxford: BAR.

Roberts, B.K., 1978 Perspectives on prehistory. In Dodgshon, R.A. & Butlin, R.A. (eds), 1-27.

Sopwith, R., 1833 *Alston Moor, Weardale and Teesdale*.

Young, R., 1978 Aspects of the bronze age archaeology of Weardale. *Journal of Weardale Field Study Society* 1, 15-29.

Young, R., 1980 An inventory of barrows in County Durham. *Transactions of the Architectural and Archaeological Society of Durham and Northumberland* (new series) 5, 1-16.

Young, R., 1986 Destruction, preservation and recovery: Weardale, a case study. In Manby, T.G. & Turnbull, P. (eds), 213-27.

Young, R., 1987 *Lithics and Subsistence in North-Eastern England*. Oxford: BAR.

Young, R., 1988 Barrows, clearance and land-use: some suggestions from the north-east of England. *Landscape History* 9, 27-35.

Young, R., 1992 Fieldwork and excavation at the Crawley Edge, Cairnfield, Stanhope, Co. Durham. *Durham Archaeological Journal* 8, 27-49.

Young, R., 1993 Three earthwork sites in Weardale. *Durham Archaeological Journal* 9, 9-17.

Young, R., 1994 Polished stone axes between the Tyne and the Tees. *Durham Archaeological Journal* 10, 1-12.

Young, R., 1995a Destruction is only one facet: A study of formation processes and the generation of distribution patterns for later prehistory in Northern England. *Landscape History* 16, 5-16.

Young, R., 1995b Recent fieldwork in Weardale and the formation of the archaeological record. *Journal of the Weardale Field Study Society* 8, 1-9.

Young, R. & Webster J., 2006 Survey and excavation on Bollihope Common. *Archaeology County Durham* 1, 14-19.

Young, R. & Welfare, A.T., 1977 An interim note on excavations at Crawley Edge, Stanhope in Weardale, Durham. *Council for British Archaeology, Regional Group 3, Series* 1, 15, 3-5.

Young, R. & Welfare, A.T., 1978 Excavations at Crawley Edge, Stanhope in Weardale, Co. Durham 1976-77. *University of Durham Archaeological Reports for 1977*, 8-11.

20

A MONUMENTAL CONTRIBUTION? SIR JOHN GARDNER WILKINSON'S NEGLECTED SURVEYS OF 'BRITISH' SITES IN PERSPECTIVE

C. Stephen Briggs

INTRODUCTION

The purpose of this note is to draw attention to the little-known fieldwork and interpretations of early monuments and landscapes in Britain made by the nineteenth-century antiquary, Sir John Gardner Wilkinson (1797-1875). Wilkinson is moderately well known for his books and pioneering records on Egypt – and arguably the founder of Egyptology in Britain (Thompson 1992; 2004). That scholarly esteem rests on travel and explorations abroad undertaken earlier in life, mainly during the 1830s, but sporadically thereafter until the mid-1850s. It is not now so well appreciated that the type of accurate records he first made of Egyptian monuments, and the sort of topographical recording he later undertook during extensive travels in Europe and in the Mediterranean, were later adopted and applied to upland archaeology in Britain, mainly between *c.*1855 and 1870. Over those years, with unfaltering curiosity but against slowly failing health, he visited and surveyed a number of early sites and landscapes in England and Wales of varying interest and importance. The subject-matter that attracted him, mainly, though by no means all of it, prehistoric in origin, will be introduced briefly here. A more comprehensive discussion of the site plans and drawings Wilkinson produced for a variety of monument types in Britain is in preparation.

RESIDENCE AND FIELDWORK IN GLAMORGAN

Most of Wilkinson's fieldwork in Britain was accomplished after he married in 1855. At first the couple lived in Tenby, then in 1866 they leased a house called Brynfield at Reynoldston in Gower (Briggs forthcoming (1); Gabb 2007; Thompson and Lucas 1995). Cefn Bryn was right on the doorstep, so his immediate outlook was a curious archaeologist's dream. As he would later show, Rhossili Down's moorland heath was also covered in early land-clearance features complemented by two or three Neolithic megalithic tombs and a handful of cairns or circles, probably Early Bronze Age in date (Wilkinson 1862; 1870).

Having closely examined the archaeology of the area for up to a decade before moving there, Gardner Wilkinson knew the value of the archaeological source so close to his new home. Engravings of its most arresting monuments and a report on his excavations there had been included in his 'Dartmoor' paper probably soon after he had examined them around 1860. Among several features then described, was a circular cairn made up of three concentric rows of stones, the outer one 31ft in diameter (Wilkinson 1862, 39; Briggs forthcoming (1)). Nearby, a mound of earth and stone surrounded by a circle of large stones, some 33ft in diameter, was excavated. Within its mass was a hearth of flat stones which showed evidence of burning. Similar hearths and burning were found to be common to other cairn sites in the locality. Wilkinson's better-known 1870 paper on Gower included a distribution map showing megaliths, circles, clearance and burial cairns on Cefn Bryn, and though this plan was overlooked by RCAHMW in their 1976 *Inventory* (it was missing from the office copy of *Archaeologia Cambrensis*), this and Wilkinson's other work in the locality usefully informed a valuable programme of field survey and excavation by Anthony Ward (1985; 1987; 1988; 1989) of which Thompson and Lucas (1995) were apparently unaware (Briggs forthcoming (2)).

DARTMOOR

Outside Wales, Wilkinson's best-known published surveys were centred on prehistoric Dartmoor (Wilkinson 1860a; 1861; 1862). His first two papers were concerned to explain the varied detail of building techniques observable in the wall construction of virtually all early upland field monument structures. He was also greatly exercised by the morphology and location of primitive huts (Wilkinson 1860a passim). But he could not appreciate that they were possibly Bronze Age or Iron Age in origin. Even if a little short on any novel analysis of the Dartmoor walls, it is significant to the development of early land-division studies (cf. Fleming 1979) that he at least recognised 'boundary walls, which stretch for hill and dale on Dartmoor, and which are found in Cornwall, Wales and other parts of the island … built of stones of … large dimensions … in like manner of blocks placed upright, or on their edges, or flat on their sides, generally in a single row' (Wilkinson 1861, 6). By 1862 he was venturing to expand this study to include pounds and settlements (Wilkinson 1862, 115-21).

The 1862 paper was important because Wilkinson not only used it to summarise all his ongoing researches in Devon and in Wales, but also to propose a remarkable research strategy for the future study of upland field monuments. This he achieved

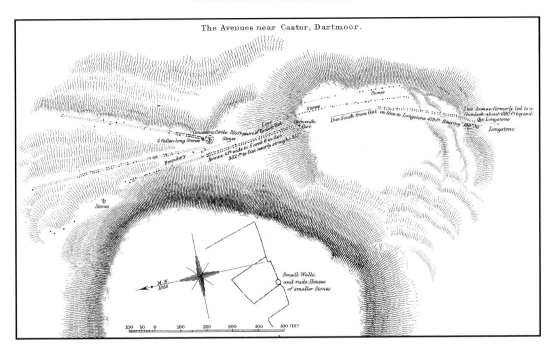

61 Shovell Down, Dartmoor. This accurate survey clearly shows the relationship between a major reave, a structured cairn and ritual or ceremonial avenue, and nearby fieldwalls and huts. *From Wilkinson 1862*

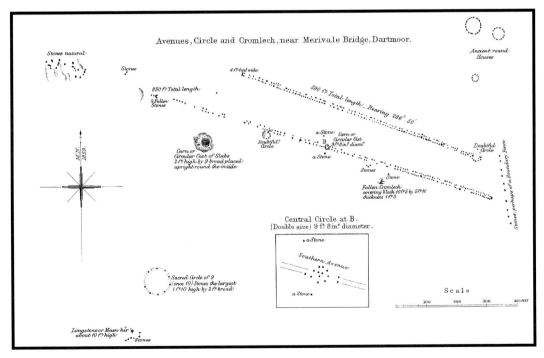

62 Sites near Merrivale Bridge, Dartmoor. An early survey plotting the ceremonial avenues, stone circles and cairns in relation to a major reave and hut circles. *From Wilkinson 1862*

through a classification incorporating almost every conceivable type of (mainly upland) monument into 18 groups. His accompanying discussion, some of it prescient for its day, suggested how some of the features had been agricultural clearances as well as land boundaries, a deduction which was to catch Andrew Fleming's eye when researching the Dartmoor reaves over a century later (Fleming 1988, 19). Indeed, Wilkinson's plans of Shovell Down (*61*) and of the Merrivale area (*62*) must be among the earliest large-scale surveys to show how major reaves were related to ritual and settlement monuments on the ground.

MEGALITHIC TOMBS

Besides publishing plans and sections of the Rhossili tombs from his Glamorgan fieldwork campaigns, Wilkinson also visited and described 14 megalithic tombs in Pembrokeshire (1871b). He printed plans and sections of a dozen (*63, 64*) and listed another 13 tombs in the county which he had not visited, and apparently also visited and planned the Marros megaliths in Carmarthenshire (drawings listed in Flynn 1997; plan in Wilkinson 1870, 121).

It is also apparent from the material listed in his notebooks that Wilkinson also knew several Severn-Cotswold tombs outside South Wales (Flynn 1997). They included Stoney Littleton (Somerset), Nettleton (Wiltshire), Rodmarton and Uley (Gloucestershire).

Gardner Wilkinson believed only in a pre-Roman, British Druidical society and had no concept of any further chronological subdivisions. And without these his understanding of the monuments and interpretations of any stratigraphies he might encounter, were seriously deficient. Sadly, for him, all pre-Roman monuments would remain simply 'British' for the rest of his life (Wilkinson 1871b, 239). In these beliefs, he was in good company among the older antiquarians. Although Daniel Wilson had publicly embraced the concept of a chronological succession from stone to bronze and iron in his *Annals of Prehistoric Scotland* of 1851, and Sir John Lubbock was successfully popularising this and other 'new' ideas in his *Prehistoric Times* (the first edition of which had appeared in 1865) many older, more conservative antiquarians were still reluctant to embrace this chronology for another 20 years (Briggs 2007; Rowley-Conwy 2007).

Another way in which Wilkinson's approach differed fundamentally from most archaeologists' views of the present day, was how he related the sites' settings to contemporary topography and to land-use history. The notion that megalithic monuments were originally built to be seen as gaunt architectural exhibits free of covering mounds probably antedates William Stukeley (1687-1765). One of Wilkinson's contemporaries, Sir James Ferguson, certainly upheld that view and lacking any sense of time perspective or of changing land-use practices since the

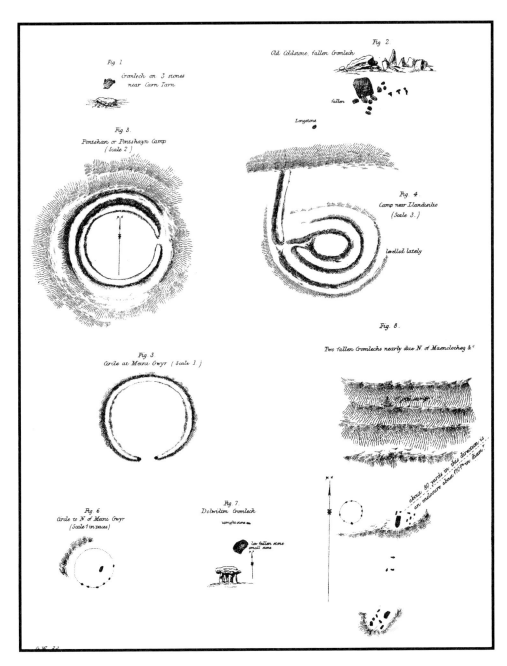

63 Megalithic tombs and stone circles in Pembrokeshire: 1: Carn Tarn, nr Ffynnonau, 2: Old Coldstone, nr St Dogwell's (fallen), 3: Pontshan or Pontshayn Camp, 4: Camp near Llandisilio, 5: Circle at Meini Gwyr, 6: Circle N of Meini Gwyr, 7: Dolwillim, Llanglydwen, 8: Two fallen cromlechs nearly due north of Maenclochog. *From Wilkinson 1871b*

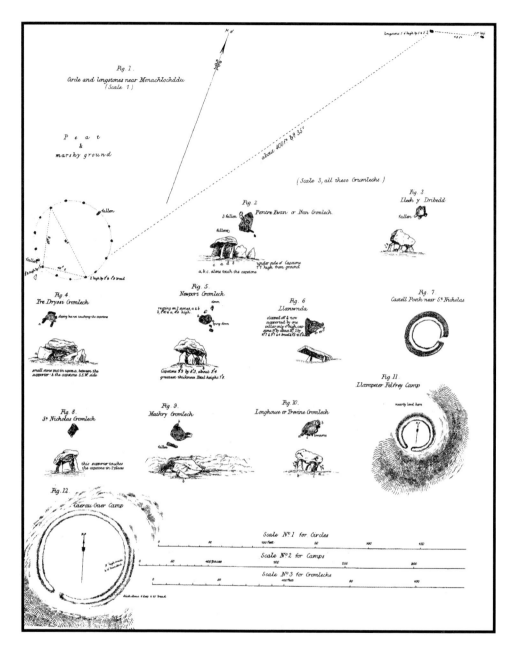

64 Megalithic tombs, small hillforts and raths in Pembrokeshire: 1: Circle and Longstones near Monchclogddu [Mynachclogddu], 2: Pentre Ifan, 3: Llech y Ddribedd, 4: Trellyffant or Trellyffan near Tre Dryssi, 5: Carreg Goetan [Coetan], Newport, 6: [Penrhiw] Llanwnda, north-west of Fishguard, 7 Castell Poeth near St Nicholas, 8: St Nicholas, south of Castell Porth, 9: Mathry Cromlech, 10: Longhouse or Trevine, 11: Lampeter Felfrey Camp, 12: Caerau Gaer Camp. *From Wilkinson 1871b*

Neolithic, he believed absences of local memory of monument denudation were sufficient to support it (Ferguson 1876, 44-5). Gardner Wilkinson apparently 'for some time … sided with [Ferguson] … but on entering more closely into the question, his sound judgement prevailed and without the slightest hesitation he acknowledged his complete concession to the side he had so long opposed' (Anon. 1876, 66). Although his original view is not obviously in evidence in print, his reversal of opinion is made plain in a discussion of Pentre Ifan and Manorbeer (Wilkinson 1871b).

In a similar vein, archaeologists in Britain are inclined to think of landscape phenomenology as a recent fashion. However, like the problem of megalith denudation, phenomenology is another notion with deep roots in earlier antiquarian literature. Indeed, interests in the relationship between natural rock outcrops and early spirituality were certainly being expressed in Stukeley's day. By the 1830s those spectacular upstanding features of differentially eroded rock outcrops, known in some parts as 'Tors', could attract as much attention as the larger man-made prehistoric sites (Evans 1994). Himself fascinated by such rock formations, and probably borrowing his engravings direct from Borlase's *Antiquities of Cornwall of 1754*, Wilkinson depicted two such 'Tors' – The Cheesewring and Mistor. These he compared to the Derbyshire 'Cakes of Bread' rock formations of similarly natural origin, in an exercise not difficult to explain of an antiquary whose prehistory was, like that of the Cornish scholar who inspired him, still well-peopled by Druids (Wilkinson 1860-61).

GARDNER WILKINSON: A BRITISH ANTIQUARIAN?

Assessing Gardner Wilkinson's place in the antiquarian community of mid-nineteenth century Britain is not easy. Whereas he did accept Fellowship to the Royal Society, unlike his father he was never elected to the Society of Antiquaries (Thompson 1992; Bernard Nurse, pers. comm.). He may have fought shy of close involvement in British archaeology after an initially bruising encounter with certain dissident members of the young British Archaeological Association in 1845. Early that year, they vainly preyed on his good name in support of a secessionist plot which resulted in the establishment of The Archaeological Institute at Winchester that September (Wetherall 1994). In the event, he was 'altogether in the dark about these differences', or of the 'war' between the older and newer factions, as he was in Egypt or Malta at the time (Anon. 1845).

The Athenaeum's account of these events mockingly underlined what journalists clearly believed was a class distinction between the two new-born national societies. It may therefore be significant that Wilkinson remained and eventually published with the more-establishment Archaeological Association, in which he also held office as a Vice-President (Briggs forthcoming). He was also to be appointed a Vice-President of the Cambrian Archaeological Association.

Gardner Wilkinson's studies of British sites have been used by only a limited number of later researchers. In Wales, his study on the megalithic sites of Pembrokeshire (Wilkinson 1871) though published rather obscurely, was known to Edward Owen and the staff of the Royal Commission on Ancient and Historic Monuments (RCAHMW 1925) and to W.F. Grimes (1963), who meticulously compared his own stone circle surveys with Wilkinson's. But the same source has escaped Burl's usually thorough bibliographies of early stone circles and alignments (the most recent in 2000) and was also overlooked in Lynch's (1972) work covering some of the same megaliths. More recently, Barker (1992) did usefully compare Wilkinson's early plans with the state of the Neolithic tombs in Pembrokeshire as he found them during the 1980s.

Wilkinson's thorough exploration of Rhossili Down is reasonably familiar to archaeologists in Wales through his 1870 *Archaeologia Cambrensis* paper (noted in Powell *et al.* 1967; RCAHMW 1976; Ward 1985; 1987; 1988). Unfortunately, however, his engravings of Rhossili's most arresting monuments and brief reports on the same excavations published in his Dartmoor 'research strategy' eight years earlier (Wilkinson 1862) have largely escaped notice both in Wales and beyond.

Traditions of accurate site and landscape survey and depiction were not strongly developed in Britain in 1860, when Wilkinson began his British investigations. Although Augustus Lane-Fox (later General Pitt Rivers) probably began planning monuments with precision in the course of the following decade, it took almost 20 years for him to get into his stride (Bowden 1991). So collectively, as a group of plans and sections, Wilkinson's published graphics of the early 1860s come quite early in the history of reliable archaeological mensuration. Whereas these have not all been checked systematically on the ground, those who have used them – particularly Barker and Grimes in Wales – seem convinced of their value. Indeed, writing soon after Wilkinson's death, Sir Samuel Ferguson (1876) enthused (that unlike Bateman's survey of the site) his engraving of Arbor Low (Wilkinson 1862) may be thoroughly depended upon. It can thus be safely concluded that Wilkinson's graphics of British monuments bear testimony to a quality of precision and presentation rare among his contemporaries in Britain before Pitt Rivers. Neglect of these important records therefore seems to be due to blanket rejection of his work because of its old-fashioned, Druidical interpretations.

It is easy to forget that although now a mainstream interest for many later prehistorians, the study of cup-and-ring marked boulders only became fashionable in Britain during the 1860s. Here, at least one researcher credited Gardner Wilkinson with being among the first to popularise that interest, taking 1835 as the first year he had observed cup-and-ring markings at Long Meg near Penrith (Astley 1911; Wilkinson 1860b).

Gardner Wilkinson's interests were broad. He would appear to have had views on cave stratigraphies, he was fascinated by all manner of later prehistoric monuments, had more than a nodding acquaintance with Roman sites and inscribed stones (Wilkinson 1871a), and sketched or planned church architecture and other medieval features. As an early conservationist he was also effective in preventing the unnecessary destruction of a medieval gate in Tenby town wall (under threat from the town's Corporation) in 1867-9 and helping to save it for posterity (Thompson 1992).

Gardner Wilkinson's greatest legacy to research on British prehistoric sites, as for the Egyptian monuments, is probably still to be found in his manuscripts. Bequeathed to relatives at Calke Abbey, an extensive collection of notebooks, drawings and surveys amassed throughout his scholarly life was eventually passed to the Bodleian Library in 1985 mainly through the good offices of the National Trust. This is now comprehensively chronicled and available online (Flynn 1997). Though already well-used by Egyptologists, his notebooks and drawings of British sites, a potentially rich source of important antiquarian records, appear to remain neglected. What is now required is a comprehensive correlation between Wilkinson's manuscript surveys, his printed articles and, where their sites are ascertainable, the monuments themselves.

ACKNOWLEDGEMENTS

In producing this article the writer gratefully acknowledges the help of Mr John Barnatt (Peak District National Park), Andrew Fleming, Gerald Gabb (Swansea Museum), Debbie Griffiths (Dartmoor National Park), Bernard Morris (Gower Society), Bernard Nurse (Society of Antiquaries), John Parkinson (National Trust, Calke Abbey), Sian Rees (Cadw), Peter Topping (English Heritage) and Anthony Ward (University of Kent).

BIBLIOGRAPHY

Anon., 1845 Our weekly gossip. *The Athenaeum* Mar 15, 269-70.

Anon., 1876 'Obituary: Sir John Gardener Wilkinson', *Archaeologia Cambrensis* 31 (Series 4,7), 66-7.

Astley, H.J. Dunkinfield, 1911 Cup-and-ring markings: their origin and significance. *Journal of the Royal Anthropological Institute* 41, 83-100.

Barker, C.T.,1992 *The Chambered Tombs of South-West Wales. Re-assessment of the Burial Monuments of Carmarthenshire and Pembrokeshire.* Oxford: Oxbow.

Bowden, M.C.B., 1991 *Pitt Rivers: the life and archaeological work of Lieutenant-General Augustus Henry Lane Fox Pitt Rivers DCL, FRS, FSA.* Cambridge: Cambridge University Press.

Briggs, C.S., 2007 Prehistory in the Nineteenth Century. In Pearce, S.M. (ed.), 226-65.

Briggs, C.S., forthcoming (1) 'An Egyptologist abroad: Sir John Gardner Wilkinson and some *British* monuments in Gower', *Gower* 2008

Briggs, C.S., forthcoming (2) *A Prehistory of the British Archaeological Association and the Royal Archaeological Institute.*

Burl, A., 2000 *Stone Circles of the British Isles.* Yale University Press: New Haven.

Evans, C., 1994 Natural wonders and national monuments: a meditation upon the fact of the Tolmen. *Antiquity* 68, 200-8.

Ferguson, S., 1872 *Rude Stone Monuments in all Countries: their age and uses.* London: John Murray.

Foster, I.L. & Alcock, L. (eds), 1963 *Culture and Environment: essays in honour of Sir Cyril Fox.* London: Routledge.

Fleming, A., 1979 Dartmoor reaves: a nineteenth century fiasco. *Antiquity* 52, 16-9.

Fleming, A., 1988 *The Dartmoor Reaves: investigating prehistoric land divisions*. London: Batsford.

Flynn, S.J.A., 1997 *Catalogue of the Papers of Sir John Gardner Wilkinson 1797-1875* [www.bodley. ox.ac.uk/dept/scwmss/wmss/online/1500-1900/wilkinson/wilkinson000.html, accessed 4 April 2007].

Gabb, G., 2007 *Swansea and its History*, Vol. I. Privately printed: Swansea.

Grimes W.F., 1963 The stone circles and related monuments of Wales. In Foster, I.L. & Alcock, L. (eds), 93-152.

Lynch, F.M., 1972 Portal Dolmens in the Nevern Valley, Pembrokeshire. In Lynch, F.M. & Burgess, C. (eds), 67-84.

Lynch, F.M. & Burgess, C. (eds), 1972 *Prehistoric Man in Wales and the West: essays in honour of Lily F. Chitty*. Bath: Adams and Dart.

Pearce, S.M. (ed.), 2007 *A Tercentenary History of the Society of Antiquaries of London, Archaeologia*. London: The Society of Antiquaries.

Powell, T.G., Corcoran, J.X.P., Lynch, F.M. & Scott, J.G., 1969 *Megalithic Enquiries in the West of Britain*. Liverpool: Liverpool University Press.

Rowley-Conwy, P., forthcoming *From Genesis to Prehistory and the Adoption of the Three Age System*. Oxford: Oxford University Press.

RCAHMW, 1925 *An Inventory of the Ancient Monuments of Pembrokeshire*. London: HMSO.

RCAHMW 1976 *An inventory of the ancient monuments of Glamorganshire, vol. 1(2): The Later Prehistoric Monuments*. London: HMSO.

Thompson, J., 1992 *Sir Gardner Wilkinson and His Circle*. Austin: University of Texas Press.

Thompson, J., 2004 Wilkinson, Sir John Gardner (1797–1875). *Oxford Dictionary of National Biography*. Oxford: Oxford University Press. [www.oxforddnb.com/view/article/29429, accessed 4 April 2007]

Thompson, J. & Lucas, R., 1995 Sir Gardner Wilkinson in Gower. *Journal of the Gower Society* 46, 6-14.

Vyner, B. (ed.), 1994 *Building on the Past*. London: The Royal Archaeological Institute.

Ward, A.H., 1985 Recent agricultural exploitation of a degraded landscape as an indicator of earlier landuse potential: the example of Cefn Bryn, Gower, West Glamorgan. *Bulletin of the Board of Celtic Studies* 32, 411-16.

Ward, A.H., 1987 Evidence for early agriculture on Rhosili Down, Gower. *Bulletin of the Board of Celtic Studies* 34, 220-7.

Ward, A.H., 1988 Survey and excavation of ring cairns in SE Dyfed, and on Gower, West Glamorgan. *Proceedings of the Prehistoric Society* 54, 153-72.

Ward, A.H., 1989 Cairns and 'cairn fields'; evidence of early agriculture on Cefn Bryn, Gower, West Glamorgan. *Landscape History* 11, 5-18

Wetherall, D., 1994 From Canterbury to Winchester. In Vyner, B. (ed.), 8-21.

Wilkinson, J. Gardner, 1860a/2001-4. *Carn Brea, near Redruth, Cornwall*. Truro: Royal Institution of Cornwall; Reprinted by Oakmagic: Penzance.

Wilkinson, J. Gardner, 1860b On the rock-basins of Dartmoor and some British remains in England. *Journal of the British Archaeological Association* 16, 102-32.

Wilkinson, J. Gardner, 1860-61 On some of the vestiges of the Britons near Hathersage. *The Reliquary* 1, 159-66.

Wilkinson, J. Gardner, 1861 On ancient British walls. *Journal of the British Archaeological Association* 17, 1-8.

Wilkinson, J. Gardner, 1862 British remains on Dartmoor. *Journal of the British Archaeological Association* 18, 22-53, 111-33.

Wilkinson, J. Gardner, 1870 Avenues and Carns about Arthur's Stone in Gower. *Archaeologia Cambrensis* 25 (Series 4,1), 23-45, 117-21.

Wilkinson, J. Gardner, 1871a The Menvendanus Stone. *Archaeologia Cambrensis* 26 (Series 4,2), 140-57.

Wilkinson, J. Gardner, 1871b Cromlechs and other remains in Pembrokeshire. *Collectanea Archaeologica* 2, 219-40.

21

ANDREW FLEMING PUBLICATIONS
(EXCLUDING BOOK REVIEWS)

1969   The myth of the mother-goddess. *World Archaeology* 1, 247-59.

1971   Territorial patterns in Bronze Age Wessex. *Proceedings of the Prehistoric Society* 37, 138-64.
Bronze Age agriculture on the marginal lands of north-east Yorkshire. *Agricultural History Review*, 19, 1-24.

1972   Vision and design: approaches to ceremonial monument typology. *Man* (N.S.) 7, 57-72.
The genesis of pastoralism in European prehistory. *World Archaeology* 4, 179-88.
Recent advances in megalithic studies. *Origini* 6, 301-15.

1973   Tombs for the living. *Man* (N.S.) 8, 177-92.
Models for the development of the Wessex culture. In Renfrew, C. (ed.), *The Explanation of Culture Change: models in prehistory*, 571-85. London: Duckworth.
(with J.R. Collis) A late prehistoric reave system near Cholwichtown, Dartmoor. *Proceedings of the Devon Archaeological Society* 31, 1-21.

1975   The implications of calibration. In Watkins, T. (ed.), *Radiocarbon, Calibration and Prehistory*, 101-8. Edinburgh: Edinburgh University Press.
Analytical approaches to the study of ceremonial monuments in N.W. Europe. In Anati, E. (ed.), *Les Religions de la Préhistoire: actes de Ueme Symposium*, 191-4. Capo di Ponte: Centre for Camunian Studies.
Megalithic astronomy: a prehistorian's view. *Nature* 255, 575.
Prehistoric land boundaries in upland Britain: an appeal. *Antiquity* 49, 215-6.

1976   Early settlement and the landscape in West Yorkshire. In Sieveking, G., Longworth, I.H. & Wilson, K.E. (eds) *Problems in Economic and Social Archaeology*, 359-71. London: Duckworth.

1977   The Dartmoor reaves. *Current Archaeology* 5, 250-2.

1978   The Dartmoor reaves. In Bowen, H.C. & Fowler, P.J. (eds) *Early Land Allotment in the British Isles*, 17-21. Oxford: BAR.
The prehistoric landscape of Dartmoor. Part l: South Dartmoor. *Proceedings of the Prehistoric Society* 44, 97-123.

Dartmoor reaves: a nineteenth century fiasco. *Antiquity* 52, 16-19.
Comments-on some developments in north European prehistory. *Norwegian Archaeological Review* 11, 17-18.

1979   The Dartmoor reaves: boundary patterns and behaviour patterns in the second millennium BC. *Proceedings of the Devon Archaeological Society* 37, 115-30.
The Dartmoor Reave Project. *Current Archaeology* 6 (67), 234-7.
(with G. Wainwright & K. Smith) The Shaugh Moor Project: First Report. *Proceedings of the Prehistoric Society* 45, 1-32.

1980   Dartmoor: the evolution of a prehistoric landscape. *The Devon Historian* 21, 25-31.
The cairnfields of north-west Dartmoor. *Proceedings of the Devon Archaeological Society* 38, 9-12.
(with J.M. Coles and B.J. Orme) The Baker site: a neolithic platform. *Somerset Levels Papers* 6, 6-23.
Prehistoric settlers on Dartmoor. In Timms, S. (ed.) *Archaeology of the Devon Landscape*, 33-42. Exeter: Devon County Council.

1982   Social boundaries and land boundaries. In Renfrew, C. & Shennan, S. (eds) *Ranking, Resource and Exchange*, 52-5. Cambridge: Cambridge University Press.
(with N. Ralph) Medieval settlement and land use on Holne Moor, Dartmoor: the landscape evidence. *Medieval Archaeology* 26, 101-37.

1983   The prehistoric landscape of Dartmoor. Part 2: North and East Dartmoor. *Proceedings of the Prehistoric Society* 49, 195-241.
Upland settlement in Britain: the second millennium and after. *Scottish Archaeological Review* 2, 171-6.
(with D. Maguire & N. Ralph) Early land use on Dartmoor – palaeobotanical and pedological investigations on Holne Moor. In Jones, M. (ed.) *Integrating the Subsistence Economy*, 57-105. Oxford: BAR.

1984   The prehistoric landscape of Dartmoor: wider implications. *Landscape History* 6, 5-19.
(with J.R. Burns) The field systems and the sluices. In Barker, G. & Jones, G.D.B. (eds), The UNESCO Libyan valleys Survey VI: Investigations of a Romano-Libyan farm, Part I, 31-42. *Libyan Studies* 15, 1-44.

1985   Dartmoor Reaves. *Devon Archaeology* 3, 1-6.
Land tenure, productivity and field systems. In Barker, G. & Gamble, C. (eds), *Beyond Domestication in Prehistoric Europe*, 129-146. London: Academic Press.
Upland settlement in Britain: the second millennium and after. In Spratt, D. & Burgess, C. (eds) *Upland Settlement in Britain*, 377-383. Oxford: BAR.

1986   Les delimitations de l'age du bronze dans la region de Dartmoor, Grande Bretagne. In Ferdiere, A. & Zadora-Rio, E. (eds) *Prospection Archaeologique et Interpretation Historique: reconstitution des territoires et paysages fossils*, 161-8. Paris: Documents de l'Archeologie Francaise.
(with J. Burns) The field system Mn51. *Libyan Studies* 17, 33-7.

1987   Coaxial field systems: some questions of time and space. *Antiquity* 61, 188-202.
Prehistoric tin extraction on Dartmoor: a cautionary note. *Reports and Transactions of the Devonshire Association* 119, 117-22.
Bronze Age settlement on the south-western moors. In Todd, M. *The South-West to AD 1000*, 111-25. London: Longman.

1988   *The Dartmoor Reaves: investigating prehistoric land divisions.* London: Batsford.

1989   The genesis of coaxial field systems. In Torrence, R. & van der Leeuw, S. (eds) *What's New? A Closer Look at the Process of Innovation,* 63-81. London: Unwin Hyman.
Coaxial field systems in later British prehistory. In Nordstrom, H. & Knape, A. (eds), *Bronze Age Studies,* 151-62. Stockholm: Museum of National Antiquities.

1990   Landscape archaeology, prehistory, and rural studies. *Rural History* 1, 1-11.
(with M. Johnson) The Theoretical Archaeology Group (TAG): origins, retrospect, prospect. *Antiquity* 64, 303-6.
Pretentious – moi? In Baker, F. & Thomas, J. (eds), *Writing the Past in the Present: contemporary debate in archaeology,* 83-86. Lampeter: St David's University College Press.

1991   Swaledale's Ancient Trees. *Dalesman* 53, 68-71.

1992   Landscape archaeology in the British uplands: opportunities and problems. In Bernardi, M. (ed.) *Archeologia del Paesaggio,* 67-88. Firenze: Consiglio Nazionale delle Ricerche: Universits degli Studi di Siena.
(with A. Woolf) Cille Donnain: a late Norse church in South Uist. *Proceedings of the Society of Antiquaries of Scotland* 122, 329-50.

1994   The two sides to Swaledale's history. *Dalesman* 56, 61-4.
Swadal, Swar (and Erechwydd?): early medieval polities in Upper Swaledale. *Landscape History* 16, 17-30.

1995   St. Kilda: stone tools, dolerite quarries and long-term survival. *Antiquity* 69, 25-35.

1996   An embarrassment of professors? *Antiquity* 70, 15-17.
The reaves reviewed. *Proceedings of the Devon Archaeological Society* 52, 63-74.
Medieval and post-medieval cultivation on Dartmoor: a landscape archaeologist' s view. *Proceedings of the Devon Archaeological Society* 52, 101-17.
Total landscape archaeology: dream or necessity? In Aalen, F. (ed.) *Landscape Study and Management,* 81-92. Dublin: Department of Geography, Trinity College Dublin/Office of Public Works.
Mystery of Swaledale's old wood pastures. *Dalesman* 58, 23-7.
Early roads to the Swaledale lead mines. *Yorkshire Archaeological Journal* 68, 89-100.
A stone cross-shaft at Lower Aish Farm, Poundsgate. *Transactions of the Devonshire Association* 128, 217-8.

1997   (with Y. Hamilakis). Peopling the landscape. *Antiquity* 71, 759-61.
Towards a history of wood-pasture in Swaledale (North Yorkshire). *Landscape History* 19, 31-47.
Patterns of names, patterns of places. *Archaeological Dialogues* 4, 199-214.

1998   The changing commons: the case of Swaledale (England). In Gilman, A. & Hunt, R. (eds) *Property in Economic Context,* 187-214. Lanham, Maryland: University Press of America.
Swaledale: valley of the wild river. Edinburgh: Edinburgh University Press.
The prehistoric landscape and the territorial imperative. In Everson, P. & Williamson, T. (eds) *The Archaeology of Landscape,* 42-66. Manchester: Manchester University Press.
Wood pasture and the woodland economy in medieval Swaledale. In Atherden, M. (ed.) *Woodland History and Management,* 26-42. Leeds: Leeds University Press.

1999   Small-scale communities and the landscape of Swaledale (North Yorkshire, UK). In Ucko, P.J. & Layton, R. (eds), *The Archaeology and Anthropology of Landscape,* 65-72. London: Routledge.

Phenomenology and the megaliths of Wales: a dreaming too far? *Oxford Journal of Archaeology* 18, 119-25.

Human ecology and the early history of St Kilda. *Journal of Historical Geography* 25, 183-200.

Swaledale: a lost vaccary and a palimpsest of place-names. *Northern History* 36, 159-62.

St Kilda: family, community and the wider world. *Journal of Anthropological Archaeology* 19, 348-68.

(with M. Edmonds) St Kilda: quarries, fields and prehistoric agriculture. *Proceedings of the Society of Antiquaries of Scotland* 129, 119-59.

2001   Dangerous islands: fate, faith and cosmology. *Landscapes* 2, 4-21.

2004   The skerry of the son of the king of Norway. In Carver, E. & Lelong, O. (eds) *Modern views – Ancient Lands: new work and thought on cultural landscapes*, 65-70. Oxford: BAR.

Hail to the chiefdom? The quest for social archaeology. In Cherry, J., Scarre, C. & Shennan, S. (eds) *Explaining Social Change: studies in honour of Colin Renfrew*, 141-7. Cambridge: McDonald Institute.

St Kilda: the pre-Improvement clachan. *Proceedings of the Society of Antiquities of Scotland* 133, 375-89.

2005   *St. Kilda and the Wider World: tales of an iconic island*. Macclesfield: Windgather Press.

Megaliths and post-modernism: the case of Wales. *Antiquity* 79, 921-32.

2006   Post-processual landscape archaeology: a critique. *Cambridge Archaeological Journal* 16, 267-80.

2007   *The Dartmoor Reaves: investigating prehistoric land divisions*, second edition. Macclesfield: Windgather.

INDEX OF PLACES AND SITES